WHAT MEN ARE LIKE

What
Men
Are
Like

by
John A. Sanford
and
George Lough, Ph.D.

PAULIST PRESS
New York / Mahwah

Library of Congress Cataloging-in-Publication Data

Sanford, John A.
    What men are like.

    Bibliography: p.
    Includes index.
    1. Men—Psychology.   2. Jung, C.G. (Carl Gustav), 1875—
1961. I. Lough, George. II. Title.
BF692.5.S26 1988   155.6'32   88-15271
ISBN   0-8091-2996-5 (pbk.)

Published by Paulist Press
997 Macarthur Blvd., Mahwah, N.J. 07430

Printed and bound in the
United States of America

Contents

Acknowledgments

The authors would like to acknowledge Helen Macey, without whose help the manuscript for this book would hardly have been possible, and George Lough would like to thank his wife Cheryl Purdue for her astute editorial assistance and loving encouragement.

To my brother, Ted Sanford, and my uncle, H.M. White,
two men who have meant much to me in my life.

J.S.

To Morton T. Kelsey,
my friend and mentor who has helped me
to a deeper understanding of myself as a man.

G.L.

Introduction

by John A. Sanford

In recent years there have been many books on feminine psychology, but few on masculine psychology. The implication is that a man's psychology isn't important, or that it is so obvious it needs no explanation. Neither of these is true. Men are as complex as women, and men, like women, need to understand themselves and take their psychological development seriously. This book is written to fill in some of the gap in the literature on masculine psychology. It is written to men in all walks of life—laymen as well as professionals—who feel the need to understand more completely what it means to be a man.

However, the book is also written with women in mind. Women need to understand the men with whom they share their lives. For women have men as fathers, sons, lovers, husbands, and, if they are psychotherapists, as clients. They are often baffled when the men in their lives act as they do. This leaves them with questions, and sometimes their inability to understand their men frustrates them. So I hope and anticipate that this book will have women readers as well as men.

The book is written from my own experience as a man, from my many years of experience counseling with men, and from my counseling experience with women and their questions about men. The basic psychological point of view is that of C. G. Jung and Fritz Kunkel. It will help the reader to know some of the ideas of Jung and Kunkel beforehand, but the book is written in such a way that someone with no prior knowledge of the thinking of these men can understand it. I do not try to be comprehensive. For instance, there is little sociological emphasis in the book. While men have the same basic psychology no matter what their social strata or ethnic origin, there can be no doubt that men from different cultures and social backgrounds present different problems in some respects. The book also describes only psychological masculine development; it does not attempt to be a book of psychiatry with its discussion of disease processes. Another important area of masculine psychology, while it is discussed in several places, is not treated in depth, and that is male homosexuality.

While men and women have their differences they also have their similarities. In many places in this book what is said about a man applies equally to a woman. A woman may find herself thinking, "But that's the way it is with women also.'' This will often be true, but it would be tedious to continually point out that an aspect of masculine psychology has its comparison in feminine psychology. So, with rare exceptions, I do not point out all the areas in which men and women are alike; I let the reader make his or her own comparisons.

Since I've just now used the expression "his or her" I also want to point out that in this book I will frequently use only masculine personal pronouns. This is not to disparage the importance of deleting sexist language. It is simply because the book is about men and it seems both appropriate and simpler in most cases to use only the masculine gender.

The reader may notice that the style in which the different chapters, or even parts of a chapter, are written may vary somewhat. For example, in Chapter 1 I adopt a personal style, but in the rest of the book I write from a more impersonal point of view. There is also the fact that the book is co-authored, most of Chapters 2, 8, and 11 being written by my friend and colleague Dr. George Lough, and he has added his own introduction.

There is so much to be said on the subject of a man's psychology that each of the chapters could be a book in itself. There is also the difficulty, as with all psychological books, that one must write in generalities, and individual differences can only be cited as examples. The reader may find himself or herself wanting further material on the subject matter of various chapters, and there are suggested readings at the end of each chapter.

Introduction

by George Lough, Ph.D.

Men of all ages in our culture are in such a sad state that it is a national crisis. They lack intimate relationships with other men because they have been taught to view them as competitors not to be trusted; they are reluctant to share their feelings because that makes them vulnerable. They also avoid intimacy with men because they fear homosexual implications, mistakenly equating liking with sexuality. Men are afraid to share their feelings with women because it makes them feel mothered, which they equate with being smothered. They don't think it manly to express their emotions in the most human of ways, by crying. They die younger than women, experience all kinds of stress without adequate release, and yet they are the last to seek professional counseling for their problems (women clients far outnumber men in counseling agencies), which is ironic, since admitting problems takes courage and courage is supposed to be the essence of manhood.

Women have gotten courage from feminism, but when men hear talk of feminism and the problems of women in our society they often respond defensively that men have their difficulties too. Sometimes this response is just a way of ignoring women's issues and of denying the reality that women have suffered terribly in our culture. But at other times this response comes because men feel that their separate problems also deserve attention. The feminist movement has resulted in important changes in the consciousness of women and men. It has helped men get in touch with their sensitive natures, with their nurturing sides; it has given them increased respect for women (after they get over their first hostile reaction to the movement). But feminism has not basically helped men understand their masculinity, and of course this was not its purpose anyway. However, there is a crying need among men, though many of them are unaware of it, to understand and tap into the more positive qualities of their own masculinity with its reservoir of inner strength, assertiveness, and caring forthrightness.

When college courses on the psychology of women first came out in the 1970's, I heard repeatedly, almost always from men, that there was no need for such courses because the psychology of women is no different from that of men. I hate to admit that I believed this myself at the time. Those courses are still being taught and there is now an entire literature on women's psychology, which has indeed proved to be worthy of a separate discipline. But, of course, this logically means that the same is true of men's psychology. Yet college courses, books and lectures on men's psychology are rare.

A few years ago I began reading the small number of available books on masculine psychology. To my disappointment they were almost all socio-political in nature and not psychological. They explored some of the problems men have in our culture, but they did so in an extraverted way, skimming the surface rather than taking a deeper look at the inner nature of men. There was nothing wrong with these books; they filled a gap in the little-studied sociology of men and men's issues. But they failed to satisfy my thirst for a deeper psychological understanding of (1) myself as a man, (2) the experiences of my male clients, (3) the experiences of my female clients with the men in their lives, and (4) the experiences of my child and adolescent clients with their fathers. Only one book had a deeper psychological orientation and spoke to my experience as a man: the now classic *He!* by Robert A. Johnson. There was also one article, an interview with the poet Robert Bly, about the "Wildman" nature in every man, which struck a true note in me and in the people with whom I shared it.*

I am excited to have co-authored the present book because I feel that it touches a deeper level of the male experience. To accomplish this our book uses examples from our own lives, from our cases, and from the lives of other men we know to illustrate the psychological development of men. Our hope is that this book will help fill the need of men and women to understand masculine psychology in ways that can be applied to their everyday lives.

---

*This article is referred to in Chapter 8 of the present book.

Chapter 1

Boyhood

I spent my boyhood in a small town in the southern part of New Jersey. People knew each other. The man at the gas station greeted you by name and would fix your carburetor for you as well as pump your gas. If there was a problem at school the principal knew the parents as well as the children. There were only two doctors in town, and while they couldn't always do much for you medically, everyone respected them. I remember the night I had a violent allergic reaction to a tetanus shot; Dr. Stokes came in the middle of the night and sat by my bed until morning to be sure I came through okay. I think the small town atmosphere would have suffocated me if I had lingered there as an adult, but as a boy it was a good place in which to grow up.

A year or so ago I went to Philadelphia to give a lecture. I was a grown man now and had been for some four decades, but when I realized how close I would be to the town of my boyhood a longing came over me to return and visit again the yards where I played, the school I attended, the old playground, the house in which I grew up, the sidewalks on which I rode my bike, the little stream at the edge of town where I built dams. There was a free afternoon at the conference, so I rented a car and made my pilgrimage to the south Jersey village and my memories of boyhood.

Had I expected very much I would have been disappointed, but I was wise enough to know that in the forty years that had passed many things would have changed in my hometown. And they had. The orchards in which I used to play were now housing developments. The farms that once surrounded the town were now bisected by freeways. The once quiet streets overflowed with noisy cars. The house in which we lived was still standing but it was now the parish house of my father's old church. The church itself looked much the same except it was much smaller somehow; strangers were in it having a wedding rehearsal and they looked at me dubiously as I poked around the inside and looked at the stained glass windows. Conroy's Drug Store, which also had a splendid ice cream and soda fountain, was now part of a shopping center, and the old Criterion Movie Theater had vanished. The school had vanished too, and the playground that had seen many a game of pickup baseball was now occupied by a new public library. I didn't find the location of the new school.

There were still vestiges of the town I once knew so well. The bumpy place in the brick sidewalk along Main Street, where I used to ride my bike en route to my friend's house, was still there, and so were the trees whose roots made the bricks so bumpy. The Buick dealership that was close to our house still sold Buicks, although the salesman told me it had changed hands four times since the old days. The big lawn of a friend's house where we boys often gathered for various games was still there, and so was a little hillock of ground known as "the mound." On the whole, though, the town I knew was gone. The worst change was the backyard where I used to play. Once my parents had a garden in it, and there was a maple tree there that God created for no other reason than that boys could climb in it, hide among its branches, and imagine all kinds of things. But now the tree was gone, and the yard was paved over, made into a parking lot.

I explored the town. I was satisfied. I would never need to go back again, for the town in which I grew up was gone and another town had taken its place. And yet the old town lived on within me in a host of memories, some of them bad, many of them good. It also lived on in my dreams. Not long after my return to California I dreamt I was again in the backyard. It was all changed. I recognized nothing. It was dim and I could hardly distinguish anything. I looked for the maple tree and it wasn't there. Or was it? No, it wasn't gone! For there in my dream I saw dimly through a kind of mist the maple tree of my boyhood! I awoke curiously strengthened and reassured: the tree was still alive within me, a symbol of a living connection between a man and the world of his childhood and imagination, a connection that somehow was still alive.

Many others have gone back to the place of their childhood as though drawn to do so by some mysterious power. It is easy to dismiss such ventures as nothing more than a regressive longing for the past. Perhaps so, but there is also the possibility that this urge to return to the place of one's origins expresses a deep need: the need for the renewal of life.

The Apache Indians, for example, believed that the place where a person was born was a "power place" for that person. This was the place where that person first emerged into this life, and it was the place where that person's life could be renewed. The birth spot was remembered by the Apache mother. She chose it carefully and made sure that she gave birth to her baby near a tree. The placenta of the child was regarded as a kind of spiritual "double," and it was placed in the branches of the tree. Whenever the leaves fell from the tree and then in the spring emerged again, the life of the person who was born there would be renewed.

The Apache warrior Geronimo tells us that Apache parents would bring the child back to the birth place once a year. They would perform a ceremony with the child, rolling the child in all the four directions from the birth-spot as a center. In this way the original "power" that had emerged with the child at birth would be with the child once again. But adults also could return to the spot of their birth. A man or woman who was weary and exhausted might make a pilgrimage to the spot of birth and there perform the sacred fourfold ceremonies that would put that person in touch again with the original life power. In fact, it was Geronimo's belief that his people on the reservation were dying because they could no longer return to their birth places in order to renew their lives.[1]

The Power of the Archetypes

In the language of Jungian psychology we would say that the power that draws a person back to the place of his birth is the power of the archetypal world. The influences on us as a child are both personal and archetypal. The personal influences consist of the effect on us of our mother and father and the other significant people and circumstances in our lives. These early influences help shape the person we will be when we are an adult. Many of them are negative influences; they damage the child and lead to damaged adults. In Chapter 3 we will look at the effect of negative childhood influences more closely. But in addition to the personal influences there are the influences of the archetypes on the growing psyche of the child. These archetypal influences are innate; we are born with them and bring them with us into the world. The archetypes also influence the course of our psychic development, and flood our imagination with their imagery. They are the

1. *Geronimo: His Own Story,* ed. by S. M. Barrett. New York: E. P. Dutton and Company, 1970, pp. 32ff.

guidelines along which all life develops, the channels through which the energy of life moves.

We are especially close to these archetypal influences in childhood. They fill the child's imagination, and shape and direct his healthy development. But by the time we are adults there is a shell around us that cuts us off from a relationship with these archetypal influences. However, the need for them remains, for these influences come from that central core of our personality that C. G. Jung called "the Self," and without a contact with this Center of our being we are cut off from our essential life.

Because of the archetypes every person can be said to have two sets of parents: there are the personal parents, and the divine or archetypal parents. Our psychological development and the kind of person we become is the result of both influences. The archetypal energies, which are the equivalent of what the Apache would have called "powers," are magical, wonderful, numinous, and also sometimes dangerous. The images they produce in the mind of the child are creative; they appear spontaneously in the child's imagination and play. This living contact with the archetypal world is experienced in a unique and pristine way in childhood and it needs to be nurtured by the parents. For from this early contact with the archetypal world emerges the later creativity of the adult.

Archetypal images are the stuff of all stories that have a natural appeal to the child's imagination. When a child sits enthralled on mother's or father's lap to hear for the one hundredth time a childhood tale, it is because the story is archetypal. Such stories nourish the connection between a child and the archetypal world, because these stories emerged from and are concerned with the imaginative world. Today it is commonly supposed that such stories are not good for the child; children should be told stories of "reality" to properly prepare them for life. But the world that we call the "real world" is in many ways less real than the imaginative world, and the preparation that we need for adult life is a long and healthy immersion in the creative world of fantasy, for which our souls have a natural and in-built propensity and need. For lack of the proper early nourishment of the soul a man may in later life become dried up and uncreative.

Fairy stories are among the best stories for children. Sometimes they are shunned by squeamish adults because they contain so much that is dark and dreadful. Yet these may be the very adults who say the child should have stories that are "realistic." The fairy stories *are* realistic. They know that life is a dark, dangerous place, full of evil circumstances and evil powers. Deep in his heart every child knows this too and is afraid of it, but the fairy story shows a boy that he can find his way through by pluck and by making contact with the helpful powers. Psychologically, nothing could be more real and true to life than stories such as these.

I recall a time when friends came to visit us from another state. They decided to go to nearby Tijuana for the usual shopping and touring and took their small son and daughter with them. When they returned many hours later they were frazzled from the traffic, the shops, the crowds, and a long wait at the border while customs officials checked the cars returning to the United States. The boy was in a terrible way. His behavior was chaotic, his humor irascible, he was a discipline problem, and he drove his tired parents to distraction. So I suggested to him that he might like to hear a story. He looked quizzical, but eventually was tempted to listen when I told him the story was about a boy like himself named Hansel, and his little sister Gretel. Intrigued, he climbed up on my lap and the story began. As I told the story of Hansel and Gretel he listened in silence. When I finished he said he wanted to hear it again, so I told it again. When I was through the second time he climbed down off my lap and began to play quietly. The story had healed him; it had reconnected him to the archetypal world.

Today many parents substitute television for stories. Television has its advantages and many good things can be said about it. Some of the programs for children are sound. It is certainly helpful to a busy parent to be able to turn on the TV and have the child entertained for a while. But it is no substitute for stories because it leaves no room for the imagination. When we are told a story we recreate it in our own minds. Our consciousness becomes like a screen on which the images of the stories are created by our own imaginative faculties. When we see something on television no such process takes place. TV, in fact, probably blunts rather than feeds the imagination, cutting a child off from an inner faculty that will be immensely helpful in later life as well as in childhood.

Stories are also extremely important and valuable in religious education. When I had my parishes I tried my best to get the Sunday School teachers to retell the Bible stories as the core of the educational process, but had little success, perhaps because they did not know how to use stories just for their own sake. My philosophy of religious education was to fill the child's soul with the living stories of the Bible. Later in life the child will find uses for these tales, and a mature religious attitude can emerge from them. At the family service I frequently dispensed with the reading of the Old Testament lesson in order to tell an Old Testament story. The children—and adults too—were engrossed. One of my own children told me years later, "You know, Dad, the only good thing you ever did in church was to tell those stories."

The Use of Imagination

Play is another example of the importance of imagination in the life of the child. I clearly remember the favorite toys of my boyhood: some one hundred pieces from broken chess sets. Where I acquired them I don't recall, but for years empires rose and fell, armies marched to and fro, kings and queens dwelt in magnificent castles built from books and blocks, as my imagination used these chess pieces to represent just about anything I wanted them to be. I much preferred the chess pieces to toy soldiers. A kneeling toy soldier firing a rifle could only be a kneeling toy soldier firing a rifle. But the bishop or knight, rook or pawn from a chess set could be anything I chose.

The best toys are the toys that leave scope for the imagination because it is the imaginative world that grips the child. Modern toys are often technological marvels, but of little value for play. Take the talking dolls that are so widely advertised around Christmas. Pull the cord and the doll says three or four different things. A marvel! Of course the child is curious and wants the doll dreadfully, but once he or she has the doll, and curiosity is satisfied, the child loses interest, precisely because the talking doll does the talking and not the child. In contrast, listen to a child playing with an ordinary doll; the child does the talking *for* the doll. The scope for imagination is much greater.

The use of the imagination has healing in it because it releases creativity and connects us with our innermost being. C. G. Jung developed the use of "active imagination" as an adjunct to the healing process. Sand play therapy with children rests on the same principle. As the child plays with the fascinating figures and toys in the sandbox he or she becomes connected to the world of the archetypes. This interaction with the archetypes through play has a healing influence on the child, and helps lead the child to the inner center, from which comes our creativity. Fritz Kunkel once noted that children play the archetypes. He said that if they are creative enough to play the whole series of archetypes it would be the best preparation for later life.*

Sometimes creative play enables a child to get through an unhappy childhood intact. In the midst of unhappy family circumstances a child's personality can become injured. However some children find a way through the unhappiness by their absorbing play. In this way they contact the inner images that see them through the difficulties of their personal lives. Such children, however, will find that later in life they are called on to continue to live close to the unconscious. It is as though the inner images will not forget them and do not want to be cast aside. "We saved you in your early years, and now we want you to continue to accept us as your companions," is the attitude the unconscious expresses to that adult who in childhood took refuge in the inner world in order to find healing from a hostile outer world.

So far we have been discussing introverted ways of playing. The games with objects such as the chess pieces or toy soldiers, little cars or trucks, are almost always played alone or with one other companion. Extraverted boyhood play takes the form of games. Some of the games may be a boyhood version of games that are part of our society, such as baseball. Other games may be invented by the boys themselves. Boys at play—when left to themselves—make up a special world in which adults are not included. The school playground has its own code of ethics. The empty lot where pickup baseball or football is played has its own rules. The woods or streams, orchards, backyards or alleys, where the boys invent their own forms of play, constitute a secret world, and if an adult shows up, his or her presence casts a distinct pall on the boys' natural expressiveness.

The Special World of Boyhood Play

In the world of boys at play the budding man is already being tested. Firm friendships are made, and so are enemies. Anything goes in this world that is honorable in the eyes of the boys. The only unforgivable sin is to be a tattletale; this offense is promptly punished by exclusion. When boys play together they are getting prepared for the

*From an unpublished lecture entitled "Psychology and Christianity."

hurly-burly world of adult life. But it is not just preparation for later life. Boys at play are living *now;* boyhood *is* life already in process.

In today's crowded, organized, and sophisticated world, the natural game-playing of boys is apt to be taken over by adults. It then becomes organized, with all the pluses and minuses that this brings about. The presence of the adults greatly changes the atmosphere. While a helpful and understanding Little League baseball coach can be a great help to a young boy in need of masculine guidance, the coach can just as likely be shallow, immature, and aggressively competitive to win—for his sake, not for the boys'. He then becomes a destructive, not constructive influence. Even at best, something is lost when life for boys becomes organized too quickly, but in today's world it is often the only way the boys can get together, for it seems that the empty lot on the corner doesn't exist today as it once did, and the parks and playgrounds are overcrowded, or have become dangerous places where a careful parent does not wish to leave the child unattended.

I have distinct memories of the vacant lot at a certain part of town where every Sunday afternoon in the fall we boys gathered who wanted to play pickup football. We chose our own teams, made our own rules, and regulated our own games. At the end of the afternoon we went home exhausted and happy. I was pleasantly surprised some years ago to read a study by psychologist Carol Gilligan of boys and girls at play that took me right back to such boyhood games.

In her book *In a Different Voice* Gilligan summarized the research of psychologist Janet Lever who in 1976 studied 181 fifth grade children at play. Lever noted several contrasts between boys' play and girls' play. Boys played outdoors more often than girls; they also played in larger and more age-heterogeneous groups than girls; their games were more competitive than girls' games and they lasted longer.

Gilligan's findings verified those of Lever. She observed:

> Boys' games appeared to last longer not only because they required a higher level of skill and were thus less likely to become boring, but also because, when disputes arose in the course of a game, boys were able to resolve the disputes more effectively than girls.

Quoting Lever, Gilligan continues:

> "During the course of this study, boys were seen quarrelling all the time, but not once was a game terminated because of a quarrel and

no game was interrupted for more than seven minutes. In the gravest debates, the final word was always to 'repeat the play,' generally followed by a chorus of 'cheater's proof.' "

Gilligan continued:

> In fact, it seemed that the boys enjoyed the legal debates as much as they did the game itself, and even marginal players of lesser size or skill participated equally in these recurrent squabbles. In contrast, the eruption of disputes among girls tended to end the game.[2]

Gilligan drew an interesting conclusion from her observations: that girls are more oriented to relationships than boys, so when the relationships break down they no longer want to play the game. On the other hand, she noted, boys are so engrossed in the game that they never sacrifice it because of difficulties with the relationships.

By happenstance, not long after reading her book, I was in Chicago. I went jogging through a park and saw, not far off, a group of boys in a game of pickup football. Maintaining a discreet distance so I would not be obtrusive, I decided to watch for a while. Several wild plays were made with much vigorous tackling and shouting back and forth but no great difficulties until one team threw a long pass downfield. The ball came down almost in the hands of a receiver, but, alas, he dropped the ball. Or—was he pushed! That was the question, and the boys from each side were immediately in an argument with cries of, "He was shoved!" . . . "Pass interference!" . . . "Pass completion!" . . . with answering cries of, "He never touched him!" . . . "He dropped the ball." The debate went on for quite some time. I'm sure it was the full seven minutes Carol Gilligan allowed for such arguments, until finally one creative boy resolved the difficulty when he called out, "The umpire wasn't looking. Come on, let's play." With that the squabble ended. All the boys seemed relieved to have an honorable end to the argument and the game went on.

Carol Gilligan's findings and my experience watching the boys at play in the park in Chicago were verified by my boyhood experience when we played our football games on the empty lot. We certainly had our arguments, but *never* did the game end because of them. I had one

---

2. Carol Gilligan, *In a Different Voice.* Cambridge: Harvard University Press, 1982, p. 9.

additional memory, however, that Gilligan did not notice. In our boy-hood pickup football games, when a boy showed up after the game had started, a debate would ensue about which team he would be on. If the boy was a good player, each team would clamor to have him on their side; if he was a poor player each team would try to pass him off on the other. There was a notable lack of sensitivity to the feelings of the boy if he was an inferior player. Girls might, perhaps, have shown more awareness of the fact that the feelings of the inferior player might be hurt by the way in which each side tried not to have him on their team. On the other hand, there was no question but that he would play; no matter how poor a player he was, he was never sent away. Here we see two typically male characteristics: a relative insensitivity to feelings, and, at the same time, a kind of masculine generosity.

Emotional Bonding with Parents

Gilligan is no doubt correct that relationships are more important for girls than for boys, but nonetheless boys *do* need their relationships. A boy needs a warm and supportive relationship with mother and father, and then, secure in this, he ventures forth manfully into the world of the boys. The small boy may be a warm and cuddly child in his mother's lap. Then when he is satisfied he jumps down to strut out into the world and play at being a man.

Later, when he is a man, he will do essentially the same thing. The roving hunter or warrior can roam the woods and plains for weeks encountering danger and overcoming hardships so long as he is secure in the knowledge that his village, with its people and warmth, awaits him on his return. The modern-day businessman or professional man or laboring man may, in a similar fashion, roam the world of competition and danger with courage as long as he knows that his heart is secure in a network of relationships at home. There was once a study made of soldiers in combat. The purpose was to try to determine which soldiers could endure that terrible stress and which ones might collapse under it. One factor that was unearthed was about the dreams of the soldiers. As long as a soldier's dreams were filled with his hometown, his mother or wife or sweetheart or children, he would make it through his ordeal. But if his dreams began to be filled with the war, he was on his way out.

The establishment of an emotional connection between the small child and the mother and father is called bonding. In the case of the mother, the bonding begins even before birth. Marie-Louise von Franz once pointed out that it is important for a woman who is pregnant to have time for her fantasy life. Her fantasies about the baby, she said in her inimitable way, "weave" the baby's psychic life.[3] The mother's experience of nursing the child will deepen the connection between herself and the infant, and increase the bonding.

If such bonding does not take place there will be serious emotional disturbances later in life. For example, in extreme cases the lack of bonding may contribute to the development of so-called psychopathic personality. Such a personality appears to be devoid of a conscience and incapable of moral behavior, or of meeting and living with the usual requirements of social reciprocity. The precise cause of psychopathic personality is not clear; there may be genetic influences too, but the cause may also be due to inadequate bonding in infancy.

There can be no doubt of the importance of this early emotional connection. Such bonding, in fact, can take place between a human being and virtually any warm-blooded creature. Puppies, for instance, who are cuddled and held by people when very small become socialized to human beings, but if they do not have such experiences within the first twelve weeks of their lives they may remain aloof and never be good companions to human beings.

For unknown reasons, it appears that some children are more reluctant to bond than others. Cases have even been reported—though they are more anecdotal than scientific—of infants who never bonded to the parents no matter how hard the parents tried. If there is such a lack of capacity for bonding, it is rare and at the present time unexplainable.

The Mother Complex

The nature of the early relationship with the mother determines the kind of mother complex that a boy will take with him into the world. The mother complex can be regarded as the continuing influence within a man of the early relationship with the mother (or mother substitute). When the relationship with the mother is basically warm and nourish-

---

3. Marie-Louise von Franz, *The Feminine in Fairy Tales*. Zurich, Switzerland: Spring Publications, 1972, p. 39.

ing, a relationship in which the boy feels loved and accepted, we speak of a positive mother complex. When the relationship is negative and rejecting so that the boy feels unwanted and unloved, we speak of a negative mother complex. Of course, in actual experience a boy will experience his mother sometimes one way and sometimes another. Nevertheless, a predominantly positive or negative pattern usually emerges.

A positive mother complex is a great gift to the boy and future man. It will endow the man with a certain feeling of confidence in himself. He will not be so prone to a life-defeating emotional need that others can never satisfy. He can sustain rejection if necessary. His unconscious attitude is: "My mother loved me; if others don't there must be something wrong with them." Such a boy will likely be close to, and appreciative of, the world of women and of the feminine, but this will not necessarily take him away from the world of the masculine if his early relationship with the father is adequate too. He will also have an enhanced capacity to love a woman later in his life.

But not everything will be rosy for the man with the positive mother complex. His confidence may be too great and may leave him with the illusion that nothing can harm him. Because of this he may underrate the dangers of life and be overcome by them. The story of Achilles is a good example. Thetis, mother of the Greek hero Achilles, desirous of guaranteeing protection for her son, besought the gods for their help. She was told to dip her infant son in the river Styx and henceforth the water would protect him from any injury. So it proved, and Achilles was invulnerable to injury even in the fierce combat of the Trojan War. However, in dipping her baby into the river, Thetis held him by the heel. This part of his body was not moistened by the water and eventually the mighty warrior Achilles was wounded in the heel by a Trojan arrow and died. Even today we say of someone who appeared to be invulnerable, but was not, that "he had an Achilles heel." During the Vietnam War a reporter interviewed some members of the Green Beret forces who volunteered for extremely dangerous combat. He was interested in why, knowing the dangers as they did, they chose this course of action. The answers he received were unanimous: to a man they said they understood the dangers, but they were sure they would be unscathed. Such are the dangers of the positive mother complex.

But there are other difficulties awaiting the man with the positive mother complex. He may be so close to the world of the mother, and hence of the feminine, that later in life he avoids it lest he become swallowed by it. This causes him to erect unconscious barriers between himself and women even though his underlying feeling is positive. He may also become so closely attached to his mother that he finds difficulty in freeing himself from his longing to be with her, and reluctant to go out to face the real world with all of its dangers and hardships. As we will see in a later chapter, he may also unconsciously compete with the father for the mother's affection and thus become estranged from him. However, this is only likely to happen if the eros between the mother and father is not correct. If the mother's love for her husband is sound, then the boy cannot intrude in their relationship; however, if there is a love problem between the man and woman, the woman's eros may engulf the son, connecting him too closely to her. This may lead later in life to sexual difficulties, in extreme cases contributing to homosexuality.

Unless a man with a positive mother complex matures sufficiently he may also have difficulty making a lasting relationship with another woman. I recall hearing a woman psychiatrist who told the case of a woman who had three sons. This woman was, she stressed, a wonderful woman and mother; she was everything that a woman and mother should be. The result was that her sons were greatly attached to her, and as a consequence all three of the sons had several divorces. The psychiatrist said it was as though they could never find another woman to measure up to their mother.

The boy with the negative mother complex has his problems too. For example, he may reach maturity with a lack of confidence in himself. Even if he has established a fairly mature and functioning ego structure he will likely have within himself an "injured child." When he becomes a man he may so distrust women, or so lack confidence in his own lovability, that he may have difficulties in relating to women. In order not to get hurt again he will likely erect unconscious emotional barriers between himself and his wife or lovers. The negative mother complex may also instill in him feelings of guilt and self-rejection. But even here there are possible compensations. If later in life he ministers to his wounded child within, he may develop a superior consciousness, sensitivity, and awareness. If he has "the right stuff" within him, he may go out into life more resolutely than his counterpart with the positive mother complex, asking from life, so to speak, no quarter. He may also as a boy compensate for his emotional isolation by establishing an early relationship with his inner, imaginative world that may stand him in good stead later. The unconscious, it seems, has innumerable ways of helping us cope with and get successfully through life no matter what the circumstances of our childhood.

In a later chapter on masculine relationships we will go more deeply into the father-son relationships. But it is appropriate here to point out that the boy has a need for bonding to the father as well as to the mother. Fathers usually bond to their sons later than mothers. The mother, feeling in her body the early connection between herself and the baby during pregnancy, naturally tends to bond earlier than the father, for whom the forthcoming baby may seem like something of an abstraction as he goes about his tasks in life. Once the father physically feels the reality of the baby, however, all of this may change. There is something about the physical contact of warm, living bodies that makes a bridge between people and establishes an emotional bond. A woman whose husband seemed indifferent to their baby brought her problem to her doctor. He said, ''Put the baby in your husband's arms so he will have to hold him.'' She did, and from then on the father and the child became close.

A boy craves masculine affection as much as feminine affection. He will want to cuddle in father's lap as well as mother's. If this need is not satisfied he may come to adult life with an unsatisfied craving for masculine affection that can, in some cases, influence his sexuality. If two men of mature age hugged and snuggled together like a small boy and his father it would be called homosexuality, but when the boy and his father hug it is a natural urge and instinct. In fact, the satisfaction of this need is a reinforcement of the boy's heterosexual development, and the lack of it produces emotional deprivation. One man, cheated as a boy of his father's love by the father's incapacity for closeness, dreamt repeatedly when he was a teenager of having sexual intercourse with his father. The unfulfilled need for masculine closeness was still trying to be met.

Later in the boy's life the relationship with the father usually develops through a shared activity. The two play ball together or the father tells stories. They work together on some joint project around the house, or go fishing, or play a game together, such as chess. In this way the boy identifies with the father, and if the father is an adequate carrier of the masculine principle this early identification nourishes the boy's developing masculinity.

But here a problem sometimes arises, for if the father and the son are different kinds of people it may be hard for them to find a common ground. Not all sons are "chips off the old block." Some of them are, genetically speaking, a throw-back to some distant ancestors. Such a boy is destined to be a radically different kind of man than his father, and the father and son seem like strangers to each other.

Freud thought that we entered into the world with an unformed personality; we were a "tabula rasa" waiting for life's experiences to etch out our personality formation. While life's experiences certainly do have their influence on our personality development, there is every reason to believe that a baby at birth is a little person in his or her own right. We are born with a certain kind of personality structure and psychological predisposition from the very beginning.

This is obvious when it comes to our physical structure. Some men are robust, thick-boned, and heavily muscled, with broad, thick shoulders, and necks that are as wide as their heads. Others are slender, with small bones, small necks, and muscles that may become stringy and sinewy but never thick and strong. Still others tend to be heavy, but not muscular. This is our innate physical constitution, but, as William Sheldon showed, a certain psychological propensity accompanies the physical structure.[4] The muscular "mesomorphs" are the athletes, physically vigorous men with a certain kind of personality to accompany it, while the slender "ectomorphs" tend toward the aesthetic and religious. Shakespeare was perhaps the first to note this. In his play *Julius Caesar* he has Caesar say to Brutus:

> Let me have men about me that are fat;
> Sleek-headed men, and such as sleep o'nights:
> Yond Cassius has a lean and hungry look;
> He thinks too much: such men are dangerous.
> (Act I, Scene 2, Line 158)

Sheldon's physiologically oriented typology is important and interesting, but C. G. Jung's typology goes much further. There will be several places in this book in which we use Jung's theory of types in

---

4. William H. Sheldon, *Varieties of Human Physique*. New York: Harper & Row Publishers, 1940.

order to throw light on certain masculine problems. Jung's typology is one of his most important psychological achievements and it has had an interesting history. Many people know about and use his typology who have little interest in the rest of his psychology. As a result it has enjoyed a life of its own and has been widely used in industry as well as in psychology because of its highly practical applications. Because his typology is now fairly well known we will assume that the reader knows enough about it to understand what will be said when we apply it to areas of masculine psychology. However, for those who are not familiar with Jungian typology there is an appendix at the back of the book that will provide an adequate summary. For now it is enough to point out that his typology has to do with three areas:

1. Whether we are extraverted or introverted, that is, whether our primary focus is on the world outside of us or the world within us.
2. Which of the four functions of thinking, feeling, sensation, and intuition is our natural (superior) function.
3. Whether we are a judgment type, who is good at getting the job done and reaching conclusions, or a perception type, who is so involved in the gathering of information that he finds it difficult to reach conclusions and make decisions.

In a later chapter we will also go more deeply into the matter of how the psychological types influence the father-son relationship. For now it will be enough to note that if the father and the son are different types, an identification and closeness between them will be potentially difficult. The difficulty will be especially great if the father wants the son to be an extension of himself, and to excel at things he thinks are important, sort of a "feather in his cap." If the father then discovers that the interests of the son are markedly different he may be inclined to reject him.

The rejection, however, may also come from the son. A boy who is, let us say, aesthetically inclined may find his exaggeratedly masculine father boorish and uninteresting. In contrast he may find his mother's personality much more to his liking. The result will be that the boy may reject his father even if the father makes what amounts to a sincere effort to establish a relationship.

One result of such a rejection will be that the son will also reject those qualities in himself that are like the father. He may then be cut off from his "chthonic masculinity," which will become a part of that secondary personality within us that we call the shadow. Much later in life such a man may find it necessary to appreciate the values of his father in order to reclaim his lost shadow and become a whole man.

The Adopted Boy

A special instance is the adopted boy. The adopted boy is almost certain to be a different type of person than his adoptive parents because of his different genetic inheritance. This difference needs to be recognized, accepted, and appreciated by the parents. It will be difficult for the adoptive parents to make the kind of ego-identification with their son that we described a moment ago. So a different kind of bridge must be found.

The adopted boy suffers from a primal rejection because the circumstances of his birth did not allow him to stay with his natural mother. He will enter into the relationship with his adoptive parents with a wound that the new parents cannot completely heal no matter how devoted they are to him. He may also have trouble being accepted into, and feeling at home with, the extended family. If there are natural children in the family, the grandparents, aunts and uncles may find him a bit of an "ugly duckling" and he may sense this on either a conscious or an unconscious level. Other boys may also tease him about his adopted status, increasing in him a sense of social isolation. If the adoption took place after the boy was many months or several years old there may also be a wound from inadequate earlier bonding to the natural or foster mother. All of this endows the adopted boy's personality with a certain amount of pain. However, this very pain may be the connection between the boy and his adoptive parents. One adoptive parent told me that he found it difficult to feel close to his adopted son until one day the boy fell on a hot floor furnace grate and burned himself painfully. As he struggled to relieve the boy's pain he suddenly thought: "There is our connection. Our pain!" For he too had suffered great pain over the inability of his wife and himself to have children. The pain proved to be the bond between them, the common element they shared that enabled the father to feel close to his adopted son.

Despite his handicaps, however, the adopted boy can and usually does make it in life. I do not know of any scientific study that shows that adopted children have more problems later in life than natural children. There are many anecdotes pointing in that direction, but there are also anecdotes in which the natural child has difficulties later in life. In fact, the adopted boy has certain advantages. Precisely because the adopted boy is not the parents' natural child he is less likely to be saddled with their desire that he live out for them various ego ambitions of their own. His very differences from them make it more likely that he will be allowed to be himself. Moreover, the parent-child archetypes work with adopted children as well as with natural children. For example, among the American Indians adoption was extremely common. A child whose parents died was immediately adopted into another family. Children from other tribes who became prisoners were also adopted. The ties of human affection are stronger than the ties of blood. The important thing is that the boy be wanted and liked for who he is—whether natural or adopted.

In the lore of mythology many heroes began life as adopted children. Moses comes to mind. His natural parents were his Hebrew parents Jochebed and Amram, but he was adopted into the palace of Pharaoh by the Egyptian princess who saw his cradle floating down the river. Jesus of Nazareth is another example. His mother was Mary, but his father was unknown and Joseph was his adoptive father. In Greek mythology most of the heroes had an earthly mother but an unknown father who often turned out to be a god. A striking example in Roman lore is Romulus and Remus: orphaned children who were adopted and raised by a she-wolf, and grew up to become the founders of Rome. Maybe this mythology is a way of saying that there is a compensation for everything, and that the forces of life find a way to compensate for the adopted boy's less fortunate start.

This is not a book on parenting; nonetheless a few comments about it might be helpful. They will also highlight some of the important aspects of boyhood.

The parent will be helped in raising his or her boy by studying Jung's typology, which we mentioned earlier. Many excellent books are available on this subject and are noted in the suggested readings. By identifying his or her own typology, and that of the son, a lot of consciousness will come to the fore that will aid in understanding the boy and the nature of the relationship between them.

Remember that the small child will also get to the weak spots of the parents. For instance, if we as a parent cannot cope with anger, the child will be unconsciously drawn to produce anger in us. This is because of the child's unconscious insecurity with our weakness. This gives the parent a unique chance to integrate his or her unresolved problem with anger.

We do well as parents to examine the weak areas in the parenting that we received. We do this not to blame our parents for our difficulties, but so these inadequate patterns will be less apt to repeat themselves. Otherwise, we will find that we are unconsciously led to pass on the kind of parenting we received. Of course this may be good parenting as well as destructive parenting. But by being conscious of the destructive aspects of our own parenting we have a chance to avoid passing those negative features on to our children.

As parents we need to be in control. It is when we do not know how to control our child effectively or cope with certain situations that we give in to rage. The child needs us to be in control. Then the child can feel secure.

To be in control, however, does not mean being controlling. We do not have to control or shape the boy's personality. There is a Center within the boy that knows what he is to become. We create as good an environment as we can for the boy. Given that, the Center within the boy will guide the emergence from within of his true personality.

We need to listen to and reflect the boy's feelings. We need to *see* the child for who he is. We need to let the child know that we do understand his feelings even if we have to reprimand him for his behavior.

Many problems that parents run into are developmental problems in the child. For many months a little boy has a sunny and compliant disposition; then almost overnight he becomes stubborn and unresponsive. Sometimes it is just that the boy is entering into a new phase of his development. Understanding this will help us as parents. A good book on child development will help us with this understanding. Some books are recommended in the suggested readings.

Finally, the most important thing we can do for our children as parents is look to our own development. We need to deal with our own injuries, become aware of our own projections, work on our relationship with our husband or wife, be involved in our own individuation process. This work on ourself is the greatest gift we can give to our child. Out of it will come everything else.

But we need to remember that not everything is up to us as parents. Many people make it in life no matter what happens to them. The human soul is tough and people have the resilience to survive the greatest difficulties. Alice Miller expressed it nicely: "For the human soul is virtually indestructible, and its ability to rise from the ashes remains as long as the body draws breath."[5]

There are people who have had the most damaging childhoods imaginable but, with help, became strong adults and led successful lives. This is partly because we have, as mentioned earlier, not only our natural parents but also our archetypal parents. From this reality comes an ancient idea that everyone has both human and divine parents. In Christian language, we are the child of certain parents but are also a child of God. For this reason, the importance in boyhood of the boy's early contact with the archetypes cannot be stressed too much. Play, imagination, freedom of expression—all of these ensure that the world of the archetypes will be lived out by the boy. In this way the provision is made for the possibility in adult life that the man will have the archetypes as his inner companions just as he did when he was a child.

Suggested Reading

Gilligan, Carol, *In a Different Voice: Psychological Theory and Women's Development*. Cambridge: Harvard University Press, 1983.

Kalff, Dora, *Sandplay*. Santa Monica: Sigo Press, 1980.

Miller, Alice, *The Drama of the Gifted Child*. New York: Basic Books, Inc., 1983.

———*For Your Own Good*. New York: Farrar, Straus, Giroux, 1983.

———*Thou Shalt Not Be Aware*. New York: New American Library, 1986. (Originally American Printing, 1984.)

Moustakas, Clark E., *Psychotherapy with Children*. New York: Ballantine Books, 1970.

von Franz, Marie-Louise and Hillman, James, *Jung's Typology*. New York: Spring Publications, 1971.

Wickes, Frances, *The Inner World of Childhood: A Study in Analytical Psychology*. New York: Appleton, Century, Crofts, Inc., 1927.

---

5. Alice Miller, *For Your Own Good*. New York: Farrar, Straus, Giroux, 1983, p. 279.

Chapter 2

Adolescence

Adolescence is the transition period between boyhood and manhood. The word "adolescence" comes from the Latin words "ad" (to) and "alescere" (grow up), and that is the main developmental task of adolescence: to grow up. Adolescence begins with the biological changes of puberty. But how long adolescence lasts depends partly on the culture. In so-called primitive societies adolescence can be a relatively brief phenomenon, lasting only a few days during which the youth undergoes specified initiation rituals. At the conclusion of these puberty rites he is considered to be a full-fledged adult member of the tribe, with all the privileges and responsibilities of a man.

However, in our culture adolescence may last five or even ten years because it takes so long to accomplish the transitions that we see as necessary for adulthood. In order for a man to find a place in today's world he must be educated or trained in such a way that gainful employment is open to him. In the tribe a boy who was to become a hunter could begin learning early to hunt, practicing on small game. But, of course, a boy in our more complex culture usually cannot practice his adult occupation. Most occupations require many years of preparation. Until this preparation is accomplished he remains financially dependent, and this slows down the transition from boyhood to manhood.

Nature does not know of such a prolonged adolescence. Lower forms of life have virtually no adolescence. The higher vertebrates, such as chimpanzees, may have a brief "adolescent" period in which they are no longer dependent on their parents but not yet quite mature. Certain birds, the bald eagle for instance, even after they are mature physically, will have a different coloring than the fully mature for a brief time. And young magpies, after they are grown and leave the nest, display a different life-style than the adult birds: they swarm together in indiscriminate flocks of male and female birds, but soon they pair off and then live as fully mature magpies. But no extended period of transitional status is observed in nature to the degree it is in technologically advanced human cultures.

The transition from boyhood to manhood in our culture has social, psychological, physical, and spiritual aspects. Socially, becoming a

33

man includes the achievement of economic independence, finding a place in the social order (or finding a creative way to rebel against the existing social order), and establishing relationships with the opposite sex. Development of an effective, yet not overly inhibiting or false, social persona is necessary so that a man feels comfortable in the various roles he must play in society, such as worker, husband, father, and friend.

Psychologically, becoming a man means that the adolescent must free himself from his infantile ego characteristics, and overcome his regressive longings to remain contained in the mother, or dependent on the father's protection. He must establish ego stability, which means he needs to acquire the capacity for sustained and directed ego activity even in the face of difficulties. He must learn how to control and properly express his masculine aggression. He must develop an awareness of himself as a person separate from his parents, outgrowing the psychological fusion with parents that characterizes the child.

The striving for separateness from parents helps explain why many adolescents adopt unconventional clothing and hair styles; the styles demonstrate for all to see how different from his parents is the adolescent. But along with separateness can come a feeling of isolation and aloneness; he may experience the "human condition," the "existential predicament." An adolescent may recoil from his first startling awareness of the essential loneliness of life; he may try to deny it by clinging to peers. He may make friendships out of a narcissistic need to replace the feeling of security he got from being fused with his parents. He becomes "inseparable" friends with an age mate. One indication of developing manhood is the capacity to have less egocentric friendships, ones in which there is a genuine concern for the other person instead of a fixation on having them meet one's own needs. But because he is in the middle of a transition period an adolescent can oscillate between concern for others and self-concern. One minute he feels sympathy for others that knows no bounds; he feels "Weltschmerz" or literally "World hurt," a deep sorrow for the sufferings of all humanity. Then the next minute he cares only about himself and may ridicule his friend for wanting sympathy. One reason for adolescent suicides is the lack of concern they get from peers who are themselves too egocentric to take the sufferings of another person seriously.

The Struggle for Ego Identity

The awareness of being a separate person helps an adolescent begin the foremost task of adolescence: the building of ego identity. Identity in adolescence is uncertain because it is an in-between time, not yet a man but no longer a boy. It is a time of serious self-questioning about who he is. One man remembered looking in his mirror at the age of fourteen and asking himself, "Who is that person?"

As part of his identity questioning an adolescent may have the fantasy that his parents are not his actual parents and that he is the offspring of royalty. And it is in adolescence that a youth who has actually been adopted may want to find the identity of his biological parents, and may even begin a formal search for them. It is really his own identity for which he searches; by finding out who his parents are he hopes to know who he is.

Psychological research on identity formation in young people by James Marcia reveals that there are four identity states:[1]

(1) "Identity Diffused" are those who have much confusion about who they are and are not yet able to focus and begin their identity search. In some cases their disorientation may be prolonged and worsened by drug use. Identity diffused youth can be seen in big cities wandering the streets; some are runaways who are just drifting. If this condition persists into adulthood serious psychological disturbance is the result; many homeless people may have become fixated in this identity state.

(2) "Identity Foreclosed" are those who have prematurely terminated their quest for identity, or who have not yet begun it, because they have substituted a parent's or other adult's identity for their own. They may seem to know who they are, but they are only imitating the adult who is their role model rather than being themselves. They may seem to know what they want, but it is really only what they think others want them to want. For example, if an identity foreclosed adolescent planned to become a dentist it could be because his father is a dentist instead of because he had analyzed his own capabilities and interests and determined that occupation for which he was best suited. Such a youth may wake up one day and say, "This isn't me. I didn't choose this. I need to find out what *I* want, who *I* am." This very thing hap-

---

1. Rolf E. Muuss, *Theories of Adolescence*. New York: Random House, 1975, pp. 69–81.

pened to the great writer of western novels, Zane Grey, whose father was a dentist and who became one himself to please his father, until, with the support of his wife, he quit to begin his writing career.[2]

(3) "Identity Moratorium" are those who postpone commitment to definite values and careers while questioning and actively searching to discover who they are. They often question authority and may rebel against social convention in an effort to differentiate themselves from the collective group. They form their identities by seeing themselves in opposition to something. They challenge parents and teachers and, though they may be seen as a nuisance by those in authority, they are on a legitimate quest for their own values and beliefs.

(4) "Identity Achieved" are those who have been through the moratorium period's searching process and its rebelliousness, and have discovered a sense of who they are. They are ready to make value, relationship, and career commitments that stem from their true desires and a deeper understanding of their unique personalities. They see themselves as people in their own right who have their own ideas and know what they believe and why. This state is more likely to occur chronologically later in adolescence.

Adolescents typically go through a progression in these identity states from confusion to insecure fixation, then through conscious searching and rebellion to the ultimate integration of the personality into a new identity.

The establishment of ego identity demands that an adolescent be self-preoccupied for a time. He may need to see himself as the center of the universe, to focus his energy on himself to get a sense of who he is. Narcissism is age-appropriate in adolescence. Consequently parents cannot realistically expect their adolescent to show much appreciation of them, or sympathy for their struggles. The adolescent expects his parents to take care of him and may take them for granted when they do so. Or he may give them double messages about his need to be taken care of. For example, one adolescent insisted that his mother tuck him in bed each night, but complained bitterly to her that she was overprotective when she wanted him to be home by midnight.

It is part of the parents' task, of course, to help their son develop a concern for others by requiring him to respect them and their rights

---

2. Frank Gruber, *Zane Grey: A Biography*. Mattituck, N.Y.: Amereon, Ltd. Reprint of 1969 edition published by River City Press.

and those of other people. But it will be natural for him to think first and foremost of himself. It will take time for him to learn social reciprocity and a genuine concern for others. In this way parents can help their son begin the task of overcoming his egocentric attitude.

Overcoming egocentricity is a vital part of psychological maturity; it involves recognizing that the ego is only a part of one's true identity and that the total personality is larger than the ego. In our next chapter we will examine the forms egocentricity can take, and later we will discuss how a man must shed his egocentricity in the process of becoming psychologically mature.

Another psychological change that occurs in adolescence is an increase in cognitive or intellectual ability. Whereas a small child is limited to concrete problem solving and is not yet capable of syllogistic reasoning, an adolescent is capable of abstract thinking and logical argumentation.[3] An adolescent may become an irritant to his parents because he practices his new mental powers on them, disputing minute points of their rules, marshaling his arguments like a defense attorney to persuade his parents to add a quarter of an hour to his curfew, for example. And a parent feels foolish stopping the argument with the standard, "I'm right because I'm the parent."

This increased argumentativeness should not be taken by the parents as a personal assault on them; it is a necessary process their son goes through in attempting to achieve independence. His new-found intellect helps him make the most of the moratorium period of which we just spoke. By challenging adult authority he begins to establish his own internal authority. He argues with his parents to differentiate his ideas from theirs and thus himself from them.

Demonstration of intellectual prowess can also be a way an adolescent tries to prove his masculinity. He may become obsessed, for instance, with beating his friends at chess. Or he may latch onto computers, trying to develop the best program in a sort of "macho" of the mind. The ectomorphs, from Sheldon's typology, known colloquially as "eggheads" (a term that may have originated because of their body type with its relatively greater head to body ratio), put their energy into mental pursuits just as ardently as the mesomorphs, or "jocks," put theirs into physical ones.

Becoming a man in the physical sense means undergoing the bod-

---

3. See Appendix B for a more thorough exposition of cognitive development.

ily changes of puberty (from the Latin *pubes,* which means pubic hair).
An adolescent's life experience is different depending on whether his
pubertal changes begin early, say eleven or twelve years of age, or late,
say eighteen or nineteen. Early maturers, for example, have more status
among their peers because they are physically stronger in a subculture
in which physical strength rules. But early maturers also experience disadvantages: because they look older adults mistakenly assume they are
also emotionally mature and expect too much of them. Also, girls are
more attracted to the early maturing boy and this may lead to emotional
involvements the boy is not ready to handle. As they reach the end of
adolescence, early maturers lose their high status among peers because
the others are catching up with them. The early maturer who was the
Big Man on Campus in high school is suddenly just another college
freshman.

But for the late maturer life is fraught with even more difficulties.
He is smaller in stature and does not yet have secondary sex characteristics such as pubic hair, underarm hair, deepened voice, and beard. His
bigger peers may mercilessly tease him about his lack of development.
He may fear taking group showers during physical education class because he will be ridiculed. He may be a victim of bullies, suffering in-
dignities such as being stuffed headfirst into trash cans or having his
head held in toilets while they are flushed. Shopping mall karate classes
are filled with desperate late maturers trying to prepare to defend themselves against bigger boys. Some compensate for late physical development by putting their energy into academic achievement. This wins
them the approval of adults but only further alienates them from their
peers; one of the least popular types in high school is the "brain."

When late maturers finally catch up in physical maturity, some not
until well into their twenties, they may have weathered a very painful
adolescence. They may be bitter about it, or their suffering may have
given them increased insight and deepened consciousness about life's
unfairness and a consequent empathy for the sufferings of others. Many
men in the helping professions have developed their nurturing abilities
partly from having these kinds of painful adolescent experiences.

For some adolescents, participation in organized team sports is a
good way to become comfortable with their changing bodies, and with
the resulting changes in body image and self-image. Sports can be a
container in which the adolescent can try himself out. He can experience the intense emotions accompanying victory and defeat. He can get

a taste of the camaraderie of a team. It may be one of the few experiences of male-bonding he can get in our culture. Many men say they have never been able to recreate the sense of companionship with other men that they had when they were involved in school athletics. One man who was just in his early twenties already nostalgically looked back on his experience when his football team won the high school championship game. He described how they cried for joy in each other's arms after the game. He wasn't sure he would ever experience that depth of emotion with other men again, because in our culture the contexts are very limited in which men may express feelings such as this.

As we will point out in Chapter 7 when we discuss men's friendships, men need activities through which to relate to each other. Sports can serve this function well for the adolescent who is gifted with strength and good coordination. It can be a crucial masculinizing experience that engenders a self-confidence that can generalize to all other areas of his life.

However, team sports participation can also produce psychological, and physical, wounds in the adolescent who is not athletically gifted. If he fails at sports he will be ridiculed and will feel humiliated. He may feel excluded from the society of men. This is painful, but it can also be the cause of the development of individuality and of distinguishing oneself from the male collective. One man recalled that in high school he was very good at sports until in his junior year he badly injured his knee. During the long rehabilitation period he discovered that he loved to read literature. Before this he had not even planned to attend college, but then he decided to become a teacher and a writer. This experience of separation from the team, painful though it was, helped him find his true self.

Organized team sports can be a microcosm of the unfairness of life. One man recalled the time he was on the high school football team and his father came to see him in a game. Since his father rarely had time in his busy schedule to come to his games it was a big event to have him there. However, he was only second string and had played only a small amount in each game so far that season. His father brought a home movie camera and he hoped the coach would have a heart and put him in the game for at least a couple of plays so his father could film him. But the coach sat him on the bench the entire game.

Another man recalled his anger at the arbitrary nature of authority when he had the following experience on his high school baseball team.

The coach had told the team never to enter the locker room with their cleats on because he didn't want the floors to be scratched. Since the floors were only raw concrete this did not make much sense, but they always dutifully took off their cleats before entering. Then one day after practice the man and two teammates had a race to the locker room, and in their excitement forgot to take their cleats off. The equipment manager reported it to the coach who came down hard on them, telling them they each must take a "swat," a notoriously forceful blow to the rear end with a large wooden paddle made for the purpose, or leave the team. The man took his swat first; it was performed by the coach with so much force that the sound of paddle striking bare flesh echoed through the locker room. He felt sick to his stomach and his bottom hurt for two days afterward. The two other players, after seeing the swat, decided they would leave the team instead of taking one themselves. The man himself was a mediocre player, but they were stars. The coach, realizing he had spoken too quickly, and that he could not afford to lose them from the team, relented and gave them no punishment. Of course the man felt the terrible unfairness of this but was powerless to do anything about it. Years later he was still angry about it; it had become to him the prototypical example of life's unfairness. Yet it prepared him for other instances of unfairness he was later to suffer, because he was able to use his anger not to let himself be taken advantage of when he *could* help it. Fortunately, experiences like this one can build ego strength and become part of a man's individuation.

Physical development includes sexual development and this means having to fulfill sexual needs and channel sexual energy. For example, most adolescents go through a psychologically painful struggle regarding masturbation; they enjoy its pleasure, but feel guilty about doing it. There is a time before an adolescent discusses it with peers when he may feel he is the only one in the world who masturbates. It would be helpful for him to hear the old joke: "Did you know that 80% of all boys masturbate; the other 20% lie."

Parents sometimes inadvertently add to the guilt about masturbation. One early maturing man said that when he was in the seventh grade his father took him aside, ostensibly to discuss the "facts of life" with him. Their "discussion" consisted of his father rhetorically asking him, "You don't masturbate, do you?" Because the question implied disapproval he lied and said he did not. That was the last time they ever talked about sex.

Fathers often feel uncomfortable bringing up the topic of masturbation with their son. One father said it was the most embarrassing conversation he had ever had, even though he brought it up simply to tell his son it was normal and for him not to feel guilty about it. The father himself probably had lingering and unresolved guilt from his own adolescent experiences.

G. Stanley Hall, the author of the classic four-volume turn-of-the-century treatise on adolescence, and the man who is called "the father of adolescent psychology," wrote candidly about his personal struggles with masturbation. He decided he would not masturbate and he was able to control himself and not do it, but he was still plagued with nocturnal emissions or "wet dreams." He wrote near the end of the sexually repressive Victorian era, but there are many adolescents who feel these same conflicts today.

Adolescent sexuality involves not only dealing with new biological urges, but also answering the question of one's sexual orientation, heterosexual versus homosexual. Actually this is a false dichotomy, since most people of either sex have some degree of attraction to both the opposite and the same sex. Although the behavior of people may be generally categorized as primarily heterosexual or homosexual, the boundaries for their feelings of attraction are not so tightly drawn. As Jungian analyst Adolf Guggenbuhl-Craig points out, "Two people in a relationship, regardless of whether they are of the same or different sex, must feel something physical for one another."[4] But because adolescence is a time of insecurity the adolescent wants to determine as clearly as possible what his sexual orientation is to help him resolve his identity crisis. Thus it is part of adolescent mentality to assume a clear dichotomy between homosexuality and heterosexuality.

It can be alarming to adolescent males that, besides having the normal feelings of homosexual attraction, they may also desire homosexual activity. For example, many engage in behaviors, such as mutual masturbation, which have obvious homosexual characteristics.[5]

On the psychological level their homosexual interest has the purpose of helping them forge their connection with the masculine world. By being physically close to other men they symbolically try to become

---

4. Adolf Guggenbuhl-Craig, *Power in the Helping Professions*. New York: Spring Publications, 1971, p. 68.

5. Shere Hite, *The Hite Report on Male Sexuality*. New York: Ballantine Books, 1982, pp. 36–46.

more masculine themselves. Adolescent homosexual behavior usually will not cause a permanent homosexual orientation, but can be a phase through which a youth passes on the way to a heterosexual orientation.

In one South Sea island tribal culture it is normal for boys to have sexual relations with men. It is the belief of this tribe that before a male can relate sexually to a woman he must first become masculine. The tribe thinks that the way to become masculine is to incorporate the masculinity of other men by ingesting their semen. The boys who engage in this practice do not become homosexual because of it, but go on to have sex with women, marry, and have families.[6] Though to our culture such a practice may sound bizarre and repulsive, in their culture it is taken for granted as the way to acquire masculinity.

Our own culture's homophobia may prevent us from seeing even any symbolic value to such a tribal ritual. As noted earlier, males in our society are uncomfortable about showing almost any kind of affection to each other for fear of being labeled homosexual. They show affection indirectly through teasing, which amounts to a kind of reaction formation: they "rag" on each other, showering immense amounts of negative attention on each other. They can always say to themselves they are just putting the other guy down, but actually they are displaying an excessive amount of interest in him and his masculinity. This ridiculing can be heard whether it is little boys or grown men—for example, when they are engaged in sports activities. Strangely, men show their love for each other by putting each other down. This is because our culture won't permit them to do it honestly in words of affection and praise, unless, of course, they are drunk; then they hug each other and even tell each other, "I love you." When a man is drunk his inhibitions are reduced and the deeper unconscious feelings surface. And because he is not in full control, a man later has an alibi that allows him to deny to himself and others the homosexual feelings that caused the display of affection.

As we have said, many adolescents engage in some form of homosexual activity. But even though they do it, they might be shocked to discover that it is indeed homosexual behavior. Most adolescent males in our culture have a strong conscious aversion to and fear of

---

6. Gilbert H. Herdt, *Guardians of the Flutes: Idioms of Masculinity.* New York: McGraw-Hill Book Co., 1980.

homosexuality, even to the point of panic. What they really fear is their own unconscious homosexual interest because it threatens their un-proven heterosexuality and their newly developing masculinity. So they repress their homosexual feelings and project them onto others, calling each other ''queer'' and ''fag.'' They mock each other with gestures and phrases referring to homosexual acts. The mockery appears to accomplish two purposes: (1) to demonstrate publicly a bond of intimacy with other males (to risk teasing in such a dangerous way one must feel close to the other person), because, as we said, teasing among men is the main way to show affection; and (2) openly to ridicule homosexuality so that no one, including themselves, can think they might desire it.

Some adolescents, for various reasons, fail to develop an adequate sense of their masculinity and so they fear their homosexual impulses. Then they try to prove to themselves that they do not have these impulses by taking on an extreme hostility toward homosexuals. There have been documented instances of adolescents in groups searching the streets of San Francisco and engaging in ''queer bashing'' or physically attacking homosexuals, sometimes killing them.

The acquisition of psychological masculinity is shown by the ability not to be threatened by men of different sexual orientations. Since adolescent males have not yet attained their manhood they use ridicule as bravado to hide from their fears that they never will. As they develop into self-confident men they have less need to be unsettled by others' sexual orientations because they feel more secure in their own. Unfortunately, in our culture it is a rare man who is able to develop this kind of security in his masculinity until he is far beyond his adolescent years, often not until he is in his forties. Our culture fails properly to guide and initiate adolescents into manhood so they must do it on their own through trial and error over a period of many years. We will explore this cultural failing in more detail later, but now we'll deal with the next aspect of the transition from boy to man: spirituality.

Spirituality and Initiation into Manhood

Spiritually becoming a man means the establishment of a relationship with his innermost Self and with the divine order. As Jung pointed out, in the personality there exist an innate need for spiritual meaning and a tendency to strive after it, which have resulted in the evolution of the world's great religions on the outer collective level, and in the individuation process on the inner individual level.

People seek spiritual experience because they want a larger perspective on life; they want a sense of greater meaning and to receive a feeling of security and protection in the face of the uncertainties of this transitory life. A spiritual perspective includes the realization of the smallness of the ego personality in relation to the Self (in psychological language), or of the person to God (in theological language). Certain universal human experiences mark the beginnings of a spiritual perspective—for example, looking at the multitude of stars on a clear night and, with a chill running down one's spine, feeling the enormity of the universe in relation to the tiny reality of oneself. The same kind of feeling can be gotten standing in a forest of giant redwood trees. Seeing that a reality greater than oneself exists means a deflating of egocentricity, of the idea that we sail our own ships unaided, and is a necessary reorientation for the personality to become mature.

Our culture makes it harder for boys to become men because we lack ways to give a mature spiritual perspective. Primitive initiation rituals have a spiritual emphasis; they focus on helping the boy have as much respect for the spiritual world as he does for the physical world. They give the boy a spiritual father so he no longer needs to cling to his mother for protection from fears, and so he doesn't need to go into a reaction formation and rebel to prove he isn't in need of her protection. He is given the spiritual tools to become an independent person, but not an egocentric inflated one; he knows his own strength, but he knows it in relation to the much more powerful spiritual world and the Will of God, or of the gods.

In primitive societies, as we said earlier, the transition from being a boy to being a man was made swiftly and was facilitated by initiation rites. While each primitive society had its own specific rites, there are features they all share in common. Typically, as the initiation rite begins, the boy is taken away from the mother's household to a special place set aside only for the men. During the time of his initiation, which may last several days, he is systematically alienated from his family, and after his initiation he is forbidden to return to his mother. The rite itself involves enduring physical pain amounting in many cases to torture, and also psychological pain engendered by the frightening and intimidating nature of the rites. The boy's ability to endure the pain and fear is a hallmark of his readiness to enter into the world of men. His entry into the world of men provides him with a new set of relationships to replace the ones he has severed. He is also initiated into the ''men's mysteries,'' a body of myth and culture known only to the men, and this gives him a new spiritual orientation.

One primitive rite had an interesting conclusion. After the initiation was completed the young man would return to his mother, holding a jar of water. The mother, as prescribed by the ritual, would ask him for a drink. Instead of giving her a drink the young man would throw the water in her face and walk away. This symbolized his new status as a man who is no longer under his mother's authority.

A widespread initiation ritual for young men (and women) among many of the Indians of the American West is known as the Vision Quest. The Sioux Indian Lame Deer described the Vision Quest he undertook at the age of sixteen.[7] The Indian youth had been taken under the tutelage of a medicine man named Old Chest. The rite began with his first experience in the sweat lodge: a cleansing ceremony intended to purge the youth of all impurities. Then Old Chest led him to a sacred spot on a hill where he was to be left in a small cave for four days and four nights without food or water and with only one blanket, made especially for him by his grandmother, to shield him from the chilly night air. It was his first time alone, for Indian children grow up surrounded by a large extended family and a whole village of people. He was frightened, but also full of anticipation, for only ninety-six hours away, at the end of his four-day sojourn on the hillside, he would be a man, and receive a man's name, leaving his childhood name behind. But first he needed his vision; in which there would appear to him a ''Power.'' This Power would mediate to him the Power of Wakan Tanka (the Great Spirit), and be a lifelong connection between himself and Wakan Tanka. Typically this Power would appear in theriomorphic (animal) form.

Alone in the dark, Lame Deer heard only the voices within himself, but eventually he became aware of the overwhelming presence of a great bird in his cramped little hole. He was deeply frightened and cried, but his fear lessened as he realized that the great bird was trying

---

7. *Lame Deer: Seeker of Visions* by John Fire/Lame Deer and Richard Erdoes. New York: Simon & Schuster, 1972, p. 15.

to speak with him. Then it seemed as though he were swept up into the
air with the birds and could look down on the earth, even on the moon
and the stars, and a voice said to him,

> You are sacrificing yourself here to be a medicine man. In time you
> will be one. You will teach other medicine men. We are the fowl
> people, the winged ones, the eagle and the owls. We are a nation
> and you shall be our brother. You will never kill or harm any one
> of us. You are going to understand us whenever you come to seek
> a vision here on this hill. You will learn about herbs and roots, and
> you will heal people. You will ask them for nothing in return. A
> man's life is short. Make yours a worthy one. (p. 15)

After the four days and nights were completed, Old Chest returned
for his spiritual protégé. He gave the boy, now a man, food and water,
and Lame Deer told the medicine man everything that had happened.
Old Chest helped Lame Deer understand his vision and what it meant
for him. Lame Deer concluded his story,

> We Sioux believe that there is something within us that controls us,
> something like a second person almost. We call it *nagi,* what other
> people might call soul, spirit, or essence. One can't see it, feel it or
> taste it, but that time on the hill—and only that once—I knew it was
> there inside of me. Then I felt the power surge through me like a
> flood. I cannot describe it, but it filled all of me. Now I knew for
> sure that I would become a *wicasa wakan,* a medicine man. Again
> I wept, this time with happiness. (p. 16)

This beautiful example of a youth's initiation into manhood tells
us a great deal about the psychological and spiritual needs of the adolescent, and about how the rituals encompassed these needs. The youthful Lame Deer had an older man as his mentor, or spiritual father, but
the man was not his personal father. The role of mentor or spiritual
guide for a youth cannot be filled by the biological father because the
father archetype and the spiritual guide archetype are different. (More
will be said about this in Chapter 8.) The youth experienced both psychological and physical pain, and had to endure his fears and discomfort
for four lonely days and nights. This helped him achieve the vital quality of ego stability that is so essential for a man. The appearance in his
vision of the great bird gave him a connection to a source of spiritual

power. In psychological language, we would say that Lame Deer found in his experience a connection to the Self. Out of this experience he also found the meaning of his life. In his case, it was to become a medicine man and be a healer to others. These factors are crucial for the successful completion of adolescence: the guidance of a wise and experienced man, the achievement of ego stability, the establishment of a connection to his inner Self, and the discovery of the purpose for which he was created.

In our culture such experiences are well-nigh impossible. Our culture does not provide for them, and the necessary religious beliefs that make them possible are lacking. In fact, there is hardly a place where one could go if he did seek such an experience, for the Vision Quest requires that one hear only the sounds of nature. And where can we go today and escape the sound of a machine? Even in the remotest mountains the sound of the airplane intrudes. As someone once said, never before have so few disturbed so many. But the hunger is still there within our youth, even though they themselves do not know it.

Our culture lacks anything like such an initiation rite. Ceremonies such as confirmation or bar mitzvah are all too often only pale vestiges of once living spiritual experiences. Fraternal initiations are awkward and sometimes comical ceremonies that seldom accomplish more than point to an unfulfilled need in the social order.

Partly because we lack a rite-of-passage, adolescence is a dangerous time. The leading causes of death among young men are from accidents and suicides, and the number of suicides appears to be increasing at an alarming rate. Drug addiction is rampant among our youth, and many serious psychological disorders have their onset at this time. Many of the disorders of our youth today can be at least partly attributed to the psychological deprivation they experience because there is no provision in our culture for meeting the deep needs they have. For instance, gangs may exist partly because there appears to be no other container available for some youths. The gangs may also seem to offer positions of responsibility within the context of the gang, and the much needed masculine approval of the older boys. The dangers of gang life may fulfill a need to develop certain masculine virtues that can only be developed by exposure to danger: a gang fight becomes a kind of rite of initiation. Suicides may arise from the inner desperation that can come when one cannot make a vital life transition. Strange religious cults may fulfill, in an ersatz way, the missing spiritual dimension to life. The worshipful adoration of certain leaders of youth, from rock stars to a variety of gurus, may be an attempt to fill the hunger for a spiritual mentor.

In addition to the lack of an initiation rite, there are other social and psychological problems in our culture that contribute to the danger of these years. First, there is no archetype for the kind of prolonged adolescence we have in our American culture. The archetype, among other things, has the function of guiding a person through a life transition or difficulty. The initiation rites that we described, for instance, are expressions of the archetype of transition from boyhood to manhood, but this archetype does not provide for or offer guidance for a prolonged adolescence. As a result, the psyche of a young man is like a ship without a rudder; without the inner guidance of an archetype, adolescence readily becomes a time of confusion and acute psychological difficulty.

Second, we noted the need for the young man to establish ego stability. However, our society tends to withhold from young men the opportunity to assume responsibility, and for the mature work that is necessary if ego stability is to develop. The denial of such opportunities for our young men not only denies them the training ground in which to develop ego stability, it also tends to reinforce their childishness. This was not so in times past. Many of the great men of earlier times began their adult lives by assuming great responsibility at a remarkably early age. For instance, Alexander the Great was only twenty when he ruled the then known Western world. Peter the Great assumed the reins of Czarist Russia at age seventeen. His contemporary and great adversary, Charles XII of Sweden, threw aside the yoke of a regency council that ruled in his stead while he was a child, and officiated as King of Sweden at age fifteen; at age sixteen he was leading Swedish armies on the European continent, and soon brought Swedish power to its greatest height in all its history. William of Orange, later William I of England, was called to command the Dutch armies against the invading French armies of Louis XIV when he was only twenty-one, and had a distinguished military career before then. Such examples, and many more could be added, show the capacity of young men for positions of challenge and responsibility. When an enforced period of dependency ensues instead, psychological development is impaired.

Third, American culture has no viable spiritual emphasis. Our highly materialistic society emphasizes activities that lead to money making and result in material progress. This one-sided perspective sees things spiritual as of merely secondary importance. It is our culturally dominant extraverted thinking and sensing attitude that cannot tolerate contemplation for its own sake, and is not interested in looking inward. Children are not yet contaminated by this materialistic perspective. During childhood there is a heightened receptivity to the spiritual world; the child has not yet developed the ego capability of shutting off this reality. For instance, children have imaginary companions, which is an experience of the archetypes personified. Their dreams can seem more real to them than their waking experience.

Adolescents still retain some of their childhood connection to the spiritual world, but they also have a more developed ego with which to differentiate inner and outer realities. They are not yet completely out of touch with their instinctual craving for spiritual experience. What comes out in adolescence as thrill-seeking and a quest for ecstasy is, at its roots, a spiritual urge. As we said above, youth are sometimes attracted to cults; they may get involved in cults as a way of combining their need for resolution of the identity crisis and their need for spiritual experience. The cult gives them a new identity and tells them what to believe. (The film ''Split Image'' portrays the connection between cults and youth from a psychological point of view.) Young people turn to cults and other forms of non-traditional religious expression because they see traditional organized religions as just another authority, like their parents, against which to rebel.

Fourth, our culture fails to provide people with a legitimate, safe means of spiritual experience. Human beings have an instinctual need to experience altered states of consciousness.[8] Throughout history this natural need has been filled by religion. But now youths look elsewhere for an experience of non-ordinary reality.[9] For example, widespread adolescent drug use is partly an attempt to access a level of reality other than that of the normally perceived world of sense perception. The unconscious longing for initiation into the spiritual world is strong, and the young person hopes via the drugs to enter into another state of consciousness. But where Lame Deer had to purify himself and undergo

---

8. Andrew Weil, *The Natural Mind: A New Way of Looking at Drugs and the Higher Consciousness*. Boston: Houghton Mifflin Publishers, 1972.

9. For problems with modern religions' losing touch with ways of giving spiritual experience, see Morton Kelsey, *Encounter with God: A Theology of Christian Experience*. Minneapolis: Bethany House Publishers, 1972.

psychological and physical rigors, the young man of today who uses drugs for this purpose is passive, and not inwardly ready for a contact with his innermost self.

Drug use is also symptomatic of the adolescent's tendency to linger too long in childish tendencies and regressive longings. He does this partly because there is no test of his manhood, nothing in our culture that initiates and pushes him into adulthood. Unable to find a place in the social order, the young person can express his rebellion against the negative cultural values and conditions by his use of drugs. And when pain or discomfort arises there is always the drug ready at hand to dispel his anxiety or emptiness. If silence threatens to bring the young person into contact with inner realities he is afraid to face, there is the drug ready to shield him from himself. Drug use can weaken and delay the formation of ego stability and hinder maturity by permitting temporary escape from the necessary pain of emotional growth. Safer ways of approaching the spiritual world are available, such as working on one's dreams, but only if a youth has the tenacity to search for them, and is fortunate enough to meet a mentor who is able to help him.

Fifth, in our culture a false picture has emerged of what it is to be a man. The culture's emphasis on crude, macho masculinity as a status symbol causes young men to strive after the wrong type of expression of their masculinity. They think that when they can down a whole six-pack in one sitting, race a car at top speed, or have sex with a large number of women, then they are masculine.

Adolescents who try to mimic this limited image of masculinity often put themselves at risk. For example, in a small middle-class suburb of Los Angeles there are steep hills, one of them having a sharply curving road where young males go to race their motorcycles illegally. The road is notorious for claiming lives because the speeding motorcycles go out of control and go over the edge, crashing into the deep canyons below. This is a pitiful failure at initiation because many of the "initiated" are not alive to enjoy a new status.

One aspect of initiation is to prove that one has the courage to look danger in the face without succumbing to fear. But in primitive initiation rites care is also taken so that the youths are not seriously harmed. Our culture's youth-created "rites," however, are an exaggeration of challenging danger to the point where injury and death are taunted. This is an over-compensation for youth's feeling of powerlessness in a society that does not provide a legitimate means of acquiring the power of manhood early enough. It is also a reaction to the over-protective mothering of American society, which in turn is the result of the absence and abdication of men as guides and initiators of youth. Men don't know how to initiate youths because they weren't initiated themselves. So adolescent males have two bad alternatives when it comes to initiation into manhood: forget about it or try to do it their own way. Their self-styled ''rituals'' seldom truly confer adult status precisely because they are not sanctioned by the larger community. And this in turn leads them to try more outrageous and rebellious acts in an attempt to prove their manhood.

Much of male adolescent rebellion and challenging of adult authority is a misbegotten attempt at self-initiation. Talking back to teachers, putting them down in order to build oneself up in peers' eyes, is rebellion to gain status. If there were other, culturally sanctioned ways of helping boys advance to manhood, much of this rebellion could be eliminated and the jobs of school teachers and parents would be easier. As we have noted, parents and teachers who understand rebellion in the context of attempted initiation don't have to take it personally; they are not being personally attacked, but are seen as symbols of authority that have to be challenged by the youth to make himself feel bigger, older, and more manly.

There are times, of course, when rebellion against unfair adult authority is appropriate, for there is such a thing as ''righteous anger'' that comes directly from the Self. Where there is true social injustice this anger is essential. However, much of today's youthful rebellion does not fall into this category, but is instead a frustrated attempt to prove one's masculinity.

The irony is that excessive rebellion as an attempt to become independent is actually a proof of continued dependency. This is true because in excessive rebellion one does just the reverse of what the authority tells one to do. Whereas an independently-functioning person does what *he* decides to do, the dependent but rebellious person doesn't make up his own mind but bases what he does on what others *don't* want him to do. The truly independent youth does not need to rebel excessively. He knows what he wants, and even if it coincides with what his parents want of him, that will not deter him from it because he is secure in himself. But this kind of security in youth is hard to come by, so we see much compensatory rebellion, the extreme of which may be the punk culture with its ''grossing-out'' behavior and extolling of the polar opposite of acceptable manners and appropriate social behaviors.

Some young men seek initiation by joining the military. This method can accomplish at least part of the goal of initiation: to separate them from family attachments. But the military institution can also become just another mother. Bootcamp can serve as a successful initiation for some men, but for others who are more sensitive it can be a demeaning experience that retards a feeling of self-confident masculinity. Romantic treatments of the military such as Clint Eastwood's ''Heartbreak Ridge'' do not accurately portray the negative effects of the lack of provision for individuality and continued dependency that the military can engender.

Other attempts at initiation are seen when college men join fraternities with the unconscious hope that through ''male-bonding'' they will achieve independent manhood. But too often they find they must simply conform to the collective group identity instead of realizing and exercising their unique individuality. Some of them lose their identity to the group so thoroughly that they become susceptible to group influence to the extent that they do things with the group that are against their morals and they would not do alone, such as ''gang rape'' of women. The influence of the group separates them not only from their identities, but also from their consciences. The occurrence of an action like gang rape, which irrevocably injures a woman emotionally, is a reflection of a culture that fails to provide adequate initiation rituals. Such an act reflects the culture's general devaluation of women, and is an attempt by the men to make themselves feel more like men, and to prove to their comrades that they are indeed men by demonstrating to them, in however unmanly a manner, that they can have sex with a woman.

Some grown men, long since past the period of adolescent initiation, seek weekend initiation experiences with other men. Our culture failed to provide it for them at the appropriate time and they still feel the lack. One writer reported on his experiences at one of these groups, which took place in the woods, where men got into their ''Wildman'' nature by beating drums, chanting, engaging in ritualized wrestling, and sharing their gut feelings with each other.[9a]

Finally, we may note that there is often no social container for our

---

9a. ''Robert Bly Wants to Make a Man of You'' by L.M. Kit Carson, October 1984 issue of *GQ*, Vol. 54, p. 300.

adolescents. For some, college may provide a social container in which they can live a viable life while they mature and ripen, but for many young people this is not possible. It also seems as though college as a container is breaking down in our present era. Many students move from campus to campus; others live off campus for a variety of reasons. The value of the college-age years as a psychological container in which a young man may live while he matures seems pretty well lost today. However, college may still provide youth with a moratorium period during which they do not yet have to make firm commitments to career and identity. They may experiment with clothing styles or growing a beard, and this can be done without the liabilities they would face as full-fledged adults out in society. The identity of "college student" is more flexible than, say, "insurance salesman." This period of relative freedom from commitment can be useful for experimentation with different majors and for trying out various part-time jobs, internships, and volunteer positions. Since, in college, a young man is living with peers, he has the chance to socialize on a large scale. Even if he is an introvert, he will find ample opportunity to meet new people in casual circumstances. Social life is such a big part of college, however, that the young man may neglect his studies in favor of socializing.

In fact, the only container for many adolescents is the company of others like themselves. We noted earlier that young magpies flock together for a brief time until they pair off and live like the other adult magpies. We could say that the "flocking time" for our young men goes on too long. This creates too much peer pressure among our young people, and tends to exclude positive adult influences from reaching them.

These factors, and others as well, mitigate against the prompt achievement by our young men of both psychological maturity and economic independence, and so hinder the successful transition from boyhood to manhood that is the task of the adolescent.

Parenting of the Adolescent

For parents, the adolescent period of the lives of their son may be a frightening and difficult time. The young man will swing back and forth from childish to mature behavior. The parents will still have many legal and financial responsibilities, as well as social expectations from the surrounding community, but less and less control or influence. The young man must turn away from the influence of the parents in order to find himself, even if this means making mistakes. Because the peer influence is so strong and lasts for so long, the influence of the parents is increasingly diminished.

Complicating the picture is the fact that parents of adolescents are usually going through their own midlife transitions. They may be struggling with career and relationship changes. They are reluctantly having to accept an identity of ''middle-aged'' in a society that prizes youth. They are probably having to deal with the problems of their own aging parents. They may be going through a ''second adolescence'' themselves, in which they attempt to live out those aspects of life they have neglected because of career and family commitments. Both adolescence and midlife mean an increased narcissistic concern. Parents' own problems and conflicts can preoccupy their energies to the point where it feels like just too much for them to have to deal with the problems of their son.

However, because the parents are still partly responsible for the young man they may have to make decisions about the life he is to lead. Often the parent will find there are no ''good'' decisions, only a choice of decisions all of which will be more or less unsatisfactory. Sometimes all the parent can do is to work on his or her own inner development. The more the parent understands himself or herself, the more the parent exerts an invisible, psychological, and positive influence on the adolescent. In our extraverted culture, where we believe in ''doing things'' and ''taking action,'' it is hard for a parent to realize that *who* he or she is as a person may be of more importance for the adolescent than what he or she does.

It is also important for parents to see the reality of their son as he is, as opposed to their idea of how he should be. For example, one father who was a professional man had difficulty accepting the fact that his son wanted to become an automobile mechanic. His son was naturally gifted at working on cars and loved it; he had no intention of going to college and following in his father's footsteps. Father and son were growing distant from each other until the father finally was able to accept his son for the person he was.

Precisely because we have no established rite of transition, parents may also find they are experiencing an undue amount of rejection from their son. In a primitive initiation ritual we mentioned earlier the young man could throw water in his mother's face; since it was prescribed by the ritual the mother did not have to take it personally. In our culture, a young man may symbolically by his actions and words "throw water in his mother's face" for a period of several years.

It takes all of a parent's wisdom to realize that such actions may be part of a deep need within the young man to separate from his mother and find himself, and the actions are not because he dislikes her personally or because she has not been an adequate mother. The adolescent's rejecting acts have an archetypal reality and an inner necessity. By definition the son cannot be tactful about this rejection of the parent's way. He will bristle with surly defensiveness as a compensation because he feels so little power in himself. He may go overboard with his rebellion, like Parsifal in the legend of the search for the Holy Grail, who captures the Red Knight's huge horse, leaps atop it and gallops away, but he doesn't know how to stop it and so rides all day.[10]

But parents do not need to feel they should continually submit passively to having "water thrown in their faces" either. In fact, if they allow him to humiliate them it defeats the purpose of his rebellion. It's not much of a rebellion if they just give in all the time. He needs something to fight against, and their rules and regulations, such as a reasonable curfew and completion of homework before going out, are good targets. Some rebellion is designed to test whether the parents really care enough to stop it. This rebellion may be a cry for help from an adolescent who is not able to control his own impulses and wants help from his parents but is too embarrassed to ask directly for it. For example, an adolescent son in one family was getting bad grades at an exclusive private school, not because he wasn't bright enough, but because he was failing to do his homework. At first the parents took a *laissez faire* approach, hoping to help him grow up by allowing him to experience the unpleasantness of failure. But it didn't work; after he failed he felt depressed and this further reduced his motivation. So the parents became firm and wouldn't allow him to watch TV or to use his computer or the telephone until he had finished his homework to their satisfaction. He put up a tremendous fuss, accusing them of treating him like a baby. But he did his homework and his grades improved. He felt better about himself; perhaps he was not so depressed because he was able to express his anger directly in arguing against his parents' rules instead of turning his anger inward against himself. Of course he

---

10. Robert Johnson, *HE!* King of Prussia, Pa.: Religious Publishing Co., 1974, p. 29, now published by Harper & Row, San Francisco, 1983.

never admitted to them that they helped him by setting limits and sticking to them. But it was clear that it was what helped him. Parents cannot expect to receive awards of appreciation or even slight recognition from their adolescent. They must have the courage to do what they think is best, based on who their adolescent is and their honest inspection of their own motives as being for his best interest.

Adolescence and the Journey Toward Wholeness

Jung once said that the journey toward wholeness that he called individuation was for the second half of life, that the first half of life called for a young man to find a place in the world, to deal with outer reality. This is only partly true. The other part of the truth is that a young man may not be able to deal with the world if he does not have a connection to his innermost Self. For some young men this inner contact needs to be made at the beginning of adult life. While a rite such as the Vision Quest is no longer available, some young men may benefit by the right kind of analysis. The analyst then fulfills the role of spiritual mentor, and the young man's dreams help establish a connection to the Self. Such a process does not take a young person away from the demands of life, but helps him fulfill those demands. Analysis can help fortify his ego so he can deal effectively with both the world within and the outer world; he can receive aid from the unconscious in the living of his outer life. Analysis can also be an initiatory experience; it may be modern-day technological society's equivalent of the Vision Quest.

From what we have said it may appear that adolescence is a time of painful struggle; this is basically true. But it can also be a time of joyful living, of emerging potentialities, and of a life that is increasingly adult but not yet over-burdened with adult responsibilities. It can also be a time of life when important psychological and spiritual experiences take place spontaneously.

The experience of the anima, for instance, first comes up in a man's adolescence, and her original appearance is apt to have a kind of pristine purity to it. The "anima," as we will see later, is a word that refers to a man's inner feminine, soul-like quality. Typically, the anima is first experienced in an expressed or unexpressed love affair with a young woman. Ask a man who was the first girl with whom he was in love, and he will likely get a strange faraway look in his eyes, a gentle smile will cross his face, and, sure enough, he can tell you who was the first object of his eros and admiration—this even though the girl herself may never have been aware that in this youth's inner life she was for the time being the carrier for him of extraordinarily beautiful qualities and feelings. Later, when his eros is clouded over by all kinds of egocentric desires and goals, such a pristine experience may not be possible.

One man described his beautiful yet painful first love experience as follows:

> I was fourteen years old and I reluctantly accompanied my parents on a week-long vacation to a lake a few hours from our home. I separated myself from them as soon as we got there, going down to the lake for an afternoon of diving from a diving board set up on a raft out in the lake. On my way back to my parents' trailer I heard a sweet voice behind me say, "I saw you diving; you're sure a good diver."
>
> I looked around to see a pretty young girl, about sixteen years old, smiling at me. We walked together along the path and she continued her flattery, which I lapped up. She asked me if I wanted to go to a party with her that evening at the Lake Clubhouse. I told her yes.
>
> It was a warm summer evening and as the sun was setting in the west and the full moon was rising in the east, I went to her trailer to pick her up. She met me in front of it and reached out to hold my hand. We walked down towards the lake, but not in the direction of the clubhouse. We sat on a rock and watched the moon rise and reflect off of the lake. She looked pretty before but now she became beautiful. But as time passed I asked if she thought we'd be late for the party. She said there really wasn't any party, as she leaned close and kissed me on the mouth. My heartbeat doubled. I couldn't believe how great I felt. We spent the rest of the week in almost constant companionship. Nothing more than kissing happened, but for the first time in my life I was in love.
>
> At the end of the week we said goodbye. I asked for her address so I could write to her, but instead she said she'd write to me; so I gave her my address. I should have suspected something was wrong right then.
>
> I couldn't eat for days. My parents thought I had contracted some strange bug from swallowing too much lake water. When I got home I went to the mailbox every day to look for a letter from my love. But no letter came. Then I began to realize that maybe I

was the one who was in love and not she. I remembered her talking about another guy and realized I was just a passing fling, a way for her to pass a boring week with her grandmother at the lake. I was wounded to the core. I felt as bad as I had felt good before. It was my initiation into the pleasures and pains of love. When later as a young man I read about Parsifal (in *HE!* by Robert Johnson) coming into Blanche Fleur's tent and thinking the table was set for him when actually it was for her husband, I knew how Parsifal must have felt!

Some adolescents also remember brief quasi-visionary experiences of an enormous beauty and wholeness. They may come in unexpected times, or in dreams that leave the youth filled with a sense of incredible beauty and peace. Later, under the duress of life, with the dismantling of childhood's purity, and with the onset of his egocentric strivings, even the memory of this experience may be well-nigh forgotten. But it is still there, and lives on within him as a kind of inspiration but also as a kind of wound. Robert Johnson has this to say of such an experience: "A boy in his early adolescence touches something of the Christ nature within himself, but he touches it too soon, is only wounded by it, and drops it."[11] Such an experience, and the woundedness that comes from it, may later in life supply the hidden impetus for that longing that comes up in a man to be at one with his soul.

Summary

In summary, adolescence is a period of great change in the personality. It is a period of trial and initiation into manhood, whether the culture provides for it or not. It is a time when a sense of oneself as a man is formed that will have to last a lifetime. Out of the limbo world of adolescence a man is supposed to emerge. Many men do not feel adequately initiated into manhood and never do feel in possession of their masculinity. They feel passive when they need to be assertive; they are unable to say with certainty what they want out of life; they make choices then second-guess themselves; they oscillate between weakness and macho brutality; they feel such a lack in their masculinity that, as we said in the introduction, it amounts to a national crisis.

---

11. Ibid., p. 10.

Macho masculinity arose out of men's need to compensate for feelings of inferiority about their masculinity. Since they never became initiated they feel they must repeatedly prove themselves as men. And these problems basically begin during adolescence.

Initiation is more difficult in contemporary society because it needs to occur in education, profession, and relationships with the opposite sex. This is complex because occupations take years of training and education, and the opposite sex has different expectations of a man now than it did twenty or even ten years ago.

In his quest for manhood a youth receives little help from other men, most of whom are competitive with him. He can't accept much help from his parents because he is trying to establish an identity separate from them. Analysis may work as a modern form of initiation for the youth who is open to it, more likely the introverted intuitive or feeling-oriented type of youth. But for the sensing type more concrete experiences may be necessary. (See Appendix A for a description of these types.) For some, sports may work, and, for others, intellectual pursuits. But for each adolescent who is trying psychologically to develop into a man, something initiatory is needed, and it is important for him to seek and find it in a culture that does not automatically offer it to him.

Suggested Reading

Erikson, Erik H., *Childhood and Society*. New York: W. W. Norton and Co., Inc. Second Edition, 1963.

————*Identity: Youth and Crisis*. New York: W. W. Norton and Co., Inc., 1968.

John Fire/Lame Deer and Richard Erdoes, *Lame Deer—Seeker of Visions*. New York: Simon and Schuster, 1972.

Johnson, Robert A., *He!* King of Prussia, Pa.: Religious Publishing Co., 1974.

Muuss, Rold E., *Theories of Adolescence*. New York: Random House, 1975.

Neihardt, John G., *Black Elk Speaks*. Lincoln, Neb.: University of Nebraska Press, 1961.

Chapter 3

The Tyranny of the Ego

We noted in the first chapter that by the time a boy becomes a man a shell has been built around his ego which, to a greater or lesser extent, cuts him off from that innermost core of his personality that Jung called the Self. Our personalities have two centers: the lesser center of the ego, which can be thought of as roughly equivalent to the center of the conscious personality, and the greater Center, the Self, which embraces our total personality, both conscious and unconscious. Ideally speaking the two centers should be closely related. Then the power and energy of the Self flows into and through the ego, bringing about the fulfillment of both ego and Self in a life that is creatively lived and fulfilled. The sad fact is, however, that although at birth there is a natural relationship between ego and Self, by the time the boy has reached maturity this natural relationship is lost. In its place is an isolated ego that is more or less entirely cut off from the Self.

While the life that is lived from the Self is positive and fulfilling, the life that is lived from the ego alone is negative and uncreative. When the ego tries to "go it alone" in life, with no relationship to its greater Center, the Self, we say that it is "egocentric." Because of the negative consequences of the egocentric ego we can speak of the "tyranny of the ego."

In this chapter we will describe the creative life of the Self and contrast it with the negative life that is lived by the isolated ego. We will see how and why this psychological state of affairs came about, and will describe some different patterns of egocentricity. We will also have a few things to say about how the original relationship of ego to Self can be restored, although for the most part this issue will be taken up later.

Our mentor in this chapter will be Fritz Kunkel. Kunkel followed Jung's lead when it came to an understanding of the archetypes of the collective unconscious. However, Kunkel felt that it was as important to explore and understand the workings of the ego as it was to understand the unconscious. In his many books Kunkel explored the structure of the ego and the origins and nature of egocentricity. Kunkel's writings went out of print not long after his death in 1956, but the most important of them were republished in 1984 by Paulist Press. In this section I will follow Kunkel's thought closely and in many cases will use some of his actual wording. The reader who is interested in Kunkel's own, much more detailed presentation is referred to the book *Fritz Kunkel: Selected Writings.* [1]

Kunkel believed that the essential quality of the Self is its creativity and that a life lived from the Self is first and foremost a creative life. Even when we are not aware of it, this creativity works in the innermost center of our being. It does not cease even when we are asleep; its creativity manifests itself in the extraordinary inventiveness and profundity of our dreams. To say that the Self is creative must be taken in a broad sense. It does not mean that we must all paint pictures or play musical instruments, unless, of course, we are meant to become creative artists or capable musicians. What it means is that our lives themselves are to become works of art and that we are to be capable of making creative responses to the many difficult and perplexing problems and situations that life will bring to us. The kind of creative life we lead will be different for each one of us, for the Self, being ceaselessly creative, never expresses itself in the same way twice.

The Self wants to be lived, and it hungers for those experiences that will enable it to be lived creatively. When the Self is not being lived and is denied those experiences, its creativity may turn negative and the inner powers become destructive. The experiences we need in order that this creativity can be expressed will be those that call forth our hitherto unused talents, abilities, courage, love, and potential, in whatever way is uniquely appropriate for us as individuals.

A life lived from the Self has intensity. It makes life alive, significant, and colorful. Even if things are going badly the Self can endow our experiences with a sense of the presence of something of immediate value. In fact, it is often when we are under pressure from the difficult experiences of life that the Self is felt most keenly, and its creative energies emerge most splendidly. This is why it is under duress that people achieve the heroic, for when the ego is in touch with the Self, it is always capable of making a creative ego response to even the most difficult of circumstances. No matter how bad the outer circumstances of life they cannot cut us off from the Self; only our hidden egocentricity and inner divisions can do that.

---

1. *Fritz Kunkel: Selected Writings,* ed. and with a commentary by John A. Sanford. New York: Paulist Press, 1984.

Precisely because the Self is creative it can never be made into an object. We cannot predict how the Self will act because it is creative and therefore unpredictable. We cannot contain the Self in any box built of words because it will not be contained in our conceptual formulations. If we try to possess it, it will elude us. If we try to calculate how it will react, it acts in a way that is not calculable. If we try to say "it is always this way or that way" it will contradict our expectations. If we try to harness it to goals of personal power, it will leave us. In short, we cannot manipulate the Self to our egocentric advantage.

Even though we usually say that the Self is "within us," in the final analysis it cannot be located. It is *within* us as the core of our being, but it is also *among* us as the creative element and function in relationships between and among people. When it appears in this way it brings the capacity to love other people—for who they are, not for who we want them to be. For out of the Self there pours something akin to divine love.

The Self is like God's creative energy at work in us, and a sense of the Self at work within us and within our lives is like a sense of God's presence. To do the will of the Self is, experientially speaking, the same as doing the Will of God. However, living from the Self may have little or nothing to do with our consciously espoused theological beliefs. What matters is the relationship that exists between the ego, as the center of our conscious personality, and the Self, as the Center of our total personality.

The Self is always genuine, and because it is always genuine we may sometimes refer to it as the "Real Self" in order to distinguish its life clearly from that of the ego which, to the extent it is egocentric, is a sham.

The Nature of the Egocentric Ego

In contrast to a life that is lived from the Self, a life that is lived from the ego alone is cramped and narrow. As mentioned, when the ego lives out of itself alone we say that it is egocentric. What follows is a brief description of the general nature of egocentricity and the way it distorts our life. But some words of caution are in order. First, what follows are general statements. Each individual is a separate and unique case. One limitation of psychology is that it must talk in generalities when in actual life each person is a unique example. No two people are ever exactly alike in either their creative or their egocentric qualities. However, it must be said that egocentric patterns are far more stereotyped than the genuine qualities of the Self. We are very much like others in the way we are egocentric, but unique in our Selfhood.

Second, it must be remembered that no one is completely egocentric. We are all of us at any given time a mixture of egocentric qualities and attributes of the Real Self. Sometimes we vacillate between one set of qualities and the other, even in the course of a single day. In a crisis, for instance, we may find ourselves acting heroically from the Real Self; later we may collapse into our egocentric fears. Some people may be almost completely encapsulated in their egocentricity, others relatively free of egocentricity. The reader must keep all this in mind as he reads what follows, for we are forced to write in generalities and cannot keep mentioning all the innumerable exceptions.

Third, the reader will note that egocentricity is identified with a form of evil. But some egocentric people bring about far more evil than others. One person's form of egocentricity may lead him to inflict on others great evil—we can take Adolf Hitler as an example. Another person's evil may seem mild in comparison; for instance, he may not so much originate evil as simply go along with it. Still another may seem more the victim of evil than its originator. Nevertheless, to the extent that we go along with evil, or in one way or another give the lie to life, we participate to some degree in evil. For all egocentricity, in the last analysis, is a betrayal of the creative potential within us and therefore of life's purposes.

It is also worth noting that everything said in this chapter is as descriptive of women as it is of men. There is some reason to believe that egocentric patterns in women may be somewhat different than they are in men, and we will note examples of this further on in this chapter, but men do not have a corner on egocentricity.

Finally, it must be understood that the negative qualities ascribed in the pages that follow pertain to the ego in its egocentric manifestation only. The ego in its proper function as the representative of the Self is a noble and essential aspect of the psyche. It is only when it fails to be what it is meant and created to be that it must be described in negative terms.

The difference between the creative life of the Self and the narrow life of the ego can be represented in the following diagrams:

Diagram No. 1:
The ego and Self in
harmonious relationship

Diagram No. 2:
The ego isolated from a
relationship with the Self

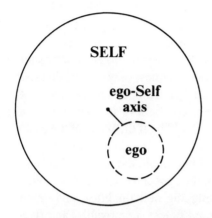

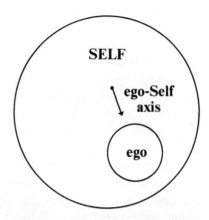

In Diagram No. 1, the Self is represented by both the dot at the center of the circle and by the circle itself. Of course all such schematic illustrations are only the crudest possible representations of psychological realities that would require many pages to describe. The smaller circle represents the ego, and the fact that its circle is composed of a partly broken line denotes the fact that the ego in this instance is open to the influences emanating from the Self. The flow of influences from the Self to the ego and back again is represented by the line connecting the center of the circle with the ego's circle and is called the ego-Self axis.

In Diagram No. 2, it will be noted that the ego's circle is a heavy, solid line. This indicates that the ego is not open to the influences of the Self but lives completely within the small circle surrounded by the heavy line. For this reason the influences from the Self do not reach the ego; consequently the ego-Self axis line is blocked, as indicated in the diagram.

Egocentricity may be defined as a state in which a person is concerned only with his own defense and the fulfillment of his own ambitions, which ambitions, on close scrutiny, turn out to be closely tied to his defenses.

Imagine yourself living within the walls of a castle. These walls are so high and so thick that you cannot see over them or through them. Moreover, the gate, while it exists, is bolted shut for fear of real or imagined enemies. So great is this fear that the gates are never opened. In fact you have lived within the castle so long that you have all but forgotten there is any world beyond it; you think all of your world is the small portion of it contained within the castle walls. These walls are your defense; you think of them that way, and you guard them and maintain them carefully. You do not realize, however, that these same walls have become your prison. While they seem to protect you by shutting out what you suppose are dangerous enemies, they have in fact shut you in. As a result your life is exceedingly cramped and narrow, but, since it is the only life you remember, you believe it is the norm and have no idea how expansive your life would be if the walls of the castle were torn down.

The image of the castle gives us clues about the nature of the egocentric ego. Like the walls of a castle, the egocentric ego is rigid. While the Self is constantly changing, displaying new qualities, and developing, the egocentric ego is like a rigid object, unmovable, and fixed in one place. Because it is rigid the egocentric ego resists time, aging, and anything that requires it to make a new adaptation to life. Because of its rigidity, creative responses to life situations are impossible. The creative forces are thus suppressed and turn negative; they begin to cry out from within for deliverance and become an enemy to the ego, rather than an ally.

The egocentric ego lives under a more or less constant sense of threat and pressure. Of course there are times when we are confronted by a genuine danger, and a sense of fear is an instinctive warning and protection. But the egocentric ego lives with a chronic sense of apprehension. Sometimes this fear is a "floating" anxiety, a constant sense of apprehension that is not attached to any particular object or situation. More often the fear is projected outside of us. Outer situations that are threatening or troublesome loom much larger than is necessary because our egocentricity makes it impossible for us to find the creative and courageous response to them. Frequently the fears create their own real or imagined threats. For instance, we may live with an obsessive fear that we have cancer, or a paralyzing fear of meeting other people, or an exaggerated fear of the communists taking over. There are a thousand and one forms that the fears may take, but the common denominator to them all is the inability of the rigid egocentric ego to make a creative response. Life within the castle is a fearful life, even though the walls are high and rigid.

Even though on a conscious level our fears may focus on real or imagined outer threats, the real threat to our egocentric ego comes from within: the inner powers and figures of the unconscious that have been alienated by our rigid psychological stance. We have already mentioned that the creative energies of the Self, when denied, turn dark and destructive. The creative powers of God can become the dark side of God, which seeks to tear down that which is not fit to exist, in this case, the egocentricity of our ego. The defensive posture of the egocentric ego extends to the inner world as well as the outer world. All emotions, desires, thoughts, and urges that come from within ourselves, that would, if allowed into consciousness, destroy our defensive patterns and threaten our conscious image of ourselves, must be fought against. In denying these inner powers, a great deal of psychic energy is lost to us, leaving the ego more impoverished than ever.

One of the most important of the inner figures that may threaten us from within is the shadow. The shadow consists of all those qualities in our personality that could have become part of our ego but have been denied because, if admitted into consciousness, they would dismantle our egocentricity. Later we will look at some examples of how the shadow threatens to overthrow the status quo of the egocentric ego; this will help us see why the shadow is feared, even though it actually contains highly positive attributes of the personality.

Because the egocentric ego fears the inner forces, it is inevitably extraverted. It must look only to the outside; it cannot afford to look within, for there it would find all those realities of its true Self that contradict its egocentric pattern and therefore are feared and rejected. By looking within, the egocentric ego would see that it is not an independent reality after all, as it has long supposed, but must subordinate itself to a much greater reality: that of the Self. This is one reason why serious introspection, even psychology itself, is so much disparaged in our extraverted culture. Nevertheless, we are often compelled against our will to look within. The unconscious wants us to look within so much that it forces us toward introspection. But when this introspection is resisted, and when it is unenlightened and therefore does not lead to insight, it becomes morbid.

The egocentric ego has a special relationship to both joy and suffering. Sometimes it feels a kind of joy, but it is a false joy, springing from a life situation that is temporarily going the way our egocentric goals want it to go. After the defeat of the French in World War II the

Germans signed a peace treaty in the same place where they had signed the humiliating Treaty of Versailles in 1919. There is a famous photograph of Adolf Hitler at the scene of the signing of the new peace treaty with the humiliated French in which he is dancing a little jig of joy. This was an egocentric joy which, as is always the case with such joys, did not last long. But even when things are going the way the egocentric ego wants them to go and it feels what it supposes to be joy or satisfaction, there is a nagging conscience somewhere within, and a fear that has only been temporarily covered over by the ego's successes.

As for suffering, the egocentric ego does its best to avoid it, yet it is constantly bringing suffering on itself. An egocentric person usually suffers a great deal; it is not feigned, but genuine, but it leads nowhere because the egocentric ego uses suffering for its own purposes. Suffering can purge and cleanse the soul when its burden is carried manfully. But the egocentric ego uses suffering to manipulate others, to get its own way, to glorify itself, or as a means of indulging in self-pity. This perpetuates the suffering and prevents it from cleansing the soul.

The egocentric ego is prone to certain destructive emotions and symptoms. One of these is inhibition. Since the egocentric ego lives within the castle-like walls of its defenses, the range of its life is limited. This results in a kind of psychological cramp, with resulting inhibitions of the free flow of life. We may be subject to sexual inhibitions, social inhibitions, or inhibitions of our creative life. These inhibitions will be experienced as a source of pain and perhaps humiliation.

The person who is egocentric is incapable of love because he will see other people only in terms of whether they support or are threatening to his egocentric posture. The capacity for genuine love comes from the Self, and flows through a person who has freed himself from his egocentricity.

The egocentric ego is prone to rage. A distinction needs to be drawn between creative anger and egocentric rage. Creative anger is the healthy response from the Self to an intolerable situation. When something takes place that is simply unacceptable to the human spirit, anger is a healthy response. Jesus' casting out the money-changers in the temple is an example. This kind of anger is under our control and can be constructively directed. Egocentric rage is different. It is constellated when some event or some person exposes or threatens our egocentric defenses. The resulting rage is not under our control but controls us and is invariably destructive.

The egocentric ego tends to have either little or no operative moral instinct, or a morbid and exaggerated one. The capacity to accept genuine guilt and moral responsibility comes from the Self, which endows us with a healthy moral instinct. While painful, the acceptance of any guilt for which we are responsible does not, in the long run, make us neurotic. To the contrary, it will be a painful but freeing experience. To live without any feeling of guilt, however, is an inflation of the ego, and a sign that we are cut off from those healthy concerns for the welfare and opinions of our fellow human beings that are aspects of the Self. It is equally egocentric, however, to live with an exaggerated or false sense of guilt. The ego is also inflated if it assumes too much guilt for itself. To be guilty, for instance, of the unforgivable sin of which the Bible speaks is to assume for ourselves a position of inordinate importance. The church, in its zeal to curb the human tendency to inflation, has prescribed a load of guilt and self-blame that may for many people be an overdose. Chronic self-condemnation keeps the old ego alive when it should be allowed to die so a new one can emerge. The truth is that egocentricity may be shrewdly concealed in the guise of an exaggerated or false humility.

Indeed, cleverness is one of the hallmarks of the egocentric ego. It can conceal its egocentric tendencies and motives under all sorts of disguises. We can pose as a great saint and fool others—and ourselves—and yet it may be nothing more than a way to hide from others what we are really all about. Shakespeare, one of the great psychologists of all time, knew this. In *Richard III,* the king says of himself:

> And thus I clothe my naked villainy
> With odd old ends stol'n forth of holy writ,
> And seem a saint when most I play the devil.
> (Act I, Scene 3)

Because of its cleverness the egocentric ego is a great cheat. It cheats on life and it cheats on the Self. It can master conceptually the best prescripts of religion and psychology in such a way that others are impressed, and can, in fact, be cheating God and life all the time. The egocentric ego is for this reason a master of lies and self-deception, a veritable devil, which, if not the originator of evil, at least readily becomes its ally.

But the ego pays a heavy price for its egocentricity in the form of anxiety, depression, and loneliness. Because the egocentric ego lives under a constant sense of threat, it lives with constant anxiety. Kunkel noted that while anxiety increases the intensity of life it diminishes its scope. This is because anxiety comes, as we have seen, from a Self that is turned against us. Kunkel defined anxiety as the opposite of creativity. It is as though the forces of creation flow in the opposite direction: instead of being like a centrifugal force, flowing outward, it becomes a centripetal force, flowing inward. Thus while consciousness becomes keener its contents disappear. Anxiety can also be likened to the forces of the Self trying to batter down the walls of the ego. The Self has been made into an enemy, and consequently it is greatly feared.

Depression is a frequent symptom of the egocentric ego. There are many reasons for depression. Sometimes it has a somatic, neuro-chemical or congenital basis. Sometimes it alternates naturally with the flow of creative energy. Sometimes it has a healing effect, seeking to bring us down into ourselves so we can reconnect with our innermost depths. But sometimes a chronic feeling of depression is a consequence of our egocentricity. Cut off from the Self, the ego receives little psychic energy. While the ego can learn to function on a remarkably small amount of psychic energy, it cannot do so without feeling depressed. Many people are so used to functioning with little energy that they think this is their normal state. They do not realize the creative energies that lie within them.

Loneliness comes because the egocentric person lacks for real companions. As we have noted, to the extent that we are egocentric we are not able to love other people. Thus egocentricity isolates us from genuine human warmth. Even when egocentric people band together in groups for mutual ego support—Kunkel called such groups the "Associated Egos"—there is no genuine caring among them. Since most egocentric people are boring and demanding, other people tend to shun them. Small wonder they are lonely. But egocentric people also lack inner companions because they are cut off from the creativity of the Self. A creative person can be alone and not be lonely because inner companions emerge in the form of creative musings, interesting thoughts, unusual perceptions, and energizing fantasies, but the egocentric person is locked up inside the sterility of his isolated ego.

The Origins of Egocentricity

The question before us now is: How did it get to be this way? We begin with the premise that the newborn child is not egocentric, but is naturally trustful and instinctually related to the Self. We are not meant to be egocentric. It is a deviation from our true nature, and the evils that it engenders are not at the core of our being. However, egocentricity can easily be brought about by destructive influences on the newborn child, perhaps even in certain cases by prenatal influences. Foremost among these influences are the egocentric aspects of the parents or parent substitutes. But we must also include the negative aspects of other people who are important in the life of the child: his educators, his extended family, indeed the social order itself into which he is born with its false values and injustices.

For cultures also are egocentric. For example, communism, seeing the exploitive, egocentric qualities of a capitalistic culture, tried to eliminate it with the ideal of a classless society. However, since society is composed of innumerable egocentric people, communist societies prove in practice to be as egocentric as capitalistic societies. It seems that social engineering can never root out sins that are rooted in our human nature. However, for the sake of brevity we will not emphasize the social side of egocentricity but will consider primarily the influences on the child that come from the parents.

The destructive influences on the child that force him into an egocentric posture may stem from parents who are basically well-intentioned or from parents who are actually malicious. Even parents who fundamentally love their children will have enough egocentricity of their own that their love will be incomplete and will lack sufficient wisdom. Our love inevitably tends either to pamper our children or to be too strict. We tend to be either too permissive or too demanding, to let the child run too free or make the child conform more than is necessary for the child's social development, to ignore the child too much or place on the child our own egocentric ambitions. Well-intentioned parents may also encourage the child to adopt certain egocentric attitudes in the mistaken belief that only such attitudes will enable him to succeed in this egocentric civilization in which we live. So the parent may urge the child to be at the top of his class, to strive too much for recognition, to demand that the child get into the right school, admonishing him that only the very best school will guarantee success in this world of money, status, and power. By subscribing to the false values of our civilization, and encouraging or demanding that the child subscribe to them also, we encourage egocentric rather than creative adaptations to life.

The influence of the parents is especially pronounced in our culture because of the relative isolation in which parents and children live. In primitive societies the whole tribe acted as a kind of parent for all of the children in the tribe. In the morning a child would emerge from lodge or tipi to be greeted by a wide world of relationships. But in our culture we have something called the nuclear family. Children and parents live together in a tightly knit, often confined relationship. Inevitably, even with the most loving parents, the time will come when an impatient mother or father breaks the natural trustfulness of the child and pushes the child into an egocentric posture.

Let us say, for instance, that it is the end of a hard week for your mother and father, and they have gone out to dinner, leaving you and your little sister with the baby-sitter. Unfortunately, the dinner did not go well; the service was slow, the dinner was cold, and when they return home neither mother nor father is in a good frame of mind. They send the baby-sitter home and come into the living room where you and your sister are playing. The truth is, they really need to be alone; they have little energy left for the demanding task of being a parent. It so happens that just before they enter the room little sister reaches over and grabs your favorite truck, the one with which you were about to play. Angry at this theft of what is rightfully yours, you pull her hair to make her give it back, which sends her into paroxysms of pain and anger—and at this precise moment mother and father come into the room. They did not see the provocation that led to this attack on your little sister; all they saw was an older and stronger brother making his little sister cry. Too tired and upset to ask questions, your parents scold you and send you off to your room. They are angry and your father doesn't come up to read you a story as usual, and your mother doesn't come to say good-night. Alone in your room you feel rejected, isolated, and unworthy of your parents' love. You also feel hateful toward your little sister, who is a born actress, and got off scot-free in the incident thanks to her skill at crying at the right moment and with the right volume.

It was not your fault that all of this happened but nevertheless you feel unlovable. In your mind, if your parents hate and reject you it's because you are an unlovable person. At this point you begin to reject yourself. You also come to believe that your anger is an enemy. You don't ever want to be isolated and rejected like this again, and it was your anger that got you into trouble. "Angry-self" has to go; in his place must come Compliant-self. So you are split. You become seemingly compliant, anxious to please, even ingratiating; the angry part of you goes underground, that is, into the unconscious, where it becomes part of that secondary personality within us that we call the shadow. The incident deepened the breach between your conscious personality and your natural wholeness, or Self. Your means of coping with this situation is to defend yourself against further injuries of this kind by adopting a conscious personality that is not really you, at the price of cutting off a part of yourself, your capacity for righteous anger, which is basically healthy and is something you will need as life goes on.

Multiply such an incident by a hundred, or even a thousand, and we can see how the child loses a relationship with the Self and is forced into an egocentric posture. Alice Miller, in her several books,* does a masterful job of telling us about such childhood tragedies. She helps us understand how parents and others, in ways that are sometimes subtle and sometimes overtly brutal, injure the child and force the child to develop defensive ego postures that split him and bring about a loss of contact with the Self.

The inevitable formation of our egocentricity is a tragedy of life. But the tragedy is complicated by the fact that when we reach adult years we pass on our egocentricity to others. We begin life as the victim of evil; we wind up being its perpetrators. For this reason the Bible is psychologically correct when it says that the sins of the fathers are visited upon the children from generation to generation (cf. Ex 20:5, KJV). For by the time we reach adulthood our egocentric ego, sham though it is, has become so firmly entrenched that it is now our cherished possession. In fact, we think this sham ego of ours *is* our true nature. We have come to rely on it with all of its machinations, cleverness, or brutality, in order to make our way through a dangerous world. We cannot imagine what we would be like without it. Therefore we expend a great deal of effort maintaining it, even though this means that we will have to inflict our egocentricity on others in order to do so. Our efforts to maintain, protect, defend, and perpetuate our egocentric ego will, even under the best of circumstances, become demonic, for, as we have seen, our egocentric ego is a sham, and the creative forces

*See suggested readings.

of the Self, unable to be expressed because they are blocked by the ego-centric ego, turn dark and destructive. It is as though our egocentricity puts a tragic and destructive twist in us that goes through our whole personality.

Fortunately, all will not be lost. Only in severe cases will the loss of contact with the Self be complete. Most of us will sometimes operate out of our egocentricity and sometimes, or at least occasionally, from the Real Self. When the latter happens we will be genuine, capable of creative responses to life, and able to love others. The extent to which we will remain in some kind of contact with the Real Self will depend on how early in life, and how violently, the loss of contact with the Self took place. If a child is exposed to exceedingly destructive treatment very early in life, that child will very likely be forced into a more or less complete loss of contact with the Self as an adult. For most of us, fortunately, the break is not that complete.

The Four Types of Egocentricity

As mentioned earlier, a drawback in discussing psychology is that one must speak in generalities, but people are individuals. Each person is a unique mixture of egocentricity and Self, with an egocentric pattern that is peculiar to him. Nevertheless, we can identify four relatively clearly defined egocentric patterns, and we will examine these now in the hope that they may throw some light on our particular way of being egocentric.

Which of these four patterns is predominant in any given individual will depend on two factors: first, the kind of personality that is the native endowment of the child; second, the kind of destructive influence to which the child has been subjected.

We are all born into this world with a certain psychological endowment. Some of us have a great deal of vitality, some have less; some have many natural gifts, some not so many; some are phlegmatic, others more sensitive; some are like strong, sturdy plough-horses, some like fleet thoroughbreds; some are born to be red-blooded men who need and crave adventure, and others are pale-blooded Hamlets inclined to reflection and probing into the meaning of things; some are extraverted, and some are introverted. Also we were born into an environment that was either too harsh and unyielding, or too soft and indulgent; and our parents had either less or more natural vitality than we did. If we compare the relative vitality of the child to the harshness or softness of the environment into which the child is born we get four possible combinations:

1. A sensitive child of relatively low vitality who is born into an environment that is too soft and indulgent.
2. A child of superior vitality who is born into an environment that is too soft and indulgent.
3. A child of superior vitality who is born into an environment that is too harsh and demanding.
4. A sensitive child of relatively low vitality who is born into an environment that is too harsh and demanding.

Out of these four combinations arise the four main egocentric patterns. We will begin with number one: the sensitive child of relatively low vitality who is born into an environment that is too soft and indulgent.

Such a child will be overwhelmed by what appears to be love, but unfortunately the overly protective and shielded environment will keep the child from discovering his own powers to explore and cope with his world. Yet it is exactly this kind of initiative that he needs to develop, for the world into which he has been born is not soft and indulgent, but hard and demanding, and it will require all of his courage and resourcefulness if he is to cope with it successfully. However his parents, without consciously intending to do so, have taught him that if he is weak and dependent he will be protected and helped. He has learned that the more he displays his inability to do things on his own the more indulgent his parents will be. If he comes up against a difficulty at school, for instance, he finds out that if he pleads illness his parents will keep him at home; in this way the difficulty does not have to be faced. Gradually, through a thousand and one experiences, he learns that the more needy and apparently deserving he is of help the more he can count on his parents, and later other people as well, to be a source of strength for him.

So when he reaches maturity his egocentric posture is to be needy, helpless, and deserving of support from others. Not only does he have to make others believe this, he has come to believe it himself. His view of himself is that this is his *true* self, when in fact it is a sham self. Of course he will suffer a great deal. To a certain extent his suffering will be a pose for the benefit of others, but in time he comes to believe in his own suffering and then it is real enough. But sadly, his suffering is used for an egocentric purpose: to make others be his source of strength, a shield against life's demands and difficulties.

He may also identify himself with the victim archetype. In nature there are predators and there are victims. Coyotes are predators; rabbits and mice are victims. In human life there are those people who prey on others and those who are their victims. So we can speak of the archetype of the predator and the archetype of the victim. If someone identifies with the victim archetype, that person unconsciously places himself time and again in a position in which he will be victimized. Being a victim is another way in which this kind of person can perpetuate this particular form of egocentricity.

This dependent kind of person will naturally seek people on whom he can depend. He may marry a strong woman and become the weak, dependent husband. She may rave and rant at him and secretly or openly despise him, but it will be worth it to him because she also protects him. (Of course she marries such a man in the first place because of egocentric needs of her own.) The kind of work he likes is a position devoid of responsibility, in which he can carry out the orders of a strong person who will reward him with protection. It is even better, however, if he can attach himself to an institution. Religious institutions often serve his purposes nicely. What better protection and shield from life could there be than the confines of certain church institutions? He may even succeed in passing off his weakness as a form of saintliness. Clergy are his natural prey. Because of their proneness to feelings of guilt, and their need to appear good and loving in the eyes of others, the clergy attract this kind of person. If the clergyman offers the required protection and support, he is rewarded with a "faithful and adoring follower," which may suit the pastor's own egocentric needs nicely.

However, as time goes on the stakes get higher, for people get tired of propping someone up, especially a boring person. Consequently, in order to persuade people to continue supporting him, this kind of person must display an ever greater and greater need and helplessness. His suffering must continue unabated, in spite of everyone's efforts to help him, yet it must never be his fault. In severe cases, his efforts to keep people supporting him may consume virtually all his time and energy and completely dominate his life.

Because of his clinging qualities this person can be dubbed a

"Clinging Vine." His form of egocentricity will profoundly affect his relationships with others. He will be an ingratiating follower and admirer of those who prop him up in life. Those people who do what he wants he will see as "White Giants," that is, powerful people who are helpful and protective. He will reward them accordingly. But if someone refuses to help him he becomes churlish and mean, and if they are threatening he will see them as "Black Giants," that is, powerful people who are dangerous.

The goal of the Clinging Vine is to surround himself with White Giants in order to allay his fears of being left on his own in a hostile world, but even when he has found enough people to give him ample support he lives in fear, for nothing can save him from the haunting anxiety that one day he will be left on his own. Nor can anything save him from the anxiety that comes from having turned his innermost Self into an enemy, an inevitable consequence of his denial of his own vital life forces. What he does not realize is that this Self within him contains all the resources he needs in order to live life courageously. But this courageous part of himself must be repressed, for if it emerged it would require him to give up his egocentricity, and this, he has come to believe, is all he has to rely on. So his most courageous qualities become part of his shadow, of which he is deathly afraid, since his shadow would urge him to face life on his own.

In the Bible, examples of Clinging Vines are the disciples, prior to the resurrection of Christ. They are not completely dominated by this form of egocentricity of course, but some of it is there. The Lord himself becomes their Center and they lean on him, unconsciously, for support and sustenance. This is why they all desert him when he is arrested and goes to his crucifixion. Their egocentricity is the source of their cowardice in this moment of crisis. Fritz Kunkel said that it was necessary for Christ to be crucified in order that the disciples could become free of this kind of egocentric dependency and learn to stand on their own. Only in this way could their relationship with Christ achieve creativity and maturity.

The next example is from situation number two: a child of superior vitality who is born into an environment that is too soft and indulgent. This child exceeds his parents in gifts and vitality. The unfulfilled ambitions of his parents are readily projected into him; he may even become the purpose for which the parents exist. They are quick to tell others of his exploits and to bask in their son's achievements. Since he is a gifted person he achieves marked success in certain areas. He may become an ''A'' student in school, or be the quarterback on the football team, or he may be elected class president, or be placed in the classes for gifted children, or become a child prodigy in music. For these achievements he receives abundant praise, some of it earned, but a certain amount of it much more than he deserves. Deserved or not, his parents lavish adulation on him without insight or wisdom. Small wonder that he comes to believe firmly in his own importance, and feels that he is superior to others, whom he expects to serve and please him in return for his favors. Even though he is but a child he soon dominates his parents, with their much more modest achievements, and perhaps his brothers and sisters as well. Because of his propensity for being on the center of the stage, we can dub this prima donna type of person the ''Star.''

However, there is a harsh world of reality outside of his home, filled with people who are not impressed with his talents. He fears this world, partly because it will not admire him, and partly because his ego, like that of the Clinging Vine, is too soft to deal with it. There are ways around the difficulty, however. He can avoid this harsh world and remain within the circle of his admirers. Or he can delegate to an admirer the task of dealing with the harsh world. For he is like a royal child who can depend on his courtiers to take care of certain things for him. At first it will be the parents who do this for him; later he will have to find others willing to serve him in this way.

Thus, although his life appears to be bright and shining, he too has his fears. For instance, he shuns the class in mathematics. He has painful memories of the ''C'' he received in math; it was the only ''C'' he ever received among his many ''A's.'' It was a detestable teacher who gave it to him in spite of the phone call his parents made about it. Since then he has done everything possible to avoid ever again taking a course in the dreaded mathematics. The grade he received made him feel ordinary, and for him that means inferior, and this is something he cannot tolerate.

Indeed, his greatest fear is that, after all, he will turn out to be just an ordinary person. To protect himself against this seeming disaster he denies in himself all his ordinary human feelings such as the desire to be loved for just who you are, the enjoyment of simple pleasures in life, and the feeling of camaraderie with your fellows when you are on an equal basis with them. All of these feelings must be denied because they conflict with his cherished idea of himself: that he is a great and fabulous person who must be admired.

These fears are especially intense under certain circumstances. If, for instance, he finds himself in the presence of someone whose achievements match or exceed his own, he finds himself distinctly uneasy, and jealous as well. He also fears facing any task or situation in life for which his talents are only modest, or inadequate, lest people—God forbid!—should laugh at him. As mentioned, he will also fear having to face the harshness of the world without admirers around to protect him. If such a situation should develop he may change from being a Star to being a Clinging Vine.

In order to assuage these fears he gathers admirers around himself. He treats them graciously, rewarding them with smiles and a genial manner that dispenses benevolent approval of them. He counts them as his friends and may protest his love for them, but in fact he rules his admirers the way a royal person rules his vassals. If his admirers include powerful people, these become his White Giants who make him feel secure. But, of course, those who are powerful but are not among his admirers make up the cast of Black Giants of whom he is deathly afraid. In the presence of those who fail to admire him or are his detractors, his mean qualities emerge: he becomes jealous, fickle, touchy, and peevish. When offended, which happens easily, he rages, boasts, lies and scolds. If he wasn't such a coward he might go so far as to fight his real or supposed enemies, but being the person he is he tries to get his courtiers to do the fighting for him. If he should be so unfortunate as to be thrown in with a ruthless person more powerful than himself who is not at all inclined to become his admirer his fear is all the greater.

A good biblical example of this egocentric type is the young man Joseph, whose story is told in Genesis 37. A careful reading of the story of Joseph as a youth shows him as a Star who had to be center-stage. This is why, when he has two great dreams that are portents of his future destiny, he takes them the wrong way and uses them to lord it over his brothers. Perhaps Joseph's arrogance and air of superiority was nourished by the favoritism showed to him by his father because he was the son of the beloved Rachel, while his brothers were the sons of Leah. Given this fact, and the fact that Joseph told tales about them to their father,[2] it is not surprising that the brothers hated him, and Joseph's demand that everyone acknowledge his superiority only fanned the flames of their hatred. It took God quite a while to get Joseph out of his egocentricity so he could carry out God's plan and, in so doing, become a great man.

We come now to the third category: a child of superior vitality who is born into an environment that is too harsh and demanding. When this child's initial trust is broken by the brutality of his parents and others, he responds by fighting back. Having a certain innate toughness, and not being burdened with an overly sensitive nature, he is able to take on the cruelty of the world around him. His attitude may be summarized as follows: "Nobody is going to get me because I'm going to get them first. I'm going to be on top of everyone, and therefore they will not be able to hurt me anymore." Thus his egocentric aim is to protect himself by dominating others. His goal therefore is to achieve power.

Nonetheless, submerged though they are, he does have feelings. Basically he wants power over others so he cannot be hurt. Inside his tough, hard ego stance there is a certain amount of human vulnerability. This he must repress. All ordinary yearnings to give and receive affection must be denied because they threaten to soften and make malleable a hardness he depends on in his ego in order to do what he fancies he must do in order to survive. Under certain circumstances this inner softness may manifest itself as sentimentality. For instance, it was said of the Nazi leader of the Luftwaffe in World War II, Hermann Goering, that he would weep copiously when he heard the music of Wagner and Beethoven. However, this sentimentality did not keep him from raining death and destruction on tens of thousands of people.

The person in this third category must repress his conscience, for even the most ordinary human conscience would not allow him to carry out his plans for power without engendering conflict. His conscience, however, does not thereby cease to exist, but operates from the unconscious, plotting his downfall. Sooner or later such a man usually trips himself up and is compelled by life to pay for his harshness.

If such a person is endowed with enough shrewdness and strength

---

2. Gen 37:2—"Joseph informed their father of the evil spoken about them." For a study of Joseph's egocentricity, and God's cure for it, see my book *The Man Who Wrestled with God*. New York: Paulist Press 1981 and revised 1987. Originally published by Religious Publishing Co., 1974.

he may become a great success in the world. The ruthlessness of a man of this type might enable him to become a highly successful business tycoon, who thinks nothing of aggrandizing power and wealth at the expense of the misfortunes of others. The most successful men of this type have become the world's most infamous dictators, all the way from the Roman Emperor Caligula to Josef Stalin. If his ordinary human feelings are repressed deeply enough he may become a hardened criminal. But his power drive may be less obvious than the above examples. He can just as easily become a prison guard as a criminal, a dictator's favorite executioner as a dictator, a businessman's executive who carries out his boss' ruthless orders as the businessman. He might even become a successful medical doctor who assumes a godlike role with his patients and with the hospital staff, even a clergyman who rules his parish as though it were his empire.

If he is not powerful enough to qualify for some of these high places in the world, such a man may have to settle for a lesser position. So he might become a minor bureaucrat who has the power to deny the requests of others and thus cause them pain and grief. Or he may be compliant enough in the world of work, where he deals with men more powerful than himself, but at home dominate his hapless wife and children, who live in fear of him.

Because of his egocentric striving for power we can call this type of person the Tyrant or Nero (after the infamous Roman emperor by this name). Neros and Stars are sometimes confused, since both of them want to be on top. They can be distinguished by the fact that the ego of the Nero is hard and that of the Star is soft. Consequently the Nero type wants power while the Star is content with admiration. Admiration is something the Nero does not need. If he strives for it, it is only a way-station on the road to achieving power. A Nero is content to be behind the scenes and let someone else get the admiration, as long as he has the essential power. In fact, he would rather have people fear him than admire him.

But in spite of his seemingly impregnable power and apparently hard and impervious ego, the Nero also lives in fear. His fear is that he will lose his power over others, that his subjects will rebel and no longer accede to his domination. He also is riddled with fear because there is one thing he cannot control: the unconscious. Thus he is plagued with fears from within himself over which he has no control. It is said of the ruthless Roman Emperor Caligula that during the day he was a tyrant, but at night he was a prey to such fears that he could not sleep, but roamed the halls of his palace crying out for the dawn to come. In fact, it is his fears, more even than his drive for power, that make such a man so dangerous. The dictator Josef Stalin, tormented by fears of being overthrown, put millions of his fellow citizens to death. Not even his friends and supporters were spared; his victims included the highest ranking officers in the army and old comrades from revolutionary days. For such a man has no loyalty. Totally lacking in loyalty himself he does not recognize it or value it in others.

The Nero is a bully at heart, and, like all bullies, his outer harshness conceals his inner cowardice. For this reason, if such a tyrant is defeated he may switch into his opposite and become craven. Winston Churchill once noted this about the ruthless German armies of World War II when he said, "The Germans are always either at one's throat, or one's feet."[3]

An excellent biblical example of this egocentric type is Herod the Great, who slaughtered the innocent children of Bethlehem because he was afraid the newborn "king of the Jews" would take his throne from him. This story shows not only the power drive of the Nero, but also the fear in which he lives.

The opposite of the Nero is the fourth combination of factors: a sensitive child of relatively low vitality who is born into an environment that is too harsh and demanding. This child, being weaker than his parents and educators, has no way to make others serve him. His efforts to cope with life meet only with defeat at the hands of others more ruthless than himself. His defense is to retreat from life by building a protective shell around himself. So he renounces all normal desires, goals, and ambitions. His egocentric posture is: if you don't care, if you don't strive, if you don't want, if you don't risk yourself, then you cannot be defeated; if you don't try to make relationships with people, if you don't let yourself love anyone or be loved, then you cannot be hurt. Because the chief characteristic of this form of egocentricity defense is withdrawal, this person can be called the Turtle.

---

3. Paul Johnson, *Modern Times and the World from the Twenties to the Eighties*. New York: Harper and Row Publishers, 1983.

Turtles and Clinging Vines have certain similarities, since both adopt a posture of weakness in order to protect themselves. The Clinging Vine, however, does reach out to people—even if only to get them to support him. The Turtle, on the contrary, withdraws from people. Also the Clinging Vine has a basically soft ego structure, while the ego structure of the Turtle is hard. His hardness is not the brutal hardness of the Nero, but is a brittle hardness, easily shattered. The Turtle is the opposite of the Star since the latter makes a point of pushing himself forward onto the center of the stage while the Turtle does the opposite. He is also the opposite of the Nero, for the Nero emerges into the world, although in unwholesome ways, while the Turtle refuses to do so insofar as it is possible.

Many people are Turtles only in specific areas. For instance, a man at his work may function effectively, even dominating others in a Nero fashion. But at home, where he encounters people who want to meet him on an emotional relationship level, he turns Turtle. His inner emotional life is sealed off from people by his brittle shell, and if anyone tries to reach his feeling side he shrinks still further away.

If a person is a full-fledged Turtle, however, he may seek a more ultimate refuge. Sometimes these refuges are cleverly disguised; a safe sinecure in some remote area of the church might do. In extreme cases the Turtle, like the Clinging Vine, might gravitate to a hospital or some other institution. Drugs can also be a refuge for the Turtle. When a frightening or anxiety-producing situation arises the drug offers protection and relief. There are always plenty of Neros around who will be happy to sell the drugs to them.

In the Bible, an example of the Turtle is the crippled man who waited for thirty-eight years by the pool of Bethzatha without being cured. John tells the story in the fifth chapter of his Gospel. It was the belief of people at that time that the waters of the pool at Bethzatha would be periodically stirred by an angel, and the first person to enter the waters after the angel had troubled them would be cured. Consequently the pool of Bethzatha was surrounded with the ill and the crippled. This man had been there for almost four decades and had not yet succeeded in being the first to enter the pool. When Jesus came along he asked him if he wanted to be healed, and the man did not answer directly, but only made an excuse. Jesus healed him on the spot. However, this did not win the man's gratitude but his resentment, and he went straight to Jesus' enemies and did all he could to get him into trouble. We could say that this man was a Turtle and did not want to be forced out of his refuge.

For a full-fledged Turtle to succeed in remaining in his refuge, he must deny many of the same qualities that the Clinging Vine must deny: his courage, urge to seek adventure, capacity for feeling—all of his most manly qualities. He simply cannot establish and maintain his chosen egocentric posture and have these qualities at the same time. So all of his healthy inclinations in these directions are relegated to the unconscious where they become part of his shadow personality.

Like all egocentric types, the Turtle lives in fear. His fear is that life may drag him out of his hiding place to face the real and imagined dangers that plague him. For instance, what if he should one day feel the stirrings of genuine love for someone? He cannot love and at the same time hide. So he fears love, just as he fears the multitude of Black Giants whom he believes to be more powerful than he is. He also has a chronic feeling of inferiority, and from this he cannot run away. No matter where he hides, there it is nagging away at him and making a hell out of his life. As with all forms of egocentricity, his egocentric solution becomes in time his problem. For example, if he has succeeded in hiding too well from life he may develop agoraphobia (fear of the marketplace), a form of anxiety that so numbs a person he becomes practically incapable of leaving home. Thus do our egocentric shelters become our prisons.

Other Aspects of Egocentricity

An interesting question arises: Are men more prone to identify with certain of these egocentric types and women with others? Of the four egocentric types, two (the Nero and Star) have characteristics that are similar to traditional masculine roles, and the other two (Turtle and Clinging Vine) have characteristics similar to traditional feminine roles. In patriarchally oriented societies we might expect more men than women to become Neros and Stars, and more women than men to become Turtles and Clinging Vines. However, this is a matter of conjecture, since no scientific study is available at this time. Even if it be true that women are more inclined in one direction and men in another, it may be that as society changes, and role options become more the same for men and women, the egocentric forms will be more equally distributed between the sexes. In any event, we can find plenty of examples of women who are dominating Neros or prima donna Stars, and many examples of men who are dependent Clinging Vines or retiring Turtles.

Another interesting question that emerges from a discussion of the four egocentric types has to do with the qualities of the shadow personality. We have seen already that the qualities of the shadow are, for the most part, positive. They may not look positive to the egocentric ego because they threaten to upset the egocentric structure, but from the larger point of view they are genuine expressions of the Self, while our egocentric qualities are false representations of who we are. This is why Kunkel once said that in a showdown between the egocentric ego and the shadow, the Self always favors the shadow. Since the shadow has been forced to live a half-life in the unconscious, when it emerges it will often erupt in such a way as to seriously upset a person's life. It will manifest a destructive side, but, on closer inspection, the destructiveness of the shadow can be seen as a manifestation of that dark side to the Self that seeks to destroy everything that is not fit to exist, in this case, our egocentricity. What is really sinister about us is not the shadow, but our own hidden, cleverly disguised, and unconscious egocentricity, which, as we have seen, can verge on the daemonic. This is why Kunkel said the secret was that the ego is the devil.[4]

However, when we make this statement we must keep in mind that it is not the ego per se that is the devil, but the egocentric ego. The ego in its rightful state is, to repeat this important point, a noble instrument of the psyche and of God's purposes. It is when it is in its egocentric or "fallen" state that it turns dark and destructive.

We must also keep in mind what was said earlier—that there are innumerable variations of the egocentric theme we have discussed. For instance, none of us are completely egocentric. Our personalities are always an admixture of elements of the Real Self and egocentric elements. We may respond to life now from one side, now from another. In a crisis, for instance, some people come through with admirable qualities that neither he nor other people had ever seen in him before. We may also display one form of egocentricity in one situation and an-

---

4. For a more complete treatment of this subject, see *Fritz Kunkel: Selected Writings* (footnote 1 of this chapter), especially my chapters in the commentary found in Part IV, entitled "Kunkel, Jung, and the Ego in Individuation," and "Kunkel's Psychology and Other Jungian Concepts." See also my book *The Strange Trial of Edward Hyde*. San Francisco: Harper & Row Publishers, 1987.

other form in another situation. We have already pointed out that a man
may be a Turtle at work (where others are more powerful than he) but
a Nero at home (where he can dominate his hapless family). People can
also change from one type to another. For instance, if a Star finds himself crowded off the stage by another Star, or otherwise humiliated, he
may switch into the groveling Clinging Vine. We may also have learned
one form of egocentric defense from one set of life circumstances and
another form from another set of life circumstances. If, for instance,
our father treated us one way and our mother treated us another way,
two different egocentric patterns may have emerged. Which pattern
would be used in a specific life situation would depend on the circumstances.

There is also the startling fact that in some children the powers of
the Self are so strong that not even the most damaging life circumstances can destroy the child's relationship to the Self. For this reason,
some children emerge intact into adulthood in spite of these difficulties.
The powers of the Self appear to be inexhaustibly creative and life-re-
newing, and when a contact with the Self is maintained people get
through even the most crushing experiences of life. As mentioned earlier, Alice Miller, at the end of her book *For Your Own Good,* puts it
nicely when she says: "For the human soul is virtually indestructible,
and its ability to rise from the ashes remains as long as the body draws
breath."[5]

Nevertheless, it is clear that by the time a man reaches adult years
his original relationship with the Self has to a greater or lesser extent
been fractured, and replaced by one or more form of egocentricity that
alienates him from others, defeats the real purposes of life, and distorts
his ambitions and goals. It is not too much to speak of our egocentricity
as tyrannical—to say that the egocentric ego exerts a tyranny, a tyranny
over others, over ourselves, over our inner powers. While the egocentric ego pursues its egocentric goal, the Self pursues its goal, the goal
of removing or destroying the egocentric patterns so the real purposes
of a man's life can be fulfilled. This is part of the process called individuation by Jung and Kunkel.

The process of individuation is a psychological, spiritual, and maturational process. The psychological aspect calls for us to achieve in-

---

5. Miller, *For Your Own Good,* p. 279.

sight into ourselves, especially into our personal complexes, the influence of our early environment on the shaping of our personality, and the nature of our egocentricity. The spiritual aspect calls for us to find and live out the meaning of our lives, and to subordinate the will of our egos to the larger will within us that Jung and Kunkel called the Self, but which also can be likened to the indwelling Will of God. The maturation aspect calls for the maturing of the ego so that it can develop away from its egocentricity and achieve wisdom and centeredness. Of course these three processes are not always clearly distinguishable from each other, and they have areas where they overlap. Becoming conscious of the archetypes, for instance, has both a psychological and a spiritual dimension. So does the process of coming into contact with our hitherto unused psychological potential.

In later chapters we will touch on themes of individuation in more detail. For now suffice it to say that unless a man overcomes his egocentricity, his individuation will not properly take place. A young man on the threshold of adult life has therefore two tasks ahead of him: the earthly task of finding a place in the world, and the heavenly task of beginning his individuation. Both tasks are important and inter-related. In the next chapter we will look at one of the earthly tasks confronting a man: his relationship to his work.

Suggested Reading

Kunkel, Fritz, *Creation Continues*. Mahwah: Paulist Press, 1987.

Sanford, John A. (ed. and commentator), *Fritz Kunkel: Selected Writings*. New York: Paulist Press, 1984.

————*King Saul, The Tragic Hero: A Study in Individuation*. New York: Paulist Press, 1985.

————*The Man Who Wrestled with God: Light from the Old Testament on the Psychology of Individuation*. New York: Paulist Press, 1981, revised and updated, 1987.

————*The Strange Trial of Mr. Hyde: A New Look at the Nature of Human Evil*. San Francisco: Harper & Row Publishers, 1987.

Chapter 4

A Man and His Work

For most men, work is one of the most, if not *the* most important aspect of their lives. For better or worse, a man will typically spend fifty percent of his waking life at work, until he retires. Whether his work is satisfying or unsatisfying, rewarding or unrewarding, it will dominate his existence. Even if he is unemployed it will indirectly dominate him, since he will be preoccupied with the problems of unemployment.

In other cultures work has not played the same role for men as it has in our Western culture. An allegation often made in the nineteenth century by white men against Indians was that they were lazy and refused to work. Of course the Indians *did* work, but in their own way and according to the dictates of their own culture. Smohalla, founder of the dream religion that flourished among the Nez Perce and other Indian groups in the latter part of the nineteenth century, replied to the white man's charge with these words:

> My young men shall never work. Men who work cannot dream; and wisdom comes to us in our dreams.
>
> You ask me to plow the ground. Shall I take a knife and tear my mother's breast? Then when I die she will not take me to her bosom to rest.
>
> You ask me to dig for stone. Shall I dig under her skin for her bones? Then when I die I cannot enter her body to be born again.
>
> You ask me to cut grass and make hay and sell it and be rich like white men. But how dare I cut off my mother's hair?[1]

Smohalla had a different attitude toward work because he had a different attitude toward the world in which he lived and his place in it. The attitudes of our culture, however, are quite different from those of Smohalla. We often hear of the importance in our thinking of the so-called Protestant work-ethic, but a more important factor is that we live in a culture that is based on production. The production of goods results in wealth, and acquiring at least a certain amount of wealth is funda-

---

1. T. C. McLuhan, *Touch the Earth.* New York: Promontory Press, 1971, p. 56.

mental not only to our material well-being but also to our self-esteem. It is only work that enables us to produce. Most of us want or feel we must have those things that our production-oriented culture brings. Like it or not, we work for this culture and its material benefits.

Western style production does indeed produce material wealth, but it does not necessarily produce satisfying work. The production line worker of today cannot have the personal satisfaction in his work that must have come to the coopers, blacksmiths, cabinet makers, and other craftsmen of one hundred and fifty years ago who personally created their products. Nor can the impersonal management-labor relations that prevail in our industries compare favorably with the cottage-industries of the eighteenth and nineteenth centuries. In those days owners and workers knew each other by name, and their families lived next to each other in small villages. No doubt personal tensions arose, but the alienation between management and labor that so characterizes the workplace of today must have been much less.

Of course there are many men today who find their work satisfying, but there are many others who are dissatisfied, and who work, not for its own sake, but out of necessity, or to achieve some other goal. The other goals include such things as the desire for fame or recognition, for wealth or for power, goals that may be largely or partly egocentric. For instance, many men do not particularly like their work but they like the "game" they are playing. The favorite game in our culture is to accumulate wealth; we can call this the "money game." So a man might train himself as a financial expert not because he likes the work as such but because he is drawn into and fascinated by the money-making game.

Most professions involve a certain amount of game-playing—even professions that are supposed to stem from loftier motives. For instance, the seemingly dedicated pastor or priest may in fact be involved in a bit of ecclesiastical empire-building, and the psychotherapist may be striving as much for influence and recognition as he is to helping his clients.

There is something to be said for the games we play, for if a young man can find such a game it helps him get involved in life. A young man who does not know what his work is, and does not get drawn into any of the games that involve him in work, runs the danger of lacking enough motivation to get into life. This brings with it not only economic, but also psychological problems. Many a young man who cannot get into the marketplace of life develops disturbing symptoms until he finds out what he is all about. The fact is that even when men complain about their work they are almost always better off psychologically and emotionally when they have work to do. The man whose work is a game to him may, later in life, have to delve into the deeper and more real issues of life if he is to develop spiritually, but at least he will get started.

The Senex and the Puer Aeternus

Men have different kinds of personalities so they bring different attitudes and dispositions with them to the marketplace of work. Two such different kinds of men are known in Jungian parlance as the *senex* and the *puer aeternus*. Senex is the Latin word for old; our word "senile" comes from it. Puer aeternus is Latin for eternal boy or youth. The senex and the puer are two archetypes, that is, two typical but different ways in which a man's ego develops. The archetype shapes the ego's structure and attitudes. In the case of the senex, such a man develops an older way of thinking. It will be characterized by some important virtues. He will be a man who can make and see through a commitment; he will be able to set and work toward a goal; he will be capable of assuming responsibility and sticking to something, be it work or marriage or whatever. Working hard, responsibility, sticking to things: these are important values to him. The negative side of this archetype is that such a man tends to become increasingly rigid, unforgiving, lacking in flexibility, devoid of humor, and judgmental.

The puer is a Peter Pan type of character who maintains a boyish attitude toward life even as he becomes chronologically older. In some ways he is a more flexible person than the senex, and often is a charming and agreeable companion, especially to women. His unstructuredness and diversities of interests often make him an interesting man, although as time goes on his refusal to grow up becomes irritating to others. The puer does not want to commit himself to routine. He tends to shun conventional work because the commitment it would require would limit life's many possibilities. He likes to work at one thing and then another with lapses of time in between jobs. Others may find it hard to accept his inability to commit himself to any one goal or to long-lasting relationships. His refusal to grow up may impede his proper maturation, and his charming boyishness can degenerate into narcissistic self-interest. He may also bring to the matter of his psychological development the same impediment he brings to the world of work: a difficulty in taking himself or his life seriously.

The senex and the puer see life and work quite differently; they also tend to dislike each other. In the 1960's, senexes and puers were polarized in the political establishment on the one hand and the hippie movement on the other. The hatred between the puers of that era and the men in positions of power and authority was mutual and intense.

Both the pure senex type and the pure puer aeternus type can be frustrating to the women in their lives. A woman may admire and want the prestige and wealth that her senex-type husband can provide for her, but may find his personality increasingly boring and unrelated as he grows older. She may also find his commitment to work frustrating to their relationship. When confronted by his wife, such a man will often say in answer to her complaints that he spends too much time at work and neglects her and the family, "But I'm doing it all for you." And he really believes that, for the truth is that he does not necessarily like what he is doing, and sees himself as living a sacrificial life. He may truly believe that he is working for the sake of his family, overlooking the fact that there are other values in life that his family wants from him. The puer aeternus type may at first seem to a woman to be a charming, related, and interesting man. However, since he has difficulty staying with a relationship, he may prove to be a disappointment to her.

Both the senex and the puer overlook the fact that relationships require a certain amount of effort and attention. Many men have the attitude that relationships should just take care of themselves; it is their work, or play, that requires their special attention. For many women it's the other way around.

Fortunately, few men are entirely a senex type or a puer type. Sometimes a senex man's playful, boyish side comes out now and then with a most salutary effect on his otherwise dour personality, and the puer can often develop some of the valuable qualities of the senex without forfeiting his youthful values entirely. In fact, it could be said that the cure for each type is to partake of some of the other. Marie-Louise von Franz once argued that the puer can only be cured by working at something, be it outer work or inner work or both.[2] I suspect the senex

---

2. Marie-Louise von Franz, *Puer Aeternus*. Boston: Sigo Press, 1981. (Originally Spring Publications, 1970.)

can only be cured by playing at something, be it a game, or some avocation, or in a relationship.

Psychological Type and Work

The archetypes of the senex and the puer shape a man's general attitude toward work. What kind of work is best for a man is greatly determined by his psychological type, as is pointed out by Isabel Briggs Myers and Peter B. Myers in their book *Gifts Differing*. For instance, extraverts like organizing and relating to a life situation. They need and enjoy involvement with people; they like to be where the action is. Introverts are interested in organizing the facts and principles relative to a situation. They also need people but tend to relate to fewer people, though in more depth than the extravert. Thus an extravert might do well in business or industry, while an introvert might prefer to be an economist. An extravert might excel as a group leader or community organizer, while an introvert might be drawn to working with individuals or becoming an academically oriented sociologist.

Men with a strong thinking function like to deal with theories, principles, inanimate objects, things that do not require a feeling relationship. Law, science, or academic pursuits would be attractive to them.

Men with a strong feeling function would be drawn to work with people in some related capacity. If their feeling function is extraverted they might do well as parish clergymen, but if it is introverted they might become chaplains or pastoral counselors instead.

Men with a strong sensation function do well dealing with concrete reality, that is, with facts and situations that they can "get their hands on." If they have mechanical or technical skills they would do well as mechanics or engineers. Such men might also do well in the military or as craftsmen. With thinking as an auxiliary function a sensation type could become a good accountant; with feeling as an auxiliary function, sales work would be attractive.

Men with intuition as a strong function will be drawn to fields of endeavor that are full of possibilities; when the possibilities in a situation are exhausted they will tire of the work. An extraverted intuitive type might become a real estate developer, for this requires a man who can see the as yet unrealized possibilities in a situation. Journalists also often come from the ranks of the extraverted intuitive types. An introverted intuitive type, especially if he has thinking as an auxiliary function, might become a research scientist or a mathematician.

Psychological type tests have shown that certain fields tend to attract men of certain psychological types. For instance, many creative writers have a strong intuitive function. Internists and general practitioners are apt to be introverted intuitive types with feeling as an auxiliary function, but surgeons come from the ranks of extraverted sensation types. Feeling types with perception who enter law school tend to drop out, but a thinking type with judgment does well in the profession. An introverted attorney might like doing legal research or become a specialist in contracts, while an extraverted attorney might enjoy the process of litigation.

Like writers, artists tend to come from the ranks of introverted intuitive people. On the other hand, art therapists tend to be extraverted feeling types; they use their artistic skills in helping other people. Teachers of art tend to be introverted feeling types; their niche in life lies in transferring their perceptions of the inner world of art to others via education.

In many professions there are no hard and fast distinctions because the field is broad enough to appeal to men of varied typology. Psychology is an example. It is likely that gestalt therapists, who work with people in groups, and create therapeutic situations in the course of the therapy, tend to be extraverted. Behaviorists, with their preference for a rational and practical approach to therapy, probably tend to be thinking or sensation types. Jungian analysts, on the other hand, are almost always introverted, and favor the functions of intuition and feeling. However, there are some extraverted Jungian therapists too, and Jung himself, while introverted, was a thinking type, with a lot of intuition as well, but his wife Emma, who also became an analyst, said she was a sensation type. One reason Jung first became interested in typology was his desire to understand why he and Freud differed so much on various fundamental issues. Jung concluded that Freud worked from an extraverted thinking point of view, which was at variance with Jung's highly introverted approach.

Jung's typology is an area of his psychology that has developed a life of its own apart from the main corpus of Jungian psychology. Words that Jung virtually coined, such as extravert and introvert, are now part of the common parlance of our day. The Myers-Briggs psychological types tests are used widely in industry and elsewhere by persons who do not even know that the typology on which the tests are based was originated by Jung. These types tests are used in the process of evaluating a man for a job because of the importance of combining the right job with the right man. If a man knows his typology it can be helpful to him in finding the sort of work that will be conducive to his effective functioning. People may enjoy playing at their least developed (inferior) function; for instance, an introverted intuitive type may derive great satisfaction from becoming an amateur bird-watcher. But we get paid for what we do well with our most natural (superior) function, and that is also the kind of work that gives us the most satisfaction. The exception to this rule comes when a man has used up one side of himself and must develop other sides in order to go on living successfully. This is often part of a man's midlife crisis, which we will comment on in the next chapter.

Gods, Goddesses, and a Man's Vocation

Jung's typology alone, however, is not sufficient to account for the great diversity of human types nor for the wide variety of fields of endeavor to which men are drawn. For a further understanding we must look at the archetypes, and understand how deeply they shape and affect a man's personality. We have already noted that the archetypes are built-in or *a priori* patterns in the psyche that produce and shape psychic energy in certain typical ways. Because the archetypes are inherent in the structure of the psyche itself, and not the result of learned behavior, they are akin to the instincts. However, while we use the word instinct to refer to physically observed patterns of reaction and behavior, the idea of the archetype includes not only physical behavior patterns but also the typical emotions, fantasies, and sense of meaning that accompany that pattern of behavior. We have already examined two of the archetypes—the puer and senex—and have seen how these archetypes shape the development of a man's ego in typical ways. Now we will look at other archetypes, with a particular view to the way in which a certain archetype in a man will incline him to a certain kind of work.

Psychology did not invent the archetypes, it has simply learned to observe and study them. The archetypes have always evidenced themselves in human behavior and in all direct expressions of unconscious life, for instance in fairy tales, creative art, great literature, and, of particular importance for our present discussion, in mythology. Wherever the collective unconscious has found a more or less direct expression we will find the archetypes spontaneously representing themselves. Of all the world's mythologies Greek mythology is the most highly developed and psychologically instructive, for the gods and goddesses of the Greeks are excellent representations in imagery, poetry, art, and story, of the major archetypes of the human psyche. The gods personify specifically masculine archetypes, and the goddesses specifically feminine archetypes. Whether we are a man or a woman our psyche contains both gods and goddesses, that is, both masculine and feminine archetypes. In our chapter on a man's relationship to his feminine side we will consider the influence on his psychology of the feminine archetypes. In this chapter we will concentrate mostly on the influence in a man of the masculine archetypes, especially as they relate to his work.

The principal Greek gods include Zeus, Apollo, Hermes, Asklepius, Ares, and Hephaeustus. Since, as mentioned, each god can be taken as a representation of an archetype, we will use the words god or goddess and archetype interchangeably. No doubt each man's psyche contains all of these archetypes, but it is also true that one or more of these gods will be of central importance in the life of any particular man, and that his psychology will be especially shaped by that archetype. Which god is of the most importance in a man's psyche appears to be a matter of heredity, or, if you like, of fate. It is like being dealt a hand of cards. The cards are dealt, you pick up your hand, and whatever cards it contains are the ones with which you must play the game. So it is that certain archetypes turn up within us as "our cards" to play with.

We will begin with Hephaeustus. Hephaeustus was thrown from the heights of Olympus to the earth. There are various accounts of how this happened. One of them is that Hephaeustus was born lame and his mother, Hera, was so upset with her disfigured son that she cast him from heaven; Hephaeustus fell all day until he landed on the earth. He made his primary abode under the earth, near the great volcanoes Etna and Vesuvius. Here he had a forge and became a master craftsman. He excelled in inventing ingenious and artfully wrought devices, and a number of tales about him revolve around his creations.

In one of these stories Hephaeustus revenged himself on his mother. It seems that Hera asked the Olympians for a resplendent throne, as befitted her role of queen of the gods. As a master craftsman, Hephaeustus was given the task of building such a throne, and he made one so beautiful and wonderful that Hera was delighted with it. No sooner had she sat on the throne, however, than invisible but unbreakable chains suddenly appeared and bound her fast. Hera could not free herself, nor could any of the other gods free her. To make it worse, the throne soared into the air with the bound goddess and could not be brought down. There was nothing to be done but to implore Hephaeustus to return to Olympus and free Hera, but this he refused to do. Eventually Dionysus tricked him into returning to heaven but he only freed Hera from the marvelously wrought chains when the gods agreed to give Aphrodite to him in marriage.

However Hephaeustus' marriage only proved to be a source of grief for him, for wayward Aphrodite was not about to be faithful to a husband in marriage, much less to the crippled god Hephaeustus. One of Aphrodite's frequent amors was the god of war, Ares, and when word reached Hephaeustus of their illicit union, he plotted revenge. In his underground forge he devised a net of chains that was so marvelously light that it was almost invisible, but so marvelously strong that no one could break them. Coming upon Aphrodite and Ares in their love-making, Hephaeustus cast the net upon them, holding them fast. No matter how they struggled they could not free themselves. The gods were called to aid them in their plight but they could not free the illicit lovers either. Aphrodite and Ares were subjected to humiliation and ridicule by the onlooking gods as they lay helplessly caught in Hephaeustus' net. Eventually the gods prevailed on Hephaeustus to come and liberate his captives, which he did only after he had avenged himself on them by witnessing their humiliation. Yet it should be pointed out that Aphrodite, bound in the net though she was, never showed the slightest embarrassment; it was only Hephaeustus' enemy Ares who experienced humiliation, caught in the clever net of the master craftsman of the gods.

In Hephaeustus we have portrayed the archetype of the craftsman. A man who has this archetype within him will have the power to build devices with great skill. He may also be given the inventive powers of Hephaeustus, for Hephaeustus was both craftsman and inventor, and this will give him the ability to originate devices and creations that hitherto have not been seen among humankind. His power in life will be inventiveness and skillful craftsmanship. Such a man might become a master furniture-maker, or a great engineer, or an electronic wizard. His inventive mind will be highly valued in today's technological society. He will also be extremely useful around the house, with an uncanny ability to fix almost anything. Combined with an artistic bent he might become a sculptor. Given a problem that has to do with things, mechanics, or electronics, his inventive mind will be challenged and excited, and almost certain to come up with an ingenious solution. In contrast, a man in whom Hephaeustus is lacking may find himself baffled even by such simple problems as rewiring a lamp.

Examples of men in whom this archetype is predominant abound in our era of history. Thomas Edison, Alexander Graham Bell, and the devisers of the atomic bomb are included among them, to name just a few of the clever men who have forged for us this awesome and dangerous technological society.

Having mentioned Ares we will proceed to him next. He was the god of war and war-making. His Roman equivalent was Mars. Ares loved fighting for its own sake. Other gods might shun a fierce struggle, but Ares reveled in it. He personifies the archetypal energy that plunges men into war, strife, and conflict. A man in whom Ares is strong will relish such ferocity, even to the point of creating those occasions in which it is necessary. He may well be drawn into a military career, but not necessarily, for strife, struggle, and war of various kinds take place in many realms of life: business, various professions, even marriage.

An example of the god Ares emerging in a man as a martial spirit is General George S. Patton, of World War II fame. Patton was known as a great brawler and fighter. His Third Army was probably the hardest-driving army in the Allied Forces. Patton was so strongly identified with war and war-making that when he was at Kasserine Pass in North Africa, overlooking the plains to the north where ancient Carthage once engaged in struggles against Rome, he believed that he had once been there fighting in those ancient battles. Indeed, his central archetype, Ares, was there, and was now reincarnated in his own spirit. When World War II ended the rest of the world rejoiced, but Patton was disappointed. He openly admitted loving the excitement, glory, and blood and guts of war, and was accused, with some justification, of trying to incite a continuation of the war by making an attack on the Russians.

Next we come to Asklepius. Asklepius' father was Apollo; his mother was the mortal woman Coronis. According to the story, Apollo became enamored of Coronis and had intercourse with her, but, being a god, he never intended to remain with her and left her to continue his godlike and heavenly pursuits. However, Apollo expected Coronis to be faithful to him. Suspecting she might not be, he appointed a crow to keep watch over her. Sure enough, the crow saw her engaged in love-making with a mortal man and brought word of the betrayal to his master. In revenge, Apollo tied Coronis to a funeral pyre and proceeded to burn her to death. At the last moment, however, Apollo realized Coronis was pregnant with their child. Just in time he snatched the unborn child from her womb and saved him from death. This child was Asklepius.

Apollo entrusted the child to the care of the centaur Chiron, who was a physician. Perhaps he had been driven to his profession because he himself had been inflicted by Heracles with an incurable wound and he may have learned the healing arts in order to minister to himself. At any rate, Chiron taught the boy Asklepius all he knew about healing so that by the time Asklepius reached maturity he was a doctor in his own right. Athena, seeing his natural proclivity toward healing, gave Asklepius a marvelous gift: the blood from the torso of the slain Gorgon, Medusa. The blood that had flowed from her right side brought healing and life; the blood that flowed from her left side brought death.

Armed with his knowledge and with the saving blood of Medusa, Asklepius became a great physician. The ill among humankind found their way to him and he cured them of their many afflictions. All were delighted—except the god Hades, god of the underworld, who complained to Zeus that he was being cheated because human beings were no longer dying and his kingdom was not being replenished. Zeus had to agree with his brother god that this was an affront, and at Hades' urging he slew Asklepius with a thunderbolt. At this, however, there arose from humanity such a lament that even the hearts of the gods were moved. Zeus responded by raising Asklepius from death and placing him among the stars as an immortal, divine physician.

The Greeks believed that all knowledge, power, and skill at healing came from the divine Asklepius, and they called their physicians "Aslepiads," that is, "sons of Asklepius." From our point of view Asklepius is the archetype of the healer. When this archetype appears in a man he finds himself inclined toward and skilled in the healing profession. His healing capacity may take various forms depending on his typology. He may, for example, become a surgeon, an internist, or a neurologist. But he may also become a psychotherapist, or even a spiritual healer or herbologist. Asklepius has many sons and they are all different, except that they are healers, each in his own way.

It is significant that both Chiron and Asklepius were "wounded healers." Asklepius, as we mentioned, was saved from death twice, and Chiron suffered from an incurable wound. We find that many men who are drawn into the field of healing, especially the healing of the psyche, are wounded spirits themselves. In ministering to their own wounds they learn how to heal the wounds of others. In fact, the way such men realize their call to a healing profession is often through a distressing psychological or physical illness of their own.

Next we will consider the two brothers, Hermes and Apollo. Even though they were brothers they were quite different in their personalities. Apollo was born first, and by the time Hermes appeared on the scene he was already a well-established personality, gifted in music, and the owner of a remarkable herd of cattle in which he took great pride. When Hermes was born his very first act was to steal his brother's cattle. He misled his brother by the crafty trick of marching the cattle off backward; in this way the footprints of the cattle indicated they had gone off in the opposite direction. Thus Hermes began his life by displaying his essential characteristics: his craftiness, cleverness, and wit, and in this cunning resourcefulness lay his great strength.

As we have seen, Hephaeustus was also clever and resourceful, but while he used his cleverness with things, Hermes used his with people. For instance, Hermes was the patron god of thieves and robbers, and of all those men who gained advantage in life through trickery. Everyone who makes his living by his wits owes his gifts to this archetype, and some people with Hermes within them become quite wealthy and successful. In our culture, really great wealth is not accumulated by hard work so much as it is by making a shrewd deal. Really large amounts of money are made through someone's cleverness. Certain men have a natural shrewdness with money and in their dealings with people. If this natural shrewdness is combined with a certain amount of ruthlessness their wealth may be accumulated at the expense of those less shrewd than themselves.

In spite of his craftiness, or maybe because of it, Hermes was likable. His thievery did not involve maliciousness or brutality. An excellent portrayal of a Hermes-man is found in the film "The Grey Fox," a true-to-life account of a train-robber who found he just could not lead a straight and narrow life.

Hermes was also the god of luck and chance, and the patron of magicians. He himself had a magic wand with which he could put people to sleep and awaken them, and he also could make himself invisible by means of his cap, obtained from Hades, god of the underworld. He was a god who was friendly to humankind, and was known to be a generous giver to those in need. For instance, if a man made a happy find or had a stroke of luck he would attribute it to Hermes. Merchants put their trust in him and saw him as their patron deity, for he was the god of joyous and even unscrupulous profit. However, he could also reverse himself: if a man unexpectedly lost his profits, that too could be the work of Hermes. The bad luck as well as the good came from him and a man who was a true son of this god just had to expect that.

This complex and multi-faceted god had many other functions as well. It was Hermes, for example, who brought men dreams. He also cared for and multiplied the flocks. He also was a guide of souls and escorted the soul of a deceased person to the underworld. Among the gods he served as the messenger, which is why the United States Army Signal Corps has adopted the caduceus of Hermes (two snakes entwined on a staff) as its emblem.* But for our purposes it is enough to note the aspect of Hermes that is involved in luck, cleverness, profit-making, deception, and chance, for here is the archetype of all those men who are drawn to that field of business or profit-making that depends on shrewdness, a bit of calculating unscrupulousness, and lucky chance. Hermes might be said to be the patron saint of capitalism, which, as an economic system, allows this archetype to operate freely as long as it does not break too many laws (though these laws are necessary in order to circumscribe the activities of those men in whom this archetype is strong). The great entrepreneurs of the capitalistic world have this god as their innermost source of power. The man who makes and loses fortunes is a devotee of Hermes, even though he may never have heard about him. The lowly pickpocket on the street and the master of high finance who finds a way to deceive his fellow entrepreneurs both have within them the same archetype. Much mischief is done by this power, but there is also a certain element of creativity that comes from it. Fortunes made by a man in whom Hermes was a strong influence have sometimes redounded to the ultimate benefit of humankind, while the capitalistic system in which Hermes flourishes has proved to be a better producer of wealth than rigidly run economic systems that preclude his

---

*A staff with one serpent around it is the symbol of Asklepius. The medical profession, which is better at surgery than mythology, usually confuses the two.

activity (and so force him to go underground, for in any system the clever and the ruthless wind up victimizing their fellows).

The brother of Hermes, as we have seen, was Apollo, and among the gods only Zeus was more important. Apollo, while not the sun itself, for the sun was the god Helios, was a sun-god. Being associated with the sun, Apollo made the earth fruitful and protected the crops. However, the sun can be destructive as well as beneficent; its rays can sear and lay waste as well as warm and nourish. So Apollo also had two sides: he was an archer whose shafts could bring sudden death, but he was also a god of healing, but his healing came through purification of soul and body. He warded off illness and evil by purifying the soul of guilt and the body of impurities. He also helped a man clarify himself inwardly. His sacred shrine at Delphi, where people went to consult the oracle, had over it the ascription "Know thyself." His province therefore is the power of insight, reflection, and self-knowledge. From all of this a great gift comes from Apollo to humanity: those rules, laws, and regulations on which the orderly conduct of human life depends.

Apollo can also be regarded as the god of knowledge. His farseeing aspect, and his objective stance, undergird the qualities that make for great minds. But Apollo's insight also revealed that which was not yet visible and which had not yet come into existence. It was therefore to Apollo that great seers and visionaries owed their capacities.

Apollo was also a god of music, and the lyre was his special invention. He, along with the Muses, inspired musicians and musical inventiveness in general. He is responsible for the mathematical order and structure of music as well as its harmonious aspects, for through music all the harmonious forms of life are expressed. His music, however, is that of moderation and beauty, not of ecstasy or wild excitement (which belongs to another god, Dionysus).

To Apollo we owe all that is called Apollonian: form, order, harmony, reflection, insight, coolness, distance. Men in whom this archetype is strong lend order to life, and contain within themselves the spirit of reflection. Such men might excel as lawmakers or statesmen. With a musical gift they might become musicians, especially of the classical inclination. They would excel at administration. If drawn into a military career they would become generals whose penchant was for the organization of the army, and whose forte was grand strategy. They might become great orators with a gift for ringing phrases fraught with imposing meaning. A man in whom Apollo was strong would run his home or business well. He might make a good, though distant, father, a dependable provider but distant lover. In the business world he would not be a gambler, such as those whose god is Hermes, but might achieve success through careful administration, planning, and consistent aims. He might also be drawn into the world of science, where he would seek out the order that unites the multifarious forms and aspects of life.

The last of the gods we will consider is Zeus who was supreme among the gods. Zeus was the lord of the sky, the winds, the clouds, rain, and thunder. He dwelt in the air or on mountain tops. He knew all there was to know and governed the world of gods and men as a supreme sovereign. He meted out to humanity both good and evil, although he was usually a compassionate ruler who protected the weak, dispensed justice, and listened solicitously to human petitions. In many ways his functions corresponded to those of God the Father in Christianity.

The Olympians owed their very existence to Zeus. Originally the divine world was ruled by the Titans, chief of whom was the sky god Cronus. Cronus begat from his wife Rhea a succession of children: Hestia, Demeter, Hera, Hades, Poseidon, and Zeus. Fearful lest one of his children supplant him, Cronus swallowed them all, except Zeus, who was born in secret and kept concealed by his grief-stricken mother Rhea. When the time was ripe, Zeus avenged his brothers and sisters by tricking Cronus into swallowing a stone. When Cronus took a draught to rid himself of the stone he vomited forth not only the stone but the swallowed deities as well. Zeus then vanquished Cronus, cast him to the depths of the universe, and enchained him there forever.

Only one deity had power over Zeus and that was Aphrodite, who often filled him with all of the longing and desire that so characterized the goddess' realm of influence. As a result, Zeus had a succession of relationships with mortal women, including among them Niobe, Io, Europa, Semele, Leda and Alcmene, and from these unions there came numerous progeny. His mortal lovers suffered as a result of the god's amorous attentions because Zeus' wife, Hera, maddened with jealousy, inflicted her vengeance on them.

Zeus can be regarded as the masculine archetype par excellence. Everything that partakes of the nature of the "founding fathers" springs from this archetype. His is the archetype of the ruler and the judge, and a lawyer who has within him this archetype might become a judge. A father who rules his family with dominance but parental concern does so from the archetype personified as Zeus. A man who finds his calling that of leader and chief is a true son of Zeus. Men who are "sons of Zeus" will tend to have productive lives, and their progeny, whether they be human children or the fruits of a productive life, will be many.

The Influence of Feminine Archetypes

In addition to the masculine archetypes we have considered there are feminine archetypes that greatly influence a man's psychology. In the chapter on a man's relationship to his feminine side we will consider some of these feminine archetypes as they are manifested in mythological images. For the most part, these feminine images influence a man's emotional and relational life more than his occupational life, but there is no hard and fast line to be drawn, and sometimes it is the goddess within a man that turns out to be the determining factor in a man's choice of profession. For our present purposes, by way of illustration, we will consider the Muses.

There were nine Muses. Taken as a whole, the Muses presided over music and poetry, but each one had her own special province. Calliope, who was first in rank among her sisters, was the Muse of Epic Poetry; Clio was the Muse of History; Erato was the Muse of Love Poetry; Euterpe was the Muse of the Flute; Melpomene was the Muse of Tragedy; Polyhymnia was the Muse of Heroic Hymns and Mime; Terpsichore was the Muse of Lyric Poetry and the Dance; Thalia was the Muse of Comedy; Urania was the Muse of Astronomy.*

If a man is drawn to become a musician, to dance, to mime, to write poetry, or to be involved in the world of drama, it can be said that his inspiration comes from one or more of the Muses. For example, the word "music" comes from the Greek word μουσική which means "pertaining to the Muses." When it comes to music, even a man's interest in a certain instrument stems from a particular manifestation of this archetype. For instance, though a musician may be able to play a number of instruments, there is one instrument or group of instruments to which he is especially drawn. He might be a keyboard artist, in which case he will play the piano, harpsichord, or organ with skill, but he will not be equally skillful when it comes to playing wind instruments.

Larousse Encyclopedia of Mythology, tr. Richard Aldington and Delano Ames, 1967, p. 127. First published in France.

Some musicians so identify with one musical instrument that it becomes the focus of their entire professional lives. The contemporary pan flutist Zamfir would be an example. The Greeks would have said that the Muse Euterpe gave him this interest and skill as a gift.

The Right Work

The variety of archetypes gives us an idea of the varied kinds of work to which a man may be called. But in addition, a man may have within himself what can be called, for lack of a better word, a "knack." By this is meant a particular faculty for doing something that is within the general field of an archetype but is not identical with the whole of it.

Take the craftsman whose archetype is Hephaeustus. Artisans like to work either with wood or with metal, but seldom with both. It is as though metal has a certain spirit within it and wood has another kind of spirit, and the artisan's own spirit matches one or the other. So the knack of a cabinetmaker may not be efficacious when it comes to working with metal, and an artisan who works with metal may not be interested in working with wood.

As we have seen, the artist has been shown to be, generally speaking, an introverted intuitive type, but not all introverted intuitive types are artists. The artistic temperament may stem not only from typology but also from the combination of a man's typology with an archetype, in this case that of the Muses. But artists themselves vary greatly in the way their artistry is expressed. One may paint, one sculpt, and another may develop his own peculiar form of artistic expression.

Chess playing is a good example of a knack. Chess players are almost always introverted men with a strong intuitive or thinking function. The archetype accompanying their typology is probably that of Apollo. But chess-playing in itself is a peculiar ability. Not all introverted intuitive or thinking types whose main archetype is Apollo are interested in or are good at chess. It is as though chess-playing men have a certain genius for this particular activity. Even within their ranks there are individuals with a peculiar strength. For instance, some players can play many games of chess simultaneously, blindfolded. They are able to visualize the position of the many pieces in each of the games. However, this is by no means a gift that is common to the usual run of even expert players.

The word "genius," which we just used, has an interesting deri-
vation. The creative spirit has an unlimited variety of expressions. Our
typology and the central archetype within us shape the main areas of
life in which we function with a maximum of skill and satisfaction. But
within each man there is a peculiar gift that functions within the broader
category and shapes his skills in a way that is peculiarly his own. The
Greeks ascribed this individual skill or ability in a man to his "genius."
No two men ever had the same genius. The genius of a man gave him
his particular natural talent and creativity. We still use the word genius
today but though we apply it only to a man of exceptional capacity,
saying, for example, that Albert Einstein was a genius, the Greeks said
that every man had a genius for something, whether it was for whittling
wood or making abstruse mathematical calculations.

Therefore, the best work for a man to do is a work that is suited
for his particular typology, which draws upon his central archetype, and
for which he has a knack or genius. But finding such work is not always
easy since most young men are unaware of their psychology. Of course
there are vocational guidance tests and vocational counselors and these
may be helpful, but there are also other ways in which a man may get
an important hint about the kind of work he is intended to perform.

Sometimes the central archetype within a man shapes both inner
fantasies and outer events in such a way that his life vocation becomes
clear to him. For example, a physician who was born around the turn
of the century and practiced medicine over fifty years, until the time of
his death at the age of eighty-two, relates that as a youth he was asked
by the doctor in the small Nebraska town in which he lived to drive him
on his rounds to his patients out in the country. The young man soon
found himself keenly interested in what the doctor was doing and in the
various ailments he treated. With some encouragement from the older
man, he readily made a decision to enter medical school. He was a natural for it. The archetype of Asklepius was so strong within him that
both the outer event (being asked to drive the doctor on his rounds) and
the inner event (his ability to imagine himself doing a doctor's work)
combined to make him aware of his calling to medicine.

In the above instance, a specific activity helped the young man to
know what he wanted to do. In other cases a man may need to rely more
exclusively on his fantasies. The archetype in us tends to express itself
in fantasies. By fantasies I mean those uninvited thoughts or images that

cross our screen of consciousness. If we can "see" ourselves doing this or that work, that is a clue that we may be meant to do it. People today tend to disregard their fantasies; even if they are aware of them they do not lend them credence and tend to make their decisions more "rationally." For this reason, many people miss the mark when it comes to their work. One young man was always aware of his interest in drama. As a youth he read plays and was intrigued by the theater, especially by the lives of the playwrights. However, his father, a practical man, urged him to enter the financial world and so he became a stockbroker, investment counselor, and then a banker. He got along well enough in this occupation, but as time went on his early interest in drama emerged again, and he found himself trying to write plays. By this time he had a family to support and it was hard for him to make a change from his financially lucrative work in finance to the uncertainties of the life of a playwright. In his case the clues about his lifework were apparent in his youth, but neither he nor his parents were sufficiently psychologically aware to give them proper credence.

Sometimes our proper vocation manifests itself in childhood in the kinds of games we play. One man began his career as a professional, but later he became unhappy with this and cast about for other work he might do. Then he remembered that as a boy of about twelve years of age he used to write short stories. He recalled the keen enjoyment he experienced as he wrote his tales and the delight with which he told them to others. Without giving up his major professional life, eventually he started to write again, and he achieved some modest success with his stories. In his case it wasn't necessary for him to give up his profession; he only needed to rejuvenate his life by dipping into the unused energy of the writer within him.

People with an artistic, literary, or musical talent often find themselves drawn toward their proper field of endeavor quite naturally. If the talent is strong, and the individual is conscious of it, there is little or no difficulty in choosing a work in which that talent can be expressed. Robert Louis Stevenson tells us in his autobiographical *Over the Plains* that from the time he was a boy he knew he wanted to write. Unfortunately he came from a long line of engineers and his father would not hear of his becoming anything so abstruse and impractical as a novelist. It was necessary for the young Robert Louis to get around his father somehow, so they made a compromise: he would study law.

It was all a ruse on Robert's part, for it was only a short step for him to move from law school into writing, which, of course, remained his lifelong passion and profession.

The writer, artist or musician faces certain difficulties in establishing himself in his profession, for he often finds himself faced with the necessity of selling his skills to others in order to make a living. If he has to please someone else with his work in order to be paid for it, he may also have to dilute his creative genius. The composer Charles Ives found a way around this problem. Ives was one of the first to experiment with modern styles of musical composition. He was ahead of his time and knew that his compositions were not in the fashion of the day, but he did not want to curb his creative impulses in order to satisfy the tastes and expectations of others. So Ives decided to make his living in the insurance industry, and compose music on the side. In this way, since he did not have to make a living with his musical ability, he was free to compose exactly as he wished.

Finding the right work is a matter of psychological as well as practical importance, for if our creative energies are denied or repressed they can turn against us, making us sour on life, or even becoming destructive. They have the power to block a man completely if he persists in doing the wrong kind of work. A law student consulted a therapist because he was sure he was losing his mind. To his great distress, he was unable to comprehend what he read in his lawbooks. He could read the same page ten times and have no idea what it said. He was disconsolate, distracted, and depressed. In the course of the conversation with the therapist he happened to mention that he had read quite a bit of one of Carl Jung's books. The therapist asked him, "How could you manage to read the book by Jung when you couldn't comprehend even one page of a lawbook?" The young man had never asked himself that question. The next day when he returned to the therapist for a second appointment he was completely cured. He was free of anxiety, could read anything he wanted to, and was no longer depressed. His cure was simple: he had left the therapist's office and headed for the office of the dean of the law school and resigned. It was still a struggle for him to find the right work in life, but eventually he did, and his symptoms never returned.

Sometimes there are various kinds of work that a man can do. Various archetypes may contend within him for supremacy and no one archetype may claim the center of the stage. Nevertheless, for practical reasons such a man will choose one line of work and pursue it to the exclusion of the others. This leaves the other possibilities in himself unlived. It often works out in such cases that somewhere in midlife the energies that once were available to him for his chosen work begin to dry up. His work becomes increasingly boring and burdensome and he may begin to be depressed. He may feel as though he is now just "turning the crank." C. G. Jung once said that a man's work begins as his passion, then becomes his duty, and finally his burden. While this may not always be true, it is often the case.

The problem is that the original energy from the archetype he was using in his work has been used up. Archetypes do not necessarily remain active within us throughout our lifetime, and when they disappear the energy they gave us also disappears. Parents, for instance, who were zealous fathers or mothers when the children were growing up, may find when the children are adolescents that the parenting energy within them that once was so strong has now gone. They still love their children but wish they would finish growing up and find their own homes. When this happens to a man regarding his work, he must cast about for other energies within him that have not yet been drawn upon. He needs to find the other archetypes that belong to his personality that have fresh energy because their potential has not yet been exhausted. All of this becomes part of the midlife crisis of many men, and it is to this subject that we now turn.

Suggested Reading

Gerzon, Mark, *A Choice of Heroes: The Changing Faces of American Manhood.* Boston: Houghton Mifflin Co., 1982.

Kerenyi, Karl, *The Gods of the Greeks.* Thames and Hudson, 1979.

Myers, Isabel Briggs and Peter B., *Gifts Differing.* Palo Alto: Consulting Psychologists Press, Inc., 1980.

von Franz, Marie-Louise, *Puer Aeternus.* Boston: Sigo Press, 1981. (Originally Dallas: Spring Publications, 1970.)

Chapter 5

The Midlife Crisis

We hear a lot nowadays about something called the midlife crisis, and for good reason. There is no question that somewhere in midlife, which can be regarded as between the ages of thirty-five and fifty, many men find themselves in a psychological and spiritual crisis. It may have come upon them relatively suddenly, but more likely it has crept up on them slowly, so insidiously taking them over that a man may not have been aware of what was happening to him until he has developed definite symptoms. These symptoms include depression, boredom, a chronic fatigue that is not alleviated by ordinary rest, increasing irritability, difficulty in performing tasks that once were done with ease and enthusiasm, somatic complaints, and, with some men, excessive drinking. Our task is to see what is involved in a man's midlife crisis; why it exists, and how it can be resolved. We will approach the task in two ways. First, we will look at its narrower manifestation in the phenomenon known as "burnout." Second, we will look at the broader problem: the problem of the "exhausted ego."

Burnout

Burnout is an old term with a new meaning. The word used to be used in a situation in which an energy such as fire or electricity passed through something and left it burned or depleted. For instance, if a powerful electric current passes through an inadequate conduit, the conduit will burn out. In forestry, a forest fire that is so hot it destroys the ground cover as well as the trees and brush is said to be a burnout. But now the word is used in a new way: it is applied to people who are burned out at what they are doing in life. When this happens, the energy that once passed through a man energizing his life and work has departed, leaving him depleted and depressed. As a rule a man experiences this phenomenon in midlife; consequently burnout is a part of or even the cause of a man's midlife crisis.

When a new word appears in our vocabulary it suggests there is a new problem in society. No doubt men have always burned out at what they were doing, but the fact that the word burnout is suddenly in vogue suggests that we are confronting a psychological problem that is far more widespread today than in times past, or, at least, that the problem has been identified and come into the focus of conscious attention.

Anyone can burn out: doctors, lawyers, laborers, teachers, parents, clergymen, psychotherapists. A key element is repetition. The doctor who sees the same old illnesses again and again, the clergyman who performs the same ecclesiastical routines and deals with the same kind of problematic parishioners, the psychotherapist who has dealt with one too many chronically depressed or drug-dependent patients, the laborer who has performed the same function once too often, the teacher who has taught the same material over and over again, all of these men may have become dull, like a knife that has been used so many times it has lost its edge.

Repetitive work exhausts the ego. The creative spirits within us like fresh work and fresh challenges. When it is a matter of encountering the same old problems, then the spirit leaves us. Like an old piece of wood left high and dry on the beach by the receding tide, we can be left high and dry from our source of energy.

Repetitive work also erodes our life force. The Greeks even had a myth about it: the myth of Sisyphus. Sisyphus was a mortal man who revealed that his daughter Aegina was the mistress of Zeus. For this crime against the gods, Zeus condemned Sisyphus to the underworld, Tartarus, where he was compelled to roll a huge round stone up a steep hill. When the stone was within inches of the summit, down it rolled again. Sisyphus was then compelled to roll the stone up the hill once more. In this way the Greek myth used incessant and repetitive work as a symbol for divine punishment.

Another relevant image from Greek mythology is the story of the hydra. The hydra was a huge serpent with nine heads, and the head in the middle was immortal. It was one of Hercules' twelve labors to slay this terrible monster that was ravaging the countryside. Hercules tried to kill it by cutting off the heads with his club, but each time he struck off a head two others grew in its place. This gives us the image of a work that can never be finished, that must be done over and over, a labor that only becomes harder the more we work at it. Hercules finally won the battle by burning the monster's heads with red-hot brands, and, after he severed the head that was immortal, he buried it deep in the ground. Unlike Sisyphus, Hercules was finally able to complete his task and go on to something else, but it took a truly Herculean effort to do so.

When it is only the ego that has worn out, the problem is bad enough, but sometimes the archetype from which comes a man's energy for his work has also become depleted. We have already noted that archetypes that once were prominent in someone's psychology may disappear later in life. Then all the energy that the archetype once supplied has disappeared. The man is left with the same work to do but the energy source for doing it has gone. He has simply run out of gas, and he doesn't know where to find any more.

Let us take teaching as an example. There is an archetype for the teacher. From time immemorial there must have been men who taught others the skills they needed in life. Some men are extremely adept at this; others lack this ability. Someone who has the archetype of the teacher in him will have the instinctive sense of how to impart skills to others and develop their potential; he will also find great satisfaction in doing this work. But teaching, especially in a school system, tends to be repetitive work. A teacher usually teaches a specific subject or grade level. Each year the same material is taught over and over again. The people he is teaching differ each year, of course, but they are also similar. There are the same types of problems, the same questions, the same difficulties, and the same interactions with others. The time may come when a man simply gets worn out by this. Worse yet, the time may come when the archetype of the teacher within him has exhausted its potential energy. Then his work becomes a burden to him. Yet he may feel as though he has to continue. He has a family to support, he isn't trained to do anything else, he hasn't reached retirement age yet and still has to teach in order to make his living. He is burned out, but seems to have no choice but to continue in the old work and the old way.

One teacher who had this problem was so depleted by the end of his school day that he was virtually in tears. By the time he returned home he felt hopeless. Only one thing saved him: near his house was a modest-sized mountain, and every afternoon after school was over he would climb that mountain. Somehow that gave him the strength to go on until at last he could retire.

When a man is faced with such a dilemma there are right ways and wrong ways for him to try to solve the problem. An example of the wrong way is found in the fairy tale called "The Handless Maiden." It is a long tale involving a young woman who lost her hands in a deal with the devil, but it is only the first part of the story that concerns us.

The tale begins with a miller whose mill had once prospered but who has now fallen on hard times. The mill has become old, and it no longer produces as it should, and his business is suffering as a result. Depressed, the miller wanders through the woods where he meets the devil. "What seems to be the problem?" the devil asks him, and the miller tells him of his plight. The devil replies that the solution is simple: if the miller will promise him one thing he will see to it that his mill prospers once again. "And what is that?" asks the miller. "That you give me the first thing you see when you return home and look into your back yard." The miller thinks to himself, "There is nothing there but that old apple tree; I can easily dispense with that." So the agreement is made. But when the miller returns home and looks into his backyard, whom should he see but his one and only daughter. The miller is aghast, but there is no going back on an agreement with the devil, and he is forced to deliver his daughter into the hands of the evil one.

As Marie-Louise von Franz pointed out in her shrewd analysis of this story,[1] the mill was one of the first major technological triumphs of the human race. By a clever trick, men learned to harness the energy of streams and make the water work for them. The water turned the wheel, and the wheel, through a series of mechanical gears and contrivances, turned the millstone, and the millstone did all sorts of work that the miller wanted done. The miller was thus one of the first mechanics, and the mill one of the first mechanical operations. The fact that the miller's mill is no longer producing is an image of the depletion of a man when his purely mechanical and ego-centered way of functioning no longer works for him. The devil is the devilish side of a man's ego. The story tells us that he can keep the old mechanical work going some more—but only at a price. The price is symbolized in the story by the selling of the miller's daughter to the devil. In life, the price for finding a devilish way to keep his old mechanical life going is paid by a man through an injury to his feminine side. We are reminded of Jesus' saying, "What does it profit a man if he gains the whole world but loses his own soul?"

Sometimes a man can, by sacrificing his soul, working still harder, and summoning up all the tricks at his disposal, keep his old life working and producing for him. But the price is much greater than he imagines, for his damaged and rejected feminine side will certainly turn

---

1. von Franz, *The Feminine in Fairy Tales*, p. 74.

against him. He has made an enemy of his own soul, which is to say that the unconscious, that might have helped him out of his difficulties in a creative way, turns dark and destructive. Then, even though his business or work may still make money for him, a man may become ill, drink excessively, or fall into a depression. A better solution is to find a change of work, a new work that will draw upon new energies and bring the ego into fresh situations. Sometimes such changes of occupation are possible and sometimes they are not.

I have observed among clergymen, for instance, that there is a certain amount of coming and going. Many men enter the ministry late in their lives. Some have been teachers or engineers or have been in the military and have become clergymen when they are in their forties or even later. A number of denominations have set up special seminaries so older men who want to train for the ministry can do so while still continuing their old occupations. On the other hand, many clergy who entered the ranks earlier in life leave the work for something different. Often it is a work that is a "first cousin" to the ministry, such as teaching or counseling.

Sometimes it is possible for a man to make a radically different change of vocation and thereby get a new lease on life. For instance, a lawyer might enter politics. An engineer might buy and fix up old houses. A psychotherapist might stop his practice and begin a printing business.

At other times, the old work can be continued if a man adds an avocation that is meaningful to him. For instance, a doctor might leave the rigors of private practice for emergency hospital work. He works regular hours and then has time free to start another line of endeavor that may prove to be entirely different. The fresh energy he gets from his new avocation makes it possible for him to continue his old profession at a reduced level. Such solutions call for resourcefulness and boldness on the part of a man.

In order to produce the situation in which creative changes of work are possible, a man may have to find new attitudes. For instance, he may have to become symbolically "unmarried." A man is married to many things besides his wife. He is married to all kinds of ideas and obligations that he supposes are fixed, rigid, and unalterable, such as making a certain amount of income, having to succeed, having to have a big name, having to live in a certain place, having to please certain people. . . . In order to move on creatively with his life he may have to "divorce" himself from such fixed and rigid ideas and patterns. Unfortunately, many men divorce their wives instead and look for a younger woman, as though the youth of the new wife could make them young again. Such men change the women in their lives but keep the old mill going, with the devil's help, and with the predictable consequences.

The Problem of the Exhausted Ego

Sometimes, however, none of the usual answers to the problem of burnout work because the problem comes from a deeper level. Burnout is then only the surface manifestation of a more profound spiritual malaise. It isn't just the man's work that is worn out, it is the man himself at his deepest levels. A man is then confronted with what can be called the problem of the exhausted ego.

By the time a man is in midlife his youthful ego ambitions have either been fulfilled or not fulfilled. If they have not been fulfilled he looks at his life and sees that it has been a failure, at least to his way of thinking. Even though at the age of forty or thereabouts he may feel vigorous and strong enough, something in him knows that the sun, while at its zenith, is now going to sink toward the horizon and eventual death. His unfulfilled ambitions therefore look remote and inaccessible, and he becomes discouraged and may feel inferior to others. But even if they have been fulfilled the situation may not be much better. To be sure, he has reached the goals he set for himself years ago, he is a success in terms of his worldly achievements, but he finds his success empty. Now that he has reached his goals he finds they mean nothing to him. They mean nothing to him because they are the ambitions of his ego, not of the Self. He has lived the first part of his life too much out of the ego and not enough from the Center. Because his ambitions were largely egocentric they turn to dust in his hands. And now, with the sun of his ego beginning its descent toward death, he finds that his life is meaningless.

Nothing less than a complete renovation of personality and attitudes will suffice to cure such a man of his ever-deepening malaise. His problem is both psychological and spiritual, and can only be resolved by his undertaking the journey of individuation. It is now inner death for him to live any longer from the ego alone, with its egocentric wants and wishes and ambitions. He must find his deeper Self, and find what that deeper Self wants from him, and for the life that remains to be lived.

Now we see the consequences of the tyranny of the ego we spoke of in Chapter 3. There we observed that when a man starts adult life his ego is always more or less egocentric. Typically a man lives the first half of his life out of such an egocentric ego, but in a severe midlife crisis such as we have been describing the old egocentric ego is at the end of its rope. With such a man there is nowhere to go if he tries to continue in the old pattern. The egocentric way of adapting that once served him, after a fashion, serves him no longer. The spiritual task that now confronts him involves the destruction of the old egocentric adaptation and the reorganization of his personality around the greater center of the Self.

In his masterful study of masculine spiritual development *HE!* Robert Johnson tells the story of the Hideous Damsel. The story centers around the knightly hero, Parsifal. Parsifal and his fellow knights are having a great celebration of all their exploits, and no one has any more exploits about which to boast than Parsifal himself. In the midst of their revelry, there wanders into the camp a woman riding a mule, a woman so hideous to look at that the celebration stops cold in its tracks. Johnson quotes the description given of the Hideous Damsel in the old tales: "Her black hair was tressed in two braids, iron dark were her hands and nails. Her closed eyes small like a rat's. Her nose like an ape and cat. Her lips like an ass and bull. Bearded was she, humped breast and back, her loins and shoulders twisted like the roots of a tree. Never in royal court was such a damsel seen."[2]

The Hideous Damsel personifies the negative aspect of the unconscious, turned against a man when he has pursued his egocentric ambitions and goals too long. Her clinical manifestations would be depression, habitual moodiness, the inability to savor and enjoy life's pleasures, and a sense of meaninglessness that destroys a man's capacity to find pleasure any longer in his egocentric pursuits. Very often such a "dark anima" appears prominently in a man who has been notably successful in life. It is the way the unconscious has of pulling a man's attention away from his outer successes and toward his need to undergo his inner, spiritual journey.

---

2. Robert Johnson, *HE!* p. 71.

How Individuation Renews the Exhausted Ego

In Chapter 3 we mentioned the psychological, spiritual, and maturational aspects of the process of individuation. While it is not possible in the compass of this book to describe in detail what happens to a person who undergoes individuation, we can elaborate somewhat on these three aspects of the process and see how they help alleviate the exhaustion of the ego.

First we will consider the maturation of the ego. This process requires the breaking down of the old egocentric ego so it can be reorganized around the greater center of the personality, the Self. It calls for a reversal of values: from those of the ego to those of the Self. In the language of the New Testament, this is what is meant by *metanoia,* and it was the first thing that Jesus called for when he proclaimed the nearness of the kingdom of God.[3] Such a process necessitates a good deal of suffering. It includes facing one's worst fears, and enduring a series of crises. It is necessary that the individual face his shadow—his own dark, feared side—and pass through a time of personal darkness. This part of the individuation process has been described in considerable detail by Fritz Kunkel.[4]

A second aspect of individuation involves recognizing, coming to terms with, and realizing contents of the collective unconscious that were hitherto unknown. In so doing a man's understanding of who he is, and what life expects of him, is greatly widened. Coming to terms with various aspects of his personality that were unknown to him before will challenge a man's flexibility and creativity to the utmost, but it also has a reward: it brings fresh energy and meaning to life.

Of particular importance for a man is his coming into relationship in a conscious way with his feminine side. In fact, this is so important that our next chapter is devoted to this problem. It was C. G. Jung who described for us what we might expect to find in the collective unconscious, who discovered and described the major archetypes of the collective unconscious, and who showed how coming into relationship with the unconscious would help us form that new Center of the personality that he called the Self.

---

3. "The time has come and the kingdom of God is close at hand. Repent (metanoia), and believe the Good News" (Mk 1:15; cf. Mt 4:17).

4. John Sanford, ed., *Fritz Kunkel: Selected Writings.*

The third part of the process is the spiritual side of the work of individuation in contrast to the more psychological side. This includes the development by a man of a religious *weltanschauung,* or world outlook. In times past men carried much of the priestly functions, but in today's world most men have left the religious side of life to the official priests of the church, and to the women. Individuation will require a man to take up his own lost priesthood and to become a priest to his own soul.

A religious outlook does not mean that a man necessarily identifies with any particular religion, theology, or creed. It does mean that he cultivates a religious attitude that befits him and his experience, and that he wrestles with such existential questions of life as the problem of evil, the after-life, and life's underlying purposes. An important aspect of this spiritual process is the development of the quality of faith. Faith does not mean believing in things that can't be proven, or assenting to creedal statements about God. Rather, faith is the cultivation of the soul's movement toward God. It is faith that gives a man the courage to live when the going gets tough. The understanding of the contents of the unconscious requires insight and knowledge; but where knowledge leaves off, faith begins. The mind needs knowledge, but the soul needs faith, and the gifts of courage and perseverance that it brings.

Of course these three aspects of the individuation process are not so readily distinguishable from each other in actual practice. We are involved in all three at once, and the lines that separate one from another exist more in our minds than in our inner lives. We cannot give up our egocentricity without help from the unconscious, and we cannot make real the contents of the unconscious without surrendering our cherished egocentric power to the demands of the archetypes. None of the process of individuation will go far unless we have some faith, and our faith is at the same time strengthened by the discoveries that we make of the reality of the inner world. The knowledge we get through increased insight into ourselves feeds our faith, and our faith inspires us to persevere in the process of acquiring knowledge. Thus while we need to make distinctions in order to get a conscious grasp on the meaning of individuation, in actual practice everything blends into everything else.

People individuated long before there was anything called psychology. However, depth psychology, as presented to us by Jung, Kunkel and others, gives us many helpful hints on how in our contemporary times a man might proceed in undertaking such a journey. Since our time in history is heavily extraverted, many men will find that they must now turn inward, and develop their introverted life. The prophet Elijah is an example. In the Israel of Elijah's time, the true worshipers of Yahweh had been banished and his enemy, Queen Jezebel, plotted to take his life. Discouraged and exhausted, Elijah went on a long pilgrimage across the desert to Mount Sinai. There he crept into a cave on the flank of the mountain and waited for God to speak to him. At last God spoke in a still, small voice. Out of the ensuing dialogue, Elijah got fresh courage and energy for his life, and returned to his task in Israel. This is a story of making a journey inward, of finding out that God speaks from the inmost soul. It is also a story of learning to make a pilgrimage of life. Even vacations go better if they are also pilgrimages. Vacations are taken for pure pleasure, pilgrimages for a holy purpose—that is, for a reason that is inwardly meaningful.

Certain spiritual and psychological resources help us with this work. Keeping a Journal is one of these. Morton Kelsey and others have written helpful books giving valuable guidance on what it means to keep a Journal.* Another great help is to become aware of our dreams, and to keep a record of them in the Journal. Dreams reveal to us the state of our souls. They help forge a connecting link between ego and Self. They guide the soul and illuminate her darkness. They impart both knowledge of the unconscious, and faith that there is a meaningful process going on within us. Fortunately today there are many fine books to help us understand the importance of our dreams and how to relate to them creatively. Helpful though dreams are, many people will find it important, perhaps even necessary, to have a companion on their journey who can be a guide. This person might be an informed analyst or spiritual director. No one can make the journey entirely alone.

Keeping a Journal, recording dreams, finding a helper—all of these are ways of finding another source of energy to replenish ours as we make our journeys. We can compare our source of energy to that of a lake. A lake that stands by itself will soon dry up. A lake that is replenished because it is in contact with another source of water will stay full and fresh. The ancient Chinese book of wisdom *The I Ching* gives us a beautiful image of this in hexagram 58: Tui—The Joyous, Lake. The Image reads:

---

*See suggested readings.

Lakes resting one on the other:
The image of THE JOYOUS.
Thus the superior man joins with his friends
For discussion and practice.

The commentary reads:

> A lake evaporates upward and thus gradually dries up; but when two lakes are joined they do not dry up so readily, for one replenishes the other. It is the same in the field of knowledge. Knowledge should be a refreshing and vitalizing force. It becomes so only through stimulating intercourse with congenial friends with whom one holds singular discussion and practices application of the truths of life. In this way learning becomes many-sided and takes on a cheerful lightness, whereas there is always something ponderous and one-sided about the learning of the self-taught.[5]

The ego can be like a lake that is cut off from a source of contact with any other body of water and as a consequence has dried up. In the process of individuation a connection is made to other sources of energy. Now it is as though the lake is in contact with another lake and is replenished by the streams of water that flow from one to the other. In individuation, a contact with the unconscious enables energy to flow into the depleted ego. A meaningful relationship with a counselor, analyst, or spiritual director can also help us to renew our conscious lives. In such ways the exhausted ego can become replenished and renewed.

Suggested Reading

Clift, Walter, *Symbols of Transformation in Dreams*. New York: Crossroad, 1984.

Hall, James, *Jungian Dream Interpretation Handbook of Theory and Practice*. Toronto, Canada: Inner City Books, 1986.

Johnson, Robert A., *HE!* New York: Harper & Row, Perennial Library Edition, 1976, reissued 1986. Originally The Religious Publishing

---

5. *The I Ching*. New York: Pantheon Books, 1950, p. 239.

Company, 1974. (Subtitle: *A Contribution to understanding masculine psychology, based on the Legend of Parsifal and his search for the Grail, and using Jungian psychological concepts.*)

Kelsey, Morton T., *Adventure Inward*. Minneapolis: Augsburg Pub. House, 1980.

Sanford, John A., *Dreams and Healing: A Succinct and Lively Interpretation of Dreams*. New York: Paulist Press, 1978.

————*The Man Who Wrestled With God: Light from the Old Testament on the Psychology of Individuation*. New York: Paulist Press, 1981, revised and updated, 1987. Originally The Religious Publishing Co., 1974.

————*Ministry Burnout*. New York: Paulist Press, 1982.

von Franz, Marie-Louise, *The Feminine in Fairy Tales*. Zurich: Spring Publications, 1972.

Chapter 6

A Man and His Feminine Side

In our discussion of a man and his work we noted the importance of the masculine archetypes in the psychology of a man. Now we will concern ourselves with the feminine archetype within a man.

Jung pointed out that human beings are "androgynous," which comes from two Greek words that mean "man" and "woman." To say that we are androgynous, therefore, means that our personalities are a composite of masculine and feminine qualities. The idea of the androgynous nature of human beings is supported by mythologies all over the world which often represent the first human being as equally male and female.[1] It is also supported by the science of genetics that points out that a person's sex is determined by a plurality of one masculine or feminine gene. Thus a man's sex is determined by the fact that he has one more masculine gene than feminine gene, and vice versa in the case of a woman. It is Jung's contention that in a man his minority of feminine genes has an equivalent psychic representation in his personality, and he calls this inner feminine component in a man the anima.

The Russian philosopher Nicholas Berdyaev, who wrote most of his works in the 1920's, reached the same conclusion: "Man is not only a sexual but a bisexual being, combining the masculine and the feminine principle in himself in different proportions and often in fierce conflict. A man in whom the feminine principle was completely absent would be an abstract being . . . a woman in whom the masculine principle was completely absent would not be a personality. . . . It is only the union of these two principles that constitutes a complete human being."[2]

The idea of the anima, and its corresponding aspect in women termed the animus, is a way of saying that men and women share a common humanity but are also different. The difference is that in a man his masculinity is carried by his ego, and his feminine side functions as part of his unconscious personality, and vice versa with women.* Since

---

1. See my book *The Invisible Partners,* Chapter 1. New York: Paulist Press, 1980.
2. Nicholas Berdyaev, *The Destiny of Man.* New York: Harper Torchbooks, 1960, pp. 61–62.
*The matter is somewhat different, however, with the homosexual man, as we will observe later.

a man's feminine side is an aspect of the unconscious most men are unaware of it, even though it profoundly affects his life and personality for better or for worse. Because of the importance of the anima in a man's psychology much of his psychological development depends on his capacity to become conscious of, and give proper scope to, the feminine part of his nature. This is no simple task, if only because men find the idea that they are partly like women a strange and perhaps even threatening idea. For this reason Jung once referred to the task of integrating the anima as "the master-piece" of a man's individuation.[3]

Male–Female Differences

This is as good a place as any to go into an issue raised by Jungian psychology that sometimes meets with a good deal of resistance and misunderstanding. To say that a man's psychology is somewhat different from a woman's, and that his feminine side is an aspect of his unconscious rather than conscious personality, is to say that there are fundamental psychological differences between men and women that are not the result of social conditioning or social roles. In today's world this is not always a popular position because to some people it implies that Jung is saying that men have more value than women, and that social conditioning is not an important psychological influence. Nothing of this kind is meant. To say that men and women are psychologically different does not imply that either sex is superior to the other. To say that the psyche has an archetypal structure does not mean that social and environmental conditioning is not also an important influence in the development of personality. Certainly social attitudes and conditioning influence the way a man behaves, thinks, and acts. Nevertheless, just as a man's body is different in some important aspects from a woman's body, his psyche is also different, and vice versa.

Another misconception many people have drawn from Jung's idea of the contrasexual opposites in men and women is that Jungian psychology relegates certain social roles to men and others to women, in short, that it is socially sexist. In fact, exactly the opposite is the case. It is precisely because men and women are androgynous that men and women can and do perform in society most of the same functions and roles.

However, Jung's description of the psychological similarities and

---

3. Sanford, *The Invisible Partners*, p. 10.

differences between men and women does not always meet with hostility. For many people Jung's ideas bring a feeling of relief, a sub-
stantiation of what we all knew in our hearts anyway. The world would
be a pretty boring place if there were no psychological difference between the sexes, and a recognition of the differences between men and
women often evokes the response, "Vive la différence!" While some
women may find Jungian psychology sexist (in a negative sense), other
women find in it an affirmation of femininity because it offers them a
differentiated understanding of their nature. Perhaps for this reason
close to half of the Jungian analysts in the United States are women.
Most of Jung's earliest colleagues were also women and many of them
helped shape his ideas. Today many women Jungian writers continue
to contribute to our knowledge of the psyche, and of feminine nature
in particular, in many cogent books and articles.

Any discussion of masculine and feminine raises the question of
what is meant by these terms. Defining masculine and feminine in terms
of social roles leads us nowhere, since, as already noted, both men and
women can and do perform most of the same social roles. The best description is found in ancient Chinese thought, in the idea of Yang and
Yin, because Yang and Yin are not defined by social roles or psychological attributes but by means of images.

In the ancient Chinese way of thinking, all energy flows between
two poles, much as electricity flows between a positive and a negative
pole. One of these poles is termed Yang and the other is termed Yin.
The Yang and Yin are found everywhere in the created world, and they
also exist in a human being. When the energy of Yang and Yin are creatively and harmoniously related, all goes well and in accordance with
the Will of Heaven (Tao). When it does not, there is discord.

Yang is described as a banner waving in the sun, that is, something
shone upon or bright. It is designated by heaven, the sky, the bright,
the creative, the south side of the mountain (where the sun shines), and
the north side of the river (which also receives the sunlight). The primary meaning of Yin is the cloudy or overcast. It is designated by the
earth, the dark, the moist, the receptive, the north side of the mountain
and the south side of the river. Yang and Yin also are referred to as the
masculine and the feminine, and as the *p'o* soul, which expresses itself
as eros, and the *hun* soul, which expresses itself as logos. There is no
value judgment in Chinese thought. Yin is not superior to Yang or the
other way around. To the contrary, both are equally important, for only

if their two energies unite does the universe function properly and a human being become a higher and indestructible personality.

A Man's Inner Feminine Companion: The Anima

Another point to be clarified is this: although the anima has a feminine nature, it is not like a flesh-and-blood woman. As we will see, the anima has certain negative and disagreeable effects on a man and we will describe these shortly. This description of the anima, however, is not to be taken as a description of women. The anima may be womanlike, even womanish, but women are human beings, of course, while the anima is a powerful, but partial, autonomous part of a man's psyche.

Finally there is the misunderstanding among some people that Jung's ideas—particularly his idea of the anima—are "mystical." By mystical these people mean that his ideas are vague, unscientific, unreal, and unprovable. There is nothing vague or unreal about either the psyche or Jung's ideas, but it is a fact that the psyche confounds the rationalistic and materialistic prejudices and assumptions that dominate the collective thinking of our time. For most people, unless something is logical (in a narrow sense of that word) and occupies space (can be seen, heard, or touched), it isn't real. However, the psyche has another order of reality. It doesn't occupy space in the sense that so-called material reality does, and ordinarily it cannot be seen with our physical vision. Yet its manifestations are all around us, and its reality is so strong that the very survival of our world depends on what happens in the psyche.

The anima partakes of the nature of psyche. She can't be put into a tightly controlled laboratory experiment but she is real enough to produce profound moods in a man, appear as a central character in his dreams and myths, enlighten his consciousness, enliven or destroy his life, and complicate tremendously his relationships with women. Consequently these are the areas where we need to look for the anima: in a man's moods and relationships with women, and in spontaneous expressions of the unconscious such as we find, for instance, in dreams, fairy tales, and mythology. We will begin with a look at the anima in dreams.

In a man's dreams, the anima is personified as a feminine figure. While a dream figure that is someone from our waking life may either refer to our relationship with that actual person, or be used by the dream to symbolize the anima, a dream figure of an unknown woman is virtually certain to personify the man's inner feminine nature. The kind of relationship a man has with the feminine figures in his dreams tells him a lot about the relationship that exists between himself and the anima. This relationship, like a man's relationship with women in his waking life, changes from day to day and needs constant attention. In a later chapter we will look at some specific examples of the way the anima appears to men in their dream life.

Many fairy tales apply to a woman's psychology, many apply to a man's psychology, and some apply to both. In those fairy tales that apply to a man's psychology there is almost always a feminine figure who plays an important role. Characteristically, the feminine beings in these fairy tales are either highly positive and desirable (the princess, the beautiful woman who needs to be rescued, the woman who brings the hero a great boon, and so on) or else she is extremely negative and dangerous. The female figures who fall into the latter category are witches of one sort or another, and they have the unfortunate habit of ''doing in'' would-be heroes by cutting off their heads, poisoning them, turning them into stone, luring them into dangerous places, and other such unpleasant activities. In this way fairy tales represent the positive and negative, helpful and dangerous, aspects of the anima. Like dreams, fairy tales are enormously varied, giving us some idea of the complexity of the life of the psyche. In a later chapter we will examine a fairy tale in depth as an example of how the anima is depicted in these curious, seemingly simple yet psychologically profound, stories.

This brings us to mythology. In the conventional thinking of our day, mythology is a collection of antiquated stories that once were a kind of childish pre-science but now are virtually synonymous with something that is untrue. For instance, if someone says of a story or comment, ''Oh that's only a myth,'' that person is making a disparaging comment which implies that the item in question has no substance or validity. As a consequence, in our culture mythology has been discarded, thrown onto the trash heap where other useless artifacts of humanity's childhood have been relegated. However, Jungian psychology goes to this trash heap and finds that things of great value have been carelessly tossed aside. One of these is mythology, which, far from being without value, turns out to be a gold mine of information about the nature and structure of the psyche. Mythology is a spontaneous expression of the life of the unconscious, and in it are portrayed the archetypes that shape our psychology and destiny. It is a mirror in which we can see reflected our basic human nature.

The most highly developed mythology is that of ancient Greece. We have already seen how the gods of ancient Greece personify typical masculine patterns in the psyche. Now we will see how the goddesses personify typical feminine patterns.

The Goddesses and Masculine Psychology

The goddesses are particularly important for an understanding of feminine psychology, but they are also important for understanding masculine psychology. While the gods portray those archetypes that can directly shape a man's ego, the goddesses portray those archetypal powers that influence a man from the unconscious. Their effect on a man is more subtle but no less profound than that of the masculine archetypes. In fact, in some men in whose psyches the feminine plays an especially important role, the feminine powers may be the dominant powers. We have already seen, for instance, that in the case of a musician or other kind of artist the Muses personify determining archetypal influences. In similar fashion, while a man like General George S. Patton of World War II fame may have been a devotee of Ares, god of war, a Dr. Zhivago is a true son of Aphrodite.

Even a brief resume of the major goddesses of Greece will give us helpful insights into the psychology of the feminine in a man. We have already considered the Muses, so we will begin with Aphrodite.

Aphrodite was the goddess of the rapturous love-embrace, of union with the beloved, and of the bringing of life to fruition. It was said by Hesiod that when the god Cronus avenged himself on his father Uranus, Uranus' male member fell into the sea. White foam swirled up from the spot where Uranus' phallus floated on the water and out of the foam emerged Aphrodite. When Aphrodite came to shore, the earth bloomed, and Eros and Himeros, the gods of love and longing, escorted her joyfully to the place of the gods. Hesiod says that Aphrodite's "portion of honor among men and gods is girlish babble and deceit and sweet rapture, embraces and caresses."[4] She became the goddess who stirred all living creatures to make love and be fruitful. Only Artemis, Athena, and Hestia could resist her charms; all others, divine and human alike, were under her power, so surely could she ensnare and enchain them with her charms. She manifested herself in blooming gardens, which

---

4. Walter F. Otto, *The Homeric Gods*. New York: Pantheon Books, 1979, p. 92.

were often consecrated to her. The rose was sacred to her, as was the apple tree. The love that she inspired was no respecter of the sanctity of marriage, and under her influence a man or woman might shatter the most honorable and sacred vows for the sake of the beloved. Aphrodite was accompanied by a retinue of lesser goddesses including the three Graces, and, especially, Aidos, whose name means shame, modesty, and reticence. Not all was beauty in her eyes, however, and Aphrodite also reveled in the strife and quarreling that so often accompanies love-making. She could also be cruel, especially to women, whom she some-times inspired with an impossible love for an unsuitable man. Those who spurned her felt her wrath. Hippolytus, for example, was a young man so devoted to Artemis that he paid no heed to Aphrodite. She was so offended at his negligence that she changed herself into a monster, and so frightened the horses of Hippolytus that they dragged his chariot to destruction and him to an untimely death.

When Aphrodite stirs a man she fills him with the longing for love. He is driven by the archetypal energy that she symbolizes to seek union with the beloved. If the man is particularly unconscious she will be ex-perienced on the lowest, most grossly lustful level. On the highest level she will be the power urging him to union with the Divine. If he denies this energy in himself it will torment him all the more, manifesting itself perhaps in sexual obsessions, anxiety, or depression. In some men Aphrodite represents the most important archetype in their psychology. Such men gravitate toward, and love, the world of the feminine. They may be devoted to the graceful and beautiful side of life and shun that which is harshly masculine. As we have mentioned, they are the Dr. Zhivagos of this world for whom love, beauty, and relationships are the truly compelling things of life. This does not mean they are not mas-culine men, only that their masculinity is enlisted in the service of love rather than of war or power, science or craft.

Hera was the wife of Zeus and the queen of heaven. She resided on Mount Olympus where she presided in regal fashion over the ban-quets of the gods. She was not so much mother, however, as queen and matriarch. She was fiercely jealous of Zeus' frequent amors with mortal women and once implored Aphrodite for the loan of her golden girdle which gave to the wearer an irresistible power in love. Yet basically her province was not love, the love-embrace, and passion, but the sanctity of marriage as an honorable and necessary social institution. She per-sonifies that archetype that brings forth, guards, and protects all the social institutions that give cohesiveness to the social order and enshrine and perpetuate the highest of social values.

A man in whom Hera prevails as an archetypal power of the feminine will be drawn toward the social order and its preservation. For instance, he might become a clergyman who is devoted to the church, caring for her and her enshrined values protectively and lovingly. The institution of marriage will be important to him because of the values that it nourishes and cherishes, although his actual relationship with his wife, while correct and supportive, might lack intimacy and depth. He might well be a political conservative in his desire to protect and perpetuate the world of established values. His devotion will be to the collective order of things, rather than to the personal, to social concerns and values rather than to the individual soul.

Artemis was the goddess of free, virginal nature, with its shining brilliance and enchanting, awe-inspiring wildness. Hers was not the maternal side of nature, but its purity and remoteness, and also its harshness and cruelty. Hers were the clear air of the mountain tops, the untouched depths of virginal forests, the remoteness of flower-strewn meadows, and the sparkling clarity of clear streams and springs. She was the mistress of that which is pure, that which delights and enchants, but also that which is dangerous. She was the uniting principle that weaves together all the multitude of natural forms into a sublime whole. Wild animals were sacred to her, especially the lion and the bear. Indeed, she was called "the Lady of the wild beasts."[5] She was the goddess of distance and the vast and fascinating ranges of mountains were her special province. The migratory bird was thus an appropriate symbol for this goddess who, like Hermes, called men to distant journeys and was a good companion to travelers. Because of her chasteness she was immune to the power of Aphrodite and her passion. She was devoted instead to athletes and presided over the athletic competitions of ancient Greece.

Men in whom Artemis is predominant are likely to be constant and faithful but somewhat remote in their relationships. Their special province in relationship is not the world of sexuality and desire but that of firm, strong companionship. They will have a love for the wilderness and may make good members of environmental organizations with a passionate, holy zeal in their defense of untouched nature. A man like

---

5. Ibid., p. 83.

John Muir is an excellent example of this type of man. For him, wilderness was sacred, and its destruction a violation of all that was holy; he simply could not understand that other men (in whom there were different archetypes) could see wilderness only as something to be subdued. Such men may also have a mystical bent, a far-seeing inner vision that often gives them deep insight. The long-distance runner, content in his contemplative solitude, rejoicing in the chaste strength of his body, will likely have Artemis running beside him.

Demeter was the earth mother goddess whose passion and function was to nourish all living creatures. Hers also was the province of love, but for the child more than for the lover. Hers was the elemental or primitive feminine world, and hers was the power that caused the earth to bear fruit and the crops to grow. Like Aphrodite and Artemis she also had her dark and dangerous side, for she could devour the children to whom she gave birth, and could also neglect her divine task of bringing the earth to fruition. Indeed, when her daughter Kore was abducted by Hades, king of the underworld, she was so stricken with grief that she neglected the earth and its needs. Winter then came, and the whole earth became cold; life retreated, and nothing grew. Only when her daughter was restored to her half of the year did she relent. Spring then came, and flowering, blooming summer.

A man in whom Demeter is a strong influence will have a way with children, will be a faithful and devoted father, a protector and nourisher of all that is young and helpless. While Hera guards the sanctity of home and marriage, Demeter guards the young child, and a man who serves the archetype of Demeter will likewise serve all that needs his caring nourishment. A clergyman might turn this nourishing energy to his congregation, a politician to the city, a psychotherapist to a client, a doctor to a patient, a gardener to the seedlings in the garden, a farmer to his fields. Wherever helpless living creatures need a helping hand the man with Demeter in him will be drawn to fill the need.

Hestia is the goddess of hearth and home, but for its own sake, not simply as a place in which the children live. She is the least known of the goddesses, and indeed there is little to be told about her, but that in itself reveals her character. For Hestia is content to lead a simple and even invisible life. In a man she is that instinct that draws him away from the world and back to the safety and nourishing comfort of hearth and home. Here he is content for a while to enjoy the simple pleasures of warm fires at night and the snug comfort of home as a nest. Under the influence of all that Hestia represents he puts aside, at least for a while, his urge to fame or desire to make an impression on the world. If she is an especially strong influence in a man he may live a life known only to a few, yet will find this not a lack of fulfillment but a comfort and a joy.

Athena, like Artemis, was a virgin goddess. She was not born from a woman's womb but sprang into life from the head of Zeus himself, fully grown, and arrayed in warlike armor. For Athena was a warrior goddess. However she did not relish war for the sheer love of combat as did Ares, but waged war coolly, employing strategy, and inspiring warriors with courage. She particularly excelled in wars in defense of that which was noble and sacred, and was justly acclaimed for this by the Athenians, who named their city after her. In Homer's *Iliad,* the brawling Ajax was a son of Ares, but the clever Odysseus was the favorite of Athena.

Athena's province is intelligence and wise counsel, practical understanding, and thinking things through. She is a creative and constructive goddess who inspires men and women to creative achievement. From her comes culture. The joiners learn their art from her, the smiths also, and the potters, indeed all those who engage in artistic handicraft. Her special animal is the owl, symbol of wisdom and the capacity to see even in the darkness. Nothing pleases her more than the emergence in a man of greatness, consciousness, and heroic action. In a man, Athena personifies the capability for a larger than usual life; he will tend toward the heroic, and will be inventive and inclined to cultural achievement. While not prone to begin strife, he will be a man to be reckoned with should conflict be unavoidable.

We hope this brief resume of the most important goddesses of Greece, with descriptions of how they live on today in a man's psyche as archetypal influences, will give some idea of the scope and importance of the archetypes and particularly of the feminine archetype in a man's psychology. However, our discussion brings up another point for which Jung's psychology has sometimes been criticized: that it divinizes the psyche.

For instance, Jung sometimes uses the word "numinous" to describe the archetypes. The word numinous was coined by Rudolph Otto to describe the idea of the holiness of God.[6] Some critics of Jung say

6. Rudolph Otto, *The Idea of the Holy.* New York: Oxford University Press, 1950.

that by using the word numinous to describe the psyche Jung is divinizing it, and setting it up in the place of God.

The psyche does not take the place of the transcendent God, but it is a fact that the archetypes produce in us fascinating, awe-inspiring, and emotionally gripping effects, and that these are the qualities of numinosity as described by Rudolph Otto. The archetypes *act* like divinities, which is why they were personified as divine beings in an age in which mythology anticipated psychology. Jung does not make the psyche into a divinity; it is the psyche itself that is numinous. The numinosity of the psyche is attested to by the effect on us of a nightmare. For at least a brief time after we awaken from a nightmare we are all believers.

Projection of the Anima

All of the above-mentioned archetypal patterns are included in the image of the feminine in a man that Jung calls the "anima." If this is such an important part of a man's psychology, we may ask why her existence has not been recognized before. The answer is twofold. First, self-knowledge is not one of the hallmarks of the human race. The ego wants to go its merry, unconscious way. We have our cherished ideas and illusions of who we are, and we do not want to have these ideas disrupted by the facts. Besides, self-knowledge is an arduous task and most of us are too lazy to undertake it. Second, we have difficulty knowing our innermost human nature—and this includes especially the anima—because so much of it has been projected. This blocks self-knowledge, for, as we will see, when something is projected it is experienced as a quality belonging to something other than ourselves. For this reason it is important, if we are to understand our own psychology, to understand how the projection process works.

Projection is a psychological mechanism that operates whenever a vital aspect of our personality of which we are unaware is activated. Projection is an unconscious mechanism. We do not decide to project something; it happens automatically. If we decided to project something it would be conscious to us, and then, precisely because it is conscious, it could not be projected. Only unconscious contents are projected; once something has become conscious, projection ceases.

The anima has been projected in the past into man's mythological world. As we have seen, the goddesses of ancient Greece can be understood as projections of the manifold images of the feminine that exist in the psyche. The goddesses are personifications of these feminine archetypes because the archetypes readily lend themselves to personification. What ancient people understood as autonomous deities or spiritual powers we would understand today as autonomous unconscious contents. For this reason it can be said that the gods and goddesses have not died; they are as alive as ever as constituents of our innermost personalities. From our innermost depths, these eternal images continue to affect the course of our lives, just as the ancients supposed the gods and goddesses to affect the course of their lives.

The anima is also projected onto the screen of the world. Imagine you are in a movie theater watching a film. Of course you are looking at the screen in front of you, and this is where you see the moving images and pictures that make up the movie. The source of these images, however, is behind you in the projector that is hidden in a room at the back. So it is with psychological projection. The world is the screen, the unconscious is the projector, and the images of the unconscious are the contents of the psyche that are projected.

Many things can be the hook on which the projection of the anima gets fastened. For instance, ships have traditionally received anima projections, which is why they are given feminine names and usually referred to as "she." Young men especially may project the anima onto their cars, which is why they sometimes give them such loving, devoted attention. The church also receives the anima projection and becomes "mother church." Even hurricanes have received the projection which is why, until recent times, they have been called (by men of course) "Hurricane Emma" or "Hurricane Emily." Part of a man's individuation calls for him to withdraw these projections from the screen of the world and become conscious of them as psychological contents within himself.

The most common screen onto which the anima is projected, however, is, naturally enough, woman herself. For better or worse, women carry for men the projected image of the anima, an event that has fateful consequences for both men and women. Unless this projection is withdrawn, not only will the man be unable to be conscious of his feminine side as part of himself, the relationship as well will be made exceedingly difficult because it will be based partly on illusion. In the next chapter we will discuss how a man's relationship with women can help him withdraw his anima projections, thereby increasing his self-knowledge and enabling him to make realistic, human relationships with the opposite sex.

We have seen that the image of the anima has appeared as a character in fairy tales and in our dreams, that she has represented herself in art and literature, and that she has been projected into mythology and onto the screen of the world. But the anima can also be experienced directly, for she profoundly influences the state of consciousness in which a man finds himself. This influence may be helpful or destructive, so that we can speak of the positive and the negative aspects of the anima, the anima as soul or as witch. We will begin with a look at the negative, disagreeable ways in which the anima affects a man's conscious state of mind, the most important of which is his moods.

The Anima and a Man's Moods

Marie-Louise von Franz once said of the anima that she was "a personification of all feminine psychological tendencies in a man's psyche, such as vague feelings and moods."[8] It will be helpful to differentiate among feeling, emotion, and mood. Feeling is a relatively objective state. One has a "feeling about something." This "feeling about something" helps us evaluate events and people. Specifically, feeling is a valuing function of great importance. Emotion comes when feeling is greatly intensified. *We* have feelings but emotions *have us.* So we say we are "gripped by an emotion." Love, hate, fear and anger are perhaps the most prominent emotions. Emotions cause us to react; feelings help us to evaluate. A mood is a particular state of mind. A mood colors or alters our conscious world. If we say that we "got up on the wrong side of the bed," we are in a mood. A mood grips us, so we say, "I'm in a bad (or good) mood today." If a mood lingers on, we might say of a man that he is a moody man.

When a man falls into a mood he is possessed by it. Behind the mood is the anima, so a mood is a form of anima possession. It is as though, through the mood, the anima's subliminal emotionality has him in her grip. In such a state a man tends to become sulky, overly sensitive, and withdrawn. A poisonous atmosphere seems to surround him; it is as though he is immersed in a fog. He ceases to be objective or

8. C. G. Jung, *Man and His Symbols*. Garden City, New York: Doubleday & Company, Inc., 1964; Chapter 3 by Marie-Louise von Franz, p. 177.

related, and his masculine stance may be eroded by peevishness. If a man writes or argues when he is in this frame of mind, his peevishness will certainly manifest itself in what he writes or says. In writing, the influence of the anima can be seen in sarcasms, innuendos, irrelevancies, and poisonous jabs that reveal a subjective personalistic bias and detract from the objective quality of the work. A man in the grip of the anima acts for all the world like an inferior kind of woman who is upset with something, and that, in fact, is exactly what a man has within himself: an inner woman who is distraught or upset.

Such a mood may fall on a man in an instant. A seemingly chance remark from someone, a slight, almost unnoticed disappointment, and suddenly a man may be in a mood. Astonishingly enough, men almost invariably fail to note that something from within themselves has possessed them, that a mood has fallen on them and gripped them, and that the event has been quite autonomous. Such moods may simply make the man a bit grouchy or out of sorts for a while, or they may become dangerously dark. If the moods are chronic they may lead a man into alcoholism or severe depression. Under certain circumstances, an intense anima mood may plunge a man into such a feeling of hopelessness that he commits suicide. It is no doubt the presence of the anima within a man that explains why fewer men than women attempt suicide, but more men than women actually succeed in killing themselves. It is as though the anima says, "It is all futile!" and the man falls into utter despair.

The woman in a man's life could tell him a lot about these anima moods. She knows almost right away when a mood has her man because then he is not available for relationship. One cannot get through the mood to find the man. It is as though he has disappeared, and someone else has taken his place. This moodiness of the man has, as a result, a disturbing effect on a woman, who finds it difficult to be with a man who is in such a state.

If you can get to the bottom of a man's mood you will find that something has gone wrong, but the man may hardly realize what it is. It may be that his inner woman does not like what the man is doing. For instance she may not like his work because it drains her of life and energy, or it may keep her from her fulfillment in life. It is as though the man's inner woman also needs to be fulfilled in life, but the only way she can be fulfilled is through the kind of life the man leads. Imagine a woman who is denied her proper scope in life, who is forced to endure a way of life that leaves her no room for her emotions or her own creative powers. Such a woman would, naturally, become dissatisfied and her displeasure would be felt in the bad atmosphere she would create. It is exactly this way with the anima if she does not have enough share in the man's life.

Other Negative Anima Influences

One of the most subtly destructive effects of the negative anima is her capacity to poison a man's creative urges. When a man gets a creative idea or impulse that would lead him beyond the ordinary and mediocre, a subtle voice may whisper in his ear a destructive thought that may well stop him in his tracks. Jung gave us an example of this in his autobiography *Memories, Dreams, Reflections*. In the midst of working out his important ideas of the archetypes and the collective unconscious Jung became aware of a thought that intruded into his consciousness and said, "But it's only art." Being Jung, he stopped to examine this thought and its origin. He concluded it was not his own considered judgment in the matter but came, as it were, from something alien to himself. This was one of the experiences that led him to realize there is in a man a feminine side that can have destructive effects.

This experience is particularly apt to happen to men when they get an impulse to write. No sooner do they begin than they have whispers of poisonous thoughts going through their minds, such as: "Who are you to think you can write? . . . But it has already been written . . . No one would publish it . . . There is nothing original in what you say . . . " and on and on. These thoughts steal from a man his creative energy and confidence. It is the anima in her witch-form, the old fairy tale motif in which a witch turns a man to stone, that is, she paralyzes him.

The anima may also give a man bad advice about solving problems that have to do with relationships. Let us say that a man is confronted with a situation involving other people and that he must make a decision that will affect them. He may fall into a vague kind of thinking that tries to smooth things over, leading him to act in a way calculated to keep everyone happy without facing the reality of the situation. Of course eventually this reality catches up with him and then everyone is usually unhappy. It is an effect of the anima on his masculine judgment. Instead of facing the facts of the situation and dealing with people directly, a man under this anima influence lives in an illusion that obscures the situation. The man will scarcely be aware of what he is doing, much less that he is being influenced by unconscious factors, but if he trains himself to observe his mental processes he can become aware that he is being influenced unconsciously by some vague thinking that aims to pour oil on troubled waters in the illusory hope that the difficulties inherent in the situation will then no longer exist. If a man has difficulty in facing people and conflicts directly, he will, of course, be especially prone to taking the "advice" of the anima.

Another anima function is that of "inner secretary." The anima can act like a voice within him telling him what he is to do next, scheduling his day, and generally running his life for him. The result of this is that a man becomes driven. He lives frantically. He does not ever seem to find time for the things that are most important to him. It is as though someone within him makes up a list of things that he should and must do and nothing else is allowed until this list is finished, which, of course, never happens since new things are always being added to it.

Another aspect of the negative anima is her role in a man's power drive. The anima can be behind a man's constant wanting, a drivenness in a man that makes him chronically discontented with his lot in life and drives him on and on until he may go too far and be brought back to reality with a terrible jolt. Let us say, for instance, that a man goes by the Cadillac dealer, sees the enchanting and seductive beautiful new cars, and, acting on impulse, buys one. He feels euphoric about it (a sure sign of possession by the anima) but later, confronted by the reality of what he has done, the fact that he didn't need the car and that his bank account can't afford it, he regrets his purchase and may even become depressed. It's not too much to say in such a case that the anima bought the car and then he had to pay for it.

Sometimes the anima is behind a man's power drive in such a way that the eventual consequences for him are truly destructive. Such a power drive is represented for us in the fairy tale "The Fisherman and His Wife."[9] To summarize the story:

> There was once a Fisherman who lived with his wife in a pig-stye by the sea. Every day he fished for his living, but one day he caught

9. *The Complete Grimm's Fairy Tales*. New York: Pantheon Books, 1944; Random House, 1972. No. 19.

an especially large Flounder. As it turned out, this was no ordinary Flounder but an enchanted prince, who begged to be released back to the sea. The kindly Fisherman did so, returned to his wife, and told her what had happened. His wife was enraged. "Ah," she said. "It is surely hard to have to live always in this pig-stye which stinks and is so disgusting; you might have wished for a little hut for us. Go back and call him . . . Go at once!" So the Fisherman returned to the sea and called out to the Flounder:

"Flounder, Flounder in the sea,
Come, I pray thee, here to me;
For my wife, good Ilsabil,
Wills not as I'd have her will."

To make a long story short, the Flounder came to the man and granted him his wish. When the man returned home the pig-stye has gone and in its place was a lovely little cottage. For a short time everything was better, but before long his wife was discontented again and decided she wanted to live in a castle. Over her husband's protests, she insisted that he go back to the Flounder and tell him that now they wanted to live in a castle. Again the Fisherman called to the Flounder and again the wish was granted, only this time the Fisherman noticed that the sea seemed to be darker and angrier than it was before. Once more the woman was content, but only for a while and then she wanted a palace . . . and after that she wanted to be king . . . and then she wanted to be emperor . . . and then to be Pope. Each time the Fisherman called the Flounder with the same plea—

"Flounder, Flounder in the sea,
Come, I pray thee, here to me;
For my wife, good Ilsabil,
Wills not as I'd have her will."

—and each time the sea was darker and stormier but the wish was granted. At last the insatiable woman said to her husband, "Go to the Flounder again, for I wish to be even as God is." Once more the Fisherman returned to the Flounder. "Well," said the Flounder. "What does she want now?" "Alas," said the Fisherman. "She wants to be like God." "Go to her," the Flounder replied, "and you will find her back again in the pig-stye." And, the story concludes, "there they are still living to this day."

Notice in the story that the fisherman is portrayed as a weak but relatively innocent character. It isn't he who wants more and more, but his wife. The Fisherman knows this and laments to the Flounder that his wife, Ilsabil, "Wills not as I'd have her will." The tale is not about a man who is by nature a criminal, but about a man who might have turned out all right but falls under the power of the anima who drives him to want more and more until finally he goes too far. A successful businessman who doesn't know when to stop and makes one deal too many would be an example. So would a financial investor or specialist who is not content with making a million dollars but has to make still more and more until he finally oversteps the line of legality, is caught in criminal activity, and winds up in jail. A politician also may over-reach himself in this way—Nixon may have been an example. Such men almost always get caught because they are, basically, decent men, or, at least, not bad enough to get away with being criminals. For if a man who is more or less a decent person falls under the power of his darker side he will be in such conflict within himself that he will trip himself up and be caught.

The Proper Function of the Anima

In all of these instances it is important to notice that the anima has gotten between a man and the outer world. It is when this happens that she creates illusion and causes mischief, weaving for the man a "Maya" or world of unreality. This is why Jung stressed that the proper function of the anima is to be between a man's ego and the unconscious. Then she acts as a psychopomp or guide through the inner world, a mo-tivating factor in his individuation. This function of the anima was beautifully portrayed, for instance, by Dante in his epic poem "The Divine Comedy."

Clearly it is important that a man free himself from possession by the anima. The way to do this is to come into a conscious and correct relationship with her. If a man relates to his feminine side it works for him; if he doesn't it works against him. Relating to his feminine side is not a once-and-for-all task because a man has to work on this relation-ship on an almost daily basis, just as he has to work each day on his relationship with his wife or lover. It requires constant awareness and caring on the part of a man to relate to the feminine. He must learn to recognize the effects of the anima when they appear in his illusions, restlessness, and power-drive. He must learn to recognize the role of the anima in his sexual fantasies, a matter that is so important we will discuss it in a separate chapter. He needs to get to the bottom of his moods, that is, to the feelings that underlie them, and learn how to express these feelings honestly and appropriately.

When a man is able to come into relationship with his anima, she bestows on him her positive gifts. When the anima functions in her correct place, she serves to broaden and enlarge a man's consciousness, and to enrich his personality by infusing into him, through dreams, fantasies and inspired ideas, an awareness of an inner world of psychic images and life-giving emotions. A man's consciousness tends to be too focused and concentrated; it easily becomes dry and sterile. But if the effects of the anima are integrated, the man's consciousness can grow and flourish, like a garden after it rains.

Masculine consciousness has been likened to the sun, and feminine consciousness to the moon. At noon everything is seen in bright outline and one thing is clearly differentiated from another. But no one can stand too much of this hot, bright sun. Without the cool, the moist, the dark, the landscape soon becomes unbearable and the earth dries up and will not produce life. That is the way a man's life becomes without the fertilizing influence on him of the feminine. Without a relationship to his inner world a man can focus, but lacks imagination; he can pursue goals, but lacks the emotion that gives the goals meaning; he can strive for power, but is unable to be creative because he cannot produce new life out of his unaided ego. Only the fruitful joining of the Yin principle to the Yang principle—or, to use a more modern analogy, of the right brain possibilities to those of the left brain—can stir up his energies, can prevent his consciousness from becoming like a dry desert, and his masculine power from being eroded.

So the anima mediates to a man invaluable psychological qualities that make him alive. For this reason, Jung spoke of the anima as the "archetype of life" and said that she intensifies life in a man. She is like an elusive but vital ingredient in him that makes life worth living and gives him a sense of something worth striving for. It is the anima who gives a man *heart,* enabling him to be courageous in the face of life's burdens and afflictions.

As the archetype of life, the anima contains the element of meaning. It is not that she has the answers; rather, she embodies within herself the secret of life, and helps a man discover it by leading him to knowledge of himself. Jung wrote of her, "Something strangely meaningful clings to her, a secret knowledge or hidden wisdom, which contrasts most curiously with her irrational elfin nature.''[10] Behind her, he said, is ''something like a hidden purpose which seems to reflect a superior knowledge of life's laws.''[11] As the element from which there arises whatever is spontaneous and impulsive in human life, the anima personifies the life in the unconscious which, while it can never be completely integrated, nevertheless continually renews a man's lagging spirits and consciousness.

In short, the anima personifies that element in a man that can be called soul. It is this quality that enables a man to complete himself, to uncover his inner depths, and to make of his life a spiritual journey leading to wholeness. We noted in an earlier chapter (Adolescence) that some young men may have a beatific vision of the anima in their adolescence. This is an early appearance of the anima as soul. It is a hint of the spiritual journey that lies ahead of him. An experience of anima as soul will affect a man profoundly. The longing and passion it brings to him will have a lifelong influence. If the experience remains unconscious he will be driven obsessively by his longing, perhaps into compulsive sexual fantasies or excesses. If he can become conscious of the meaning of his experience, and suffer through it toward its inner meaning, his personality will be expanded and ennobled.

Suggested Reading

Otto, Walter F., *The Homeric Gods, The Spiritual Significance of Greek Religion*. New York: Pantheon Books, 1979. First published by Thames and Hudson Ltd. in 1955.

Sanford, John A., *The Invisible Partners: How the Male and Female in Each of Us Affects Our Relationships*. New York: Paulist Press, 1980.

Ulanov, Ann Belford, *The Feminine in Jungian Psychology and in Christian Theology*. Evanston, Ill.: Northwestern University Press, 1971.

Zabriskie, Philip, ''Goddesses in Our Midst.'' New York: *Quadrant* No. 17, Fall 1974.

---

10. C. G. Jung, *The Archetypes and the Collective Unconscious*, C.W. 9.1. New York: Pantheon Books, Inc., 1959, p. 30.

11. Ibid., p. 31.

Chapter 7

Masculine Relationships: Part One
Men as Friends and Lovers

Without relationships a man can neither know nor become himself. C. G. Jung once said: "One is always in the dark about one's own personality. One needs others to get to know oneself."[1] A relationship with a woman, for instance, gives a man an opportunity to learn about his feminine side. That hidden, unwanted side of a man that we call the shadow tends to intrude into relationships and create a disturbance; by reflecting on the negative reaction we get from other people because of the shadow we can become more conscious of it. The egocentric qualities and attitudes that we described in Chapter 3 likewise disturb our relationships; it is not too much to say that without relationships with other people, with whom we react and interact, we cannot get insight into or resolve our egocentricity.

Relationships not only help us know ourselves; they also help us become ourselves. In interaction with others we learn to love. We become vulnerable to other people and learn about our own feelings. When two people are in relationship they affect and replenish each other; together they bring up hitherto unrealized aspects of the Self.

As noted in Chapter 5, in hexagram 58 *The I Ching* describes relationship under the image of two lakes that are joined together. A single lake, it points out, "evaporates upward and thus gradually dries up; but when two lakes are joined they do not dry up so readily, for one replenishes the other." Of course it should be noted that negative, that is, egocentric relationships can drain us of energy. However, in a healthy relationship two energy systems meet and mutually affect each other in such a way that each person becomes more fulfilled and complete as a result of the contact with the other. In spite of this, many men neglect the relationship side of their lives and concentrate on their work.

A man's work may test his intelligence, strength, and perseverance; a man's relationships will test him in all of these areas but also on the side of Eros. Eros refers to the emotional side that draws us into warm, personal, concerned, and sometimes passionate relatedness. It is the cement that binds together lovers, parents and children, close

---

1. *C. G. Jung Speaking,* eds. William McGuire and R. F. C. Hull. Princeton, N.J.: Princeton University Press, 1977, p. 165.

friends, and even, or should we say especially, man to God. This side of a man is, in our culture, often under-developed and under-valued. Yet unless a man develops this emotional side of himself he cannot escape the trap of his egocentricity; his Real Self cannot be touched and emerge, and his true greatness and even heroism cannot be constellated. It is through Eros that a man becomes both vulnerable and strong, while being devoid of Eros relationships leaves a man prey to the influence of evil.

In a letter to William W., one of the co-founders of Alcoholics Anonymous, Jung pointed out that the power of evil is so strong that a man can be saved from being either its victim or its perpetrator only if his soul is filled with a spirit more powerful than that of evil, or if he lives within a framework of warm human relationships. He wrote: "I am strongly convinced that the evil principle prevailing in this world leads the unrecognized spiritual need into perdition, if it is not counteracted either by real religious insight or by the protective wall of human community. An ordinary man, not protected by an action from above and isolated in society, cannot resist the power of evil."[2] This truth is attested to by the fact that a man who becomes a wanton killer is almost always a loner, an emotionally isolated man, who lives without benefit of human closeness and companionship.

Relationships are a man's emotional anchor. He may devote the majority of his time and energy to objective pursuits in life, but unless he has an emotional base in relationships he could not perform this work effectively. The hunter can roam the wilderness for days or weeks as long as he is secure in the knowledge that his village, his people, his woman and family are waiting for him. A study of men at war showed that as long as they dreamt of home, friends, and family they were likely to remain psychologically intact in spite of the stresses of combat; but if their dream life became filled with the war itself, psychological collapse because of stress was on its way.

The need of men for relationships in order to maintain health has been demonstrated by James Lynch, M.D. in his book *The Broken Heart*. An impressive array of statistics gathered by Dr. Lynch showed that widowed, divorced, or single men had a significantly higher death rate from cancer than married men. Among white males, for instance, 4.1 times as many divorced men died from buccal cavity and pharyn-

---

2. C. G. Jung, *Letters 2*. Princeton, N.J.: Princeton University Press, 1975, p. 624.

geal cancer as did married men. In the case of heart disease, the death rate among divorced males relative to married males was over twice as great. The rate of cirrhosis of the liver among divorced men was seven times as great as among married men. One of the most interesting statistics related marital status, the death rate, and cigarette smoking. Lynch cites the work of Dr. Harold Morowitz, whose studies showed, not surprisingly, that, other factors being equal, non-smokers had a markedly lower death rate than smokers. He also discovered that the death rate among smokers who were single, widowed, or divorced was twice as high as among smokers who were married. The most interesting fact he uncovered, however, was that the death rate among married men who were heavy smokers was almost identical with that of divorced men who did not smoke at all. Dr. Morowitz concluded, "Being divorced and a non-smoker is slightly less dangerous than smoking a pack or more a day and staying married."[3]

Men's Friendships

We will begin our study of relationships with an examination of friendship. A survey in which men were asked to name their closest friend showed that the majority of men named a woman, usually their wife. It may be that for many men their wife is not only their primary relationship but virtually their only intimate relationship. Psychologically it is important for a man to have close relationships with members of both sexes. In our culture, however, many men seem to fear or be incapable of a close relationship with another man. Cultural factors may mitigate against close relationships between men. Any hint of Eros may bring up the fear that the relationship might be tainted with homosexual feelings, so that the natural warmth men can develop for each other is repressed. It is worth noting that in other times of history men showed themselves capable of deep affection for each other and it did not make them ashamed. A famous example found in the Old Testament is the friendship between David and Jonathan. David was clearly not a homosexual, yet the affection he had for Jonathan was intense. He expressed his Eros toward his friend in the immortal poem he composed at the time of the death of Saul and Jonathan, a poem that concludes:

---

3. James Lynch, *The Broken Heart.* New York: Basic Books, Inc., 1977, p. 46. Of course these are statistics, and individuals may not conform to the statistical average. Much the same facts were also found to occur with women.

O Jonathan, in your death I am stricken,
I am desolate for you, Jonathan my brother.
Very dear to me you were,
your love to me more wonderful
than the love of a woman.

How did the heroes fall
and the battle armour fail? (2 Sam 1:26–27).

Men who become friends are usually of similar psychological types. Thus two extraverts or two introverts are more likely to be friends than an extravert and an introvert. Similarly, intuitive or thinking types, feeling or sensation types, tend to seek out men of the same types to be their friends. Because of their similar typology, friends are likely to share the same points of view, for example, about matters of religion or politics, and this similarity of viewpoint will be one factor that helps create the friendship. Their relationship, however, is founded on a deeper kind of commonality than the sharing of a common viewpoint. Quite often it develops and is nourished by a shared activity, such as tennis, fishing, golf, jogging, the enjoyment of music, and so on. In this shared activity there may be little direct expression of intimacy. Exceptions are notable, but direct expressions of feeling or concern tend to be sporadic and engendered by some particular circumstance or troubling situation. Nevertheless, via the shared activity there springs up between the two men a quality of Eros that binds them together in friendship, a camaraderie that has deep roots and great emotional meaning. The Greeks would have said that the goddess Aphrodite unites them together in their affections, for she was the goddess not only of love-making, but of friends and friendship as well, and hers was the power that united men, as well as men and women, in the bond of friendship.

Friendship must be distinguished from an ego-alliance. In an ego-alliance the two men involved are mutually supportive of each other's egocentric postures. Their relationship is founded on this fact. It may look like a friendship, but if matters should change, and one of the men should break the ego alliance, enmity would soon result. Such a relationship exists solely on the level of the ego. Eros is not involved; indeed, it is specifically excluded since Eros always mitigates against egocentricity.

A friendship must also be distinguished from a business relationship. In a business or similar type of relationship the two men are joined together because they have certain common interests. Two business executives may lunch or socialize together in a convivial fashion, yet their relationship is founded on the fact that they need each other for the purposes of their business. The relationship need not be egocentric since it is natural that in worldly endeavors men find need of each other's services, but it is not to be confused with genuine friendship. The same thing is true, by the way, with relationships between nations. Nations don't have friendships, but they may have common interests. When they have common interests and prove to be trustworthy partners in these interests, a reliable relationship develops.

The threat to both business relationships and friendships is the egocentric shadow, for if this shadow intrudes, the relationship will be severely disturbed. In business the people involved guard against this as best they can with the use of a contract that spells out clearly who will do what for whom and under what conditions. The purpose of the contract is to protect the parties involved from misunderstandings and from the other person's shadow. If the shadow intrudes in a friendship, the friendship is threatened accordingly. The deeper the friendship the less likely this is to happen, since the bond of Eros mitigates against the intrusion of the shadow.

Although in a friendship neither person inflicts his shadow onto the other, there is an acceptance on the part of each person of the other person's failings. Friends are aware of each other's shadow but accept it, which they are able to do because it will not be inflicted on them. The more a man is accepted in his totality by his friend, the more he can drop his outer facade, that is, the persona, and simply be himself. Friendships are invaluable for this reason alone.

There is little, if any, room in a friendship for criticism. Even if one man sees clearly the failings of the other it usually mitigates against the friendship to bring up the matter. There are plenty of other people to criticize us; we value our friend because he doesn't have to do that, but is comfortable with us, failings and all. In some circles today it is fashionable to suppose that a friend should offer ''friendly,'' unasked-for criticisms. The fact is that when this happens we are put on guard; a friendship can survive only so much unrequested counsel, advice, and psychological analysis. The exception occurs when our friend wittingly or unwittingly injures us in some way. If this happens it can be forgiven and forgotten without comment, but sometimes the matter must be discussed. Even then the purpose of the discussion is to clear the air, and not for the moral edification or instruction of our friend.

Clearly friendships will vary widely in quality and in depth. With some men we are friends—but only to a point. A friendship may reach a certain level but go no further because the similarity of interests and level of trust do not go deep enough. Men may have many friends of a relatively superficial though amiable sort; a deep friendship is a rarity and a treasure. It is not every man who can find, or who is capable of, a truly deep friendship.

Marriage

Just as a man tends to make friends with men of a similar typology to his own, so there is also evidence that marriages between men and women who are alike are more frequent than marriages between men and women who are opposite. Type similarity in marriage makes for better communication and understanding; thus when problems arise, resolution may be easier. Also, similarity increases the likelihood that goals and values will be shared, thus creating a commonality that facilitates lifetime companionship.

On the other hand, a disadvantage to marriage partners being of similar type is that both partners lack a certain typological characteristic. For example, two intuitive types may understand each other, but, lacking sensation, they may have difficulty taking care of the mundane practicalities of life, such as making sure the oil in the car gets changed and planning ahead so there's food in the house for the week.

However, in marriages in which the man and woman are of differing typologies, more serious difficulties may exist. One of these may be the problem the two encounter in finding common interests. Men and women are naturally somewhat different in their interests, and if this difference is increased by a difference in typology, they may find too little ground in which they meet in common. This is particularly likely to be the case when one is an introvert and the other an extravert; they face in such opposite directions that the gulf between them often proves difficult to span, though not impossible. Communication may also be a problem when the two people are of different types. A thinking type and a feeling type, for instance, have different ways of arriving at conclusions and also different ideas of what is important. Similarly, a sensation type and an intuitive type concern themselves with separate areas of life and may find it hard to understand each other.

On the other hand, difference in typology may also have certain benefits. Since the opposites attract, the different typology between a man and woman may enhance the natural attraction exerted by their difference in sex. A man may find his wife's viewpoint interesting as well as baffling. He might become bored with a woman too much like himself and prefer the differences in spite of the problems they create. His wife's typology can also help him to broaden his viewpoint. In order to relate to her and communicate with her a man will find it helpful to understand her. This will involve understanding the meaning and validity of another psychological standpoint than his own. In so doing, the man will develop some of this side of himself. For instance, if the man is a thinking type, and comes to understand his wife's feeling perspective, he will develop some of that feeling side in himself and so become a more complete person.

Marriage involves not only a relationship but also the carrying out of certain life functions. Buying and caring for a house, creating financial security, maintaining a network of mutually enjoyable and meaningful social relationships, and raising a family are typical pursuits shared by a man and woman in marriage. If the two are of different typologies, each will bring his or her own unique skills and perspectives to bear on the problems that may arise in carrying out the marriage's functions. Thus the possibility for creativity both in the marriage relationship and in the pursuit of mutual goals may be increased by the existence of some psychological differences, which is compensation for the difficulties they create.

In our culture, marriages are assumed to be based first and foremost on the quality of relationship between the man and woman; in other cultures they may not be so. In the Orient, for instance, marriages were, and often still are, arranged by the parents. The relationship between the man and his wife, who has been selected for him, is not expected to be the important matter. What matters is that the man and the woman each carry out their socially prescribed functions. Customs are different in this country, however, and most people think of marriage as an extension and fulfillment of a love relationship. This attitude toward marriage has certain advantages and disadvantages, as we will see shortly.

Practically speaking the success of the marriage will depend on many factors in addition to the quality of relationship. One of the most important of these is the sharing of common goals and interests. If the man and woman both desire a family, want to own a certain kind of house, have certain types of vacations, and enjoy the same kind of people, these shared goals and interests will be like a cement holding them together. Perhaps the most important of these goals is the desire to raise a family, which may account for the fact that many marriages get into difficulty once the children are grown, for then the common goal that held them together is no longer there. Of course there are marriages that succeed quite well when neither partner wants children. The difficulty arises when one person wants children and the other does not. What the goals are is not as important as the fact that they are mutually desirable.

Enjoying the same people is another very important goal, for marriage is not an isolated relationship; it has an important social as well as personal dimension, a breadth as well as a depth. Insofar as the marriage is founded on the personal relationship of love and intimacy between a man and woman, it falls in the province of the goddess Aphrodite, but in its social dimension it falls in the province of the goddess Hera. In fact, if it were not for the social and familial dimensions of marriage there would be little reason for a man and woman to marry at all, since they can fulfill their personal relationship apart from declaring it socially by getting married.

Even with many goals and interests in common, however, the personality of a man and a woman will not overlap entirely. Like all relationships, marriage has its areas where personalities overlap and where they differ. Psychologist Verda Heisler represents the situation in the following diagrams:

 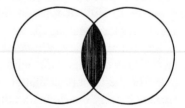

In these diagrams the shaded area where the circles overlap represents the area of common ground where the goals and interests of the man and woman meet. The unshaded portions of the two circles represent areas where they do not meet. If there is very little common ground, it will be difficult to maintain a relationship as complex as marriage over an extended period of time.

The Nature of Anima Projection

In a marriage based on a personal as well as a social relationship, the two persons involved expect that each one will love the other. The love relationship between a man and woman is a fascinating, and difficult, one. One of the main factors complicating this relationship is the natural tendency of a man to project his anima onto a woman. In the previous chapter we noted the importance of a man's feminine side, the anima, for his psychology. We saw that the anima has a positive and a negative side, and that the anima profoundly influences a man's moods and behavior. We also saw that the anima is readily projected by a man onto a woman. Now we need to look more closely at the consequences of this for their relationship.

When a man has projected his anima image onto a woman he will either make too much or too little of her, see her in an exaggeratedly and unrealistically positive way or an exaggeratedly and unrealistically negative way, depending on whether the woman carries for him the positive or the negative image of the anima, that is, whether she is perceived as soul-image or witch.

A woman who carries the image of the man's anima as soul will seem to the man to be highly desirable. She will fascinate him. He will be drawn to her. She may seem to him to be the source of all his long-hoped-for happiness. He will almost certainly have sexual-erotic fantasies about her. He may suppose that if he could only have sexual intercourse with her he would be perfectly happy. He does not realize that underlying this fascination, longing, and eroticism is his unconscious longing for union and relationship with his own soul. The man will be convinced that he loves the woman deeply, but he will not be aware of the difference between the woman as she is in herself and the anima image which she carries for him. For this reason his love for the woman will be contaminated with many unconscious factors that will complicate the relationship.

However, even if she initially welcomes the man's anima projection, she will sooner or later almost certainly live to regret it if the relationship continues long enough. His attentions to her will eventually begin to develop a negative side. She will begin to feel increasingly confined by his attentions. She will sense that the relationship has a certain "sticky" quality. She will begin to realize that somehow the man doesn't love her for herself but for some unknown reason. She may also become aware that his sexual attentions to her have a demanding and possessive quality, and that if she is disinclined toward sex on a particular occasion he is apt to become moody and resentful. Perhaps most disillusioning for the woman is her growing awareness that the man does not want her to be and become herself. Her efforts toward her own individuation may therefore be thwarted by him, especially if her own way through life leads her into directions that temporarily or partially take her away from him. If this happens she will discover that he resents it and tries to restrain her, either directly through his actions, or indirectly by "punishing" her with his passive-aggressive moods.

The woman who carries the projected anima image will be greatly affected by it. At first she may feel flattered. She will certainly feel valued, and, though she may not admit it to herself, will enjoy a feeling of power. In fact, as long as she walks around with the man's soul image she does have power over him. If the woman does not like the man, or is not attracted to him, she will find his projection on her a nuisance or annoyance. If she finds the man attractive, she will experience the initial phase of their relationship in a positive way. If the woman has her own love fantasies, perhaps of a man coming into her life who loves her completely and deeply, she may fall in love with him as much as he has fallen in love with her. Then we say they are both in love with each other, which means, psychologically, that each one fits into the other person's fantasy system.

All of these feelings of the woman are founded in reality. It is true that to the extent a man's relationship with a woman is founded only on the projection of the anima he does not see her or love her for who she really is. Because the nature of the anima is to open a man up to all the feminine world of Eros, relationship, longing, and fulfillment, the man will suppose that he loves the woman a great deal. He may protest his love often and with such apparent sincerity that the woman, beguiled by his words, will believe him. But in fact, proportionate to his state of unconsciousness, his apparent love for her will be overlaid with his blindness and egocentricity. He loves her for what she (by carrying the anima projection) does for *him*. In the final analysis, if a man loves a woman only for this reason, he has an egocentric relationship with her because he is not loving her for herself. Even though the psychological state that ensues when such projections take place is called love, there is little real love in it.

As we noted, in certain cases a man and woman may have mutual projections on each other, and this results in their "being in love." When this happens the emotions the two people experience are powerful and beautiful. For a time the man and woman may feel as though they are living in the laps of the gods, and they may promise undying love to each other. However, with the passage of time, and under the duress of ordinary life, and as the man and woman become all too familiar to each other, the projections fall away. Then the extraordinary feelings they had for each other are replaced by feelings that may be all too mundane. In certain cases the positive anima image may fall away and be replaced by the projection of a negative anima image. Hate and rejection then replace love and drawing close. Often the unconscious takes an interest in bringing about a certain degree of separation between a man and woman who have been too identified with each other through mutual projections. Only in this way can individual personality development and real human relationships come about. The problem has developed because human beings have confused themselves with gods and goddesses, and have tried to act the part in life that only the archetypes can act out. This is doomed to failure. Robert Frost has put the matter nicely in his poem "Fireflies in the Garden."[4]

> Here come real stars into the upper skies.
> And here on earth come emulating flies.
> That though they never equal stars in size,
> And though they were never really stars at heart,
> Achieve, at times, a very starlike start,
> Only, of course, they can't sustain the part.

So far I have described the negative aspect of the projection of the anima. But projection also plays a positive role, which is fortunate, for a man can never be so conscious of the mysterious nature of the anima that her image is no longer projected. Projections of the anima will continue throughout a man's lifetime. The anima projection may remain with some woman who plays a part in a man's life throughout many

---

4. *Complete Poems of Robert Frost*. New York: Holt, Rinehart, Winston, 1949, p. 306.

years, or it may consist of only fleeting projections, such as being on the waitress who serves us dinner at a restaurant.

One positive function of projection is that it initiates and draws a man into relationship with a woman, and out of this something may develop that will be important for the man and the development of his consciousness. Even when the projection falls away the relationship it initiated may continue. Many relationships between a man and woman consist partly of projections and partly of genuine human factors; in this case the projection of the anima onto the woman may be a way in which the unconscious is also included in the relationship. The projection of the anima is also one way in which a man remains aware of her, since through the projection he can see the reality of that inner feminine essence. The crux of the matter is not whether or not projections take place, but the extent of a man's egocentricity and unconsciousness.

Nevertheless, if a man is to become conscious and work out a real relationship with a woman, he needs to be aware of the projections of the anima. When he can do this he is in a position to establish a better relationship with his own feminine nature and also is better able to allow the woman to be herself. Projections are taken back by being made conscious. As we have said, we cannot keep projections from taking place, nor would it necessarily be desirable to do so, but a man can learn to recognize when a projection has taken place. For instance, whenever a woman fascinates a man we can be sure the anima has been projected, for in their all-too-human reality people are not fascinating; it is the archetypal images of the unconscious that are fascinating. In the withdrawal of his projections a man can become aware of the anima, and this recognition of her may be what the anima wants. It is as though she projects herself because she wants to be seen by the man, and this is a way for her to reach him.

Men in Relationships with Women

Once the anima is recognized a great work of psychological differentiation of the personality can begin. For instance, a man can begin to come to terms with his moods. We have already seen that a man can become enveloped in an "anima mood," that is, his feminine side may engulf him and a mood will be the result. Possession by the anima results as long as the man is unconscious of the nature and origin of his mood. We have also noted that something will usually start the mood, that it may be due to the fact that the anima does not like the kind of life the man is leading (because it leaves no room for his feminine nature). Or it may come because his feelings have been hurt or he has been angered in a relationship with a woman. When a man is in such a mood it is destructive to his relationship with a woman. She cannot penetrate the poisonous fog of the mood to get at the man himself and bring about a relationship. But if a man can learn to recognize when he is in such a mood he is in a position to do something constructive about it.

A place for him to begin is to make a distinction between a mood and a feeling. Moods come from the anima; feelings belong to the man himself. Unrecognized feelings, however, are readily taken over by the anima who translates them into moods. For instance, if a man does not feel right about his work but does not deal consciously with this problem, he becomes a moody man. In relationships, if a man has a certain hurt or angry feeling but does not express it in the relationship, or take other measures to come to terms with the feeling, then the anima gets hold of it and turns it into a resentful, hostile mood. On the other hand, if a man expresses his feelings in a relationship, they do not become moods. What happens is something like this: Let us say that the woman in his life has ignored him, or perhaps given him a painful verbal thrust or rejected him in some way, and as a consequence the man is hurt and angry. If the man were to express these feelings directly in the relationship, they would not become a mood. By expressing the feelings directly I mean telling the offending person what it is that bothers him. He doesn't insult or retaliate, but expresses directly the cause of the feeling problem. He might say, "That really made me angry when you said that." Or, "What you just said (or did) made me feel as though you don't care about me." These are related statements. They are related to the persons and issues at hand. They almost always bring out the best and most related side of the woman. As a young client of mine once said after an altercation with a woman: "I discovered that you can say almost anything you want to a woman as long as it is related."

But if the man does not express his feelings, they fall into the unconscious, and the anima gets them. It is as though the man has a basement in his house with a trapdoor. He opens the trapdoor and drops the troublesome feeling into the basement, but down there is the anima. She promptly gets hold of the hurt or angry feeling. In her hands the unexpressed feeling smolders, burns, and eats away at him. This is expressed by the man's passive-aggressive behavior, his hostile mood, and often by the retaliatory and guilt-producing behavior the man shows toward the woman who offended him. But it is all being engineered unconsciously by the anima, and so it inevitably turns out badly. Moreover, the man's hurt leads to anger. The anger, because it is unconscious and unexpressed, turns into chronic resentment. It is also like a can of gasoline that is ready to erupt into flames. If another incident comes along the man may erupt in a terrible and destructive rage. He will be overcome by raw emotion. His affect will be such that no one can relate to him. The anima has possessed him. She has dropped a match into the can of gasoline and the emotional eruption now has the man engulfed.

The anima is not deliberately being a force for evil; she is simply acting according to her nature. Jung once noted that the anima can be seen to be at work wherever emotions and affects are at work in a man. He wrote, "She intensifies, exaggerates, falsifies, and mythologizes all emotional relationships with his work and with other people of both sexes."[5] The anima does not necessarily want to carry the man's emotional life for him; she gets it by default, in the way I have described. But it is also in her nature to demand justice. Justice, in relationship, must be served. So, if the man does not deal consciously with his relationship problems and issues, the anima will take over. It is as though she says, "Why don't you say something about that irritating thing she has just done (or said) to you? If *you* don't do something about it *I* will." And the anima will proceed to keep the issue alive within the man until the disturbing matter in the relationship has been resolved.

The resolution of such problems sounds simple: bring the matter and the feelings out into the open. Unfortunately, many men have difficulty expressing their feelings. Men tend to like their relationships to be smooth, easy, and comfortable. They are reluctant to get into emotionally toned discussions or difficult relationship issues. They want peace and quiet, and want their women to maintain a pleasant atmosphere and not bring up distressing matters. A man also tends to believe, as Jung once said, that his work requires constant attention and energy but relationships should take care of themselves. (Of course women usually feel just the other way around.) Obviously this is a generalization. There are a number of men who can't stand living in an

---

5. C. G. Jung, *The Archetypes and the Collective Unconscious*, CW 9.1. New York: Pantheon Books, 1959, p. 70.

unsatisfactory relationship and will press for a quick resolution of whatever difficulties come up. They may be the ones to take the lead in relationship matters, and to draw a reluctant woman out into the expression of her feelings. Nevertheless, for various reasons, it is all too often the man who does not want to get into emotionally laden areas.

Many men are afraid of emotions and for this reason they are afraid of a woman's anger. In an effort to avoid the emotional trauma of scenes with a woman a man may do all the wrong things. For instance, he may try to appease a woman's angry animus, and her more demanding childish reactions. Appeasement is one of the worst things a man can do. It only makes the woman more a victim of her animus and childishness, and, of course, weakens the man. And in appeasing her the man will have to submerge his own genuine feelings of hurt or anger. Appeasement always sabotages relationship.

Many men who act out of fear in relationship with a woman, because they are afraid of her animus, withdraw from the relationship. But by withdrawing the man leaves a vacuum and the animus always fills this vacuum. No woman can keep her animus from filling such a vacuum because it seems to her to be an outrage. If the man retreats from a confrontation with a woman's animus, he only becomes weaker, and this guarantees that the animus domination of his woman partner will be even more complete. What is called for in the situation is that the man's masculinity become stronger than the masculinity of his wife's animus. This masculine strength must come from the man's instinctive or "lower" masculinity. A man's intellect, even if highly trained, will be of no help to him. It is his chtonic (earthy) masculinity that is needed in this kind of confrontation. Only this gives him the necessary capacity for controlled aggressiveness and strength.

If a woman is in the clutches of her animus and the man meets her head-on with his own masculine strength, and speaks with her directly and in a related (not insulting) way, she will appreciate it. At first there will be a fight, but if the man perseveres he will win the fight in a constructive way. A woman at some point may burst into tears. These tears, if they are genuine, are a sign that she is now out of the animus and into herself, and that is all for the good. Of course they may also be tears of manipulation, a device to throw the man off the track by making him feel guilty and undermining his resolve. A man in this situation should not let himself feel guilty for her tears. He must stick quietly to his guns, and the tearfulness will stop, and so will her manipulations.

Most women welcome such a confrontation with a man because it tells her that she has gone too far, and helps her get out of her own state of animus-possession. If she cares about the man she will welcome the restoration of the relationship that a man who is strong but related can bring about. Of course, "being strong" in this case means that the man must also be prepared to listen to and take responsibility for legitimate complaints about himself that his wife may have expressed. For, as we have seen, just as a man can be possessed by the anima when he has not expressed his feelings, so a woman can be possessed by the animus when her feelings have not been expressed, or when they have been expressed but have been ignored, put-down, or disparaged by the man. The worst thing the man can do is to pay no attention to a woman who has issues to bring up with him. From a woman's point of view, if a man ignores matters of relationship it is the same as ignoring her. This means to her that she and what she feels are not important to him. This sets the stage for the animus to take over and retaliate for her.

Sometimes a man is not so much afraid of the woman's anger as of his own. His rage may be something in him from which he is cut off. It may have become part of his shadow personality, of which he is largely unconscious and dreadfully afraid since his angry shadow threatens to intrude into consciousness and destroy his carefully built up ego functioning. The result is an overly passive man, whose passivity is really an egocentric form of adaptation. These Clinging Vines or Turtles live on top of volcanoes. If the volcanoes erupted they would spew destruction all around, but nevertheless within them is the fire of an anger that can be genuine and healthy.

I pointed out that when a woman's animus takes over, or when she breaks into tears, it may bring out a man's feelings of guilt and weaken him. So learning to relate to a woman also means learning to deal with feelings of guilt. Sometimes these feelings of guilt go back to a man's relationship with his mother when he was a small boy. Watch a small boy when his mother becomes angry at him. Observe how acutely unpleasant it is for him, and how a small boy will be terribly hurt, and want to do all he can to appease mother so everything will be all right again. Or how he may spew out boyish defiance in an attempt not to be overwhelmed by his own painful feelings. A woman's emotional life has a powerful effect on the people in her life. The way a woman is feeling about him can make a little boy's life happy or horrible. This will especially be the case if the mother uses her capacity to inculcate guilt as a device to control the boy. As Marie-Louise von Franz once pointed out, a woman is a master at what she called "lamenting-re-proachfulness." She doesn't even have to say "You are a bad boy." If she acts hurt, injured, or made unhappy by him, he carries away within himself a terrible feeling of rejection and unworthiness. Of course the mother must punish and correct an errant child, but she needs to do so in constructive ways that do not engender damaging feelings of guilt and unworthiness. If, in effect, mother sends the message to the boy, "If you do not do what I want I will treat you coldly and shut you out, and you will not be able to stand that," then the boy will be injured.

Such memories may be silently at work in a man's fearful response to his wife. At the least sign from her of lamenting-reproachfulness a man's guilty-little-boy may be constellated. He will need to recognize, accept, and minister to his hurt inner child in order that he not become identical with such feelings and can keep them out of his relationship with women.

Now we can see what a great help marriage, or a comparably close relationship with a woman outside of marriage, is to a man in freeing him from his mother complex. As long as a man is dominated by his mother complex he is not fully a man. We usually think that a man becomes a man by facing the world and overcoming its difficulties, and this is indeed an important part of it. But he also overcomes his mother complex and steps into his mature masculine personality by learning to express his feelings, positive and negative, with a woman, and by being able to confront the woman's animus in the ways we have examined.

Clearly, a relationship with a woman provides a man with a crucible in which his self-knowledge can increase and many of the aspects of his personality that once were unconscious to him can come to light. This is why Adolph Guggenbuhl once said of marriage that it exists not for our well-being but for our salvation.[6] That is, as long as we look at marriage only as a source of our happiness and pleasure, we will be disappointed. It is a relationship that is vital for the growth and development of many men. If it serves this function, it promotes a fundamental well-being. If some happiness now and then comes along as well, then we have a good marriage.

---

6. Adolph Guggenbuhl-Craig, *Marriage—Dead or Alive,* trans. Murray Stein. Zurich: Spring Publications, 1977, pp. 36ff.

Egocentricity in Marriage

Several times we have noted that an important influence in the quality of the marriage relationship involves the egocentricity of the man and woman. In an earlier chapter we studied the origin and nature of egocentricity and pointed out that egocentric people have difficulty in relating. Now is the time to observe how these difficulties come up in a close relationship between a man and a woman. Generally speaking we can say that to the extent the man and woman are egocentric, love in the relationship will be precluded and egocentric patterns of relating will be dominant. But when it comes to describing these egocentric patterns we come up against a difficulty that we encounter in all psychological descriptions: the need to make general statements. The difficulty is that relationships, like people, are individual. Since no two of them are alike, no general description exactly fits a particular situation. What we can do, however, is describe certain typical egocentric patterns of relating in marriage, and leave it up to each person's insight to see how he fits into the general example.

The number of general examples we need to give is somewhat limited since certain egocentric combinations will not be likely to occur in a marriage. For instance it is clear that two clinging, dependent people would be unlikely to marry each other; nor would two bullying and domineering people. Even if they did the marriage would almost certainly come to a quick and fiery end, with many mutual accusations and recriminations. Similarly two people who both wanted to be center-stage would be so competitive with each other that marriage between them would be virtually unthinkable. As for two withdrawn, protective people, it is doubtful if either one could reach out of his or her shell far enough to come into contact with the other, much less suggest marriage. Therefore the examples that follow, though they certainly do not cover all the possibilities, cover some of those that occur most frequently.

Example No. 1: *Marriage of a man who is a Tyrant to a woman who is a Turtle*

"John's" egocentric stance is to dominate others. He does this so he cannot be hurt by other people, but he is unaware both of his dominating patterns and of what underlies them. As long as he can dominate other people he feels on top and secure; he gets a certain malicious satisfaction from his capacity to bully others weaker than himself. Naturally such a man will tend to marry a woman who, for reasons of her own, is amenable to such treatment.

"Mary" is such a woman. She discovered a long time ago that the world, and other people, were frightening. She defends herself from a world she believes she cannot cope with by withdrawing from it as much as possible and finding a secure refuge. When it comes to marriage, she is willing to marry a man like John because she mistakes his domineering posture as a sign of strength and supposes that he can deal with a world that frightens her. It is true that she must submit to his domination of her and to his bullying tactics, but this seems a small price to pay in return for safety. Besides, he was the one who came along and asked her to marry him. She suspects not many men would have her, and would be frightened of one who demanded a real relationship anyway. She has been living at home with her parents, but can't stand this any longer, yet she is afraid to go it alone in life. All things taken into consideration, it seems to her as though John is the best possible bargain she can make.

So John and Mary have a workable basis for a marriage; each one fulfills the egocentric aspirations and demands of the other. This egocentric alliance, however, is not to be confused with love. In fact, the two actually despise each other. John's negative feelings toward Mary are expressed by an overbearing attitude that gets worse as the years go by. At first there was at least the pretense of affection; now even the pretense is gone. Mary feels too weak to retaliate openly, so she retaliates through being sick a lot of the time. This is an inconvenience to John, and a further refuge for her. Besides, he has to pay the bills and he hates doing that. In this way Mary manages to even the score.

Example No. 2: *Marriage of a man who is a Star to a woman who is a Clinging Vine*

"Joe" wants to be admired. His parents always told him how marvelous he was; in fact, they lived out their own mediocre lives through their son who showed from childhood certain unusual abilities. Joe graduated in the upper 1% of his class in high school. He and his parents were disappointed that someone else was the valedictorian, but there was compensation in the fact that Joe was elected president of the senior class. Joe likes being admired. As long as he is receiving adulation from others he feels good about himself. He rewards his admirers with what appears to be his friendship and affection. For this reason others think Joe is a warm and related person. Actually Joe's real devotion is to his own ego. When Joe married, he naturally chose a woman who would be one of his admirers. He certainly did not want a woman who would also be center-stage, or even have a stage of her own. So John decided to marry "Susan."

Susan has always felt inferior. She doesn't trust her own abilities; in fact, she has never thought she has abilities. Her goal in life is to find someone to whom she can cling. When she can do this she feels secure, but when she is threatened with having to stand on her own two feet, she is filled with anxiety. She soon discovered that Joe would let her cling to him as long as she admired him for what appeared to be his wonderful gifts. It is true that Joe had many other admirers, and this made Susan uneasy, but it was easy to convince herself that as long as she was faithful to the task of giving Joe what he wanted he would let her lean on him.

When Joe and Susan were first married everyone thought they had the ideal marriage. People would say, "Look how devoted they are to each other." Actually there was little love between them. It was merely an alliance of egos, and the longer they were together the more intense grew their dislike of each other. The truth was that though Susan leaned heavily on Joe, she deeply resented the way he welcomed attention from other people, especially from other women. As for Joe, he sensed this resentment and became increasingly aware that his wife did not admire him as much as she should. In fact, others were more admiring than his wife, so his attention soon turned away from the marriage relationship. This left Susan increasingly uneasy and resentful; she wasn't getting what she had bargained for. In spite of herself she retaliated by increasingly bitter attacks on Joe; this frightened her because she could see that these attacks were driving Joe further away. For what use has a man for a wife who attacks him when what he craves is admiration? Meanwhile Joe became increasingly unhappy. It was one thing to be in the upper echelons of his class at school, but another to get to the top of the real world and stay there. He is afraid the day may come when his admirers fall away and he is left only with his embittered wife. The fact is that Joe is in danger of switching from being the object of admiration to a man who becomes cravenly dependent on others.

Example No. 3: *Marriage of a man who is a Turtle to a woman who is a Tyrant*

"Bill" has never been able to make it in the world. He has always experienced others as more powerful than himself. Moreover, they have often been brutal to him. So Bill protects himself by hiding. He is especially vulnerable in the area of emotion. Easily hurt, he has withdrawn his emotions and keeps them carefully hidden and protected. Just the same he has emotional needs, which he experiences mostly as a longing for protection. So he selects for his wife a woman who seems most likely to provide this for him.

"Emily" is just the woman. Emily has never been dominated by others because she always sees to it that she dominates them. As long as she is on top, in the power position, she feels secure, so when Bill came along it was natural for her to accept his offer of marriage. In fact, she didn't wait for him to offer it but suggested it herself. Emily soon made an empire out of her home. She had children in quick succession and provided a secure home for each of them—as long as they toed the line. When they didn't she had a number of ways of enforcing her will: all the way from direct intimidation to controlling them through manipulating guilt feelings in them. One way or the other she saw to it that she ruled, and ruling Bill was no exception. Actually she despised Bill for his weakness. If a strong man had shown up in her life she would have fought him tooth and nail, but in her heart she would have hoped that he would not let her win. But a strong man was never interested in her because of her lack of femininity, so Bill was the best she could do. Soon he became less a husband to her than one of her children. She despised him all the more for this, but at least there was no doubt about her ability to remain in control. In this way her ego got what it wanted, but her soul suffered.

Other people wondered why Bill put up with his wife's domination of him, but the truth is that Bill would have put up with even more as long as he would be compensated by the presence of a strong mother-wife who would shield him from life. Besides, Emily did not want or require intimacy of him. Emotional intimacy, with all of its vulnerability, would have frightened Bill too much, but Emily settled for domination instead, and to Bill this seemed like the lesser of two evils.

Example No. 4: *Marriage of a man who is a Clinging Vine to a woman who is a Star*

"Tom" is a dependent person. He believes he can't make it in a world he perceives to be harsh and forbidding and finds the soft way out: hanging on to someone who can. His pattern is much like that of Bill. Indeed, on the surface the two seem much alike. Bill was basically hard, only his hardness was in his outer shell that concealed his inner vulnerable nature. Tom, on the other hand, is basically a soft man, pliable, and seemingly warm and friendly.

The woman he married, "Elaine," liked him at first because he seemed like such a nice man. He was apparently kind and gentle, and the fact that he was devoted to her pleased her greatly. For Elaine was a woman who went about the world lavishing on people her charms and abilities, and in return she expected their admiration. What could be better for her purposes than to marry this nice man who would never challenge her needs to be center-stage? Only as the years went by did Elaine realize that Tom wasn't really nice—only passive. His gentleness wasn't warmth; it was only a feigned gentleness that he adopted so he wouldn't have to risk himself in relating. Admiration from such a man didn't count for much, so Elaine became increasingly discontented. As she became more unhappy she became a less certain bulwark against the world for Tom. Their marriage kept on going, but it was clearly on thin ice a lot of the time and Tom became increasingly anxious. He began to drink too much, and developed some physical problems, but Elaine didn't insist that he stop the drinking, because she wasn't yet ready for the change in their relationship that this might bring about. In fact, she rather preferred him when he was drunk; then at least she didn't have to make an effort to relate to him.

Marriages such as those I have described may work quite well in the sense that they can last many years, even a lifetime. To be sure, as the years go by the two will complain increasingly about each other. The facade of love will fade away, but the marriage will continue because the two still need each other to fulfill their own egocentric desires. So the wedding anniversaries come and go, and are celebrated with due formality, but true love is not there, for love cannot develop in a relationship that is primarily an ego-alliance.

If one of the partners in such a relationship begins to emerge from his or her egocentric pattern, the marriage relationship will be disturbed. Let us say, for instance, that the clinging, dependent Susan who married the glory-seeking Joe begins to find her Real Self. She now struggles to find and become who she is, a mature person in her own right. This will entail getting a good deal of painful insight and risking herself in those areas of life of which she is most afraid. It will also entail the disruption of the marriage, but because she is now in touch with her Center she has the courage to go through this. But Joe is not changing; his needs for admiration remain as insatiable as ever. Susan might be willing to admire her husband if he deserved it, but she is no longer willing to feed his bottomless, egocentric needs for admiration just to satisfy her needs for dependency. Susan is changing and Joe doesn't like it. He accuses her of all kinds of things, and does all he can to put her back into her cramped box again, although, of course, he doesn't admit to himself what he is trying to do. If he succeeds in this endeavor, the marriage will be worse than before because it will have regressed. If he doesn't succeed, it will be because Susan insists on developing her own personality. Then Joe will have to change too or the marriage will disintegrate.

The scenario is apt to be even worse in the case of a tyrannical, domineering man like John who is married to a submissive wife like Mary who finally decides to emerge from her shell. Having contacted the Real Self, Mary is now impelled into life even though it is full of risks. Her husband will be alarmed at what he perceives as an act of rebellion. He will be all the more threatening and bullying in an attempt to force her back into her submissive state. But if she remains centered she will persevere in spite of all the fear and uncertainty it causes her. What is more, she will recognize clearly that her husband does not love her and will demand that he change or she will leave.

Unless John is able to do this the day will come when Mary will abandon him. Now there is no one for John to dominate; his game is up. The effect of all this on a once tyrannical man is sometimes pathetic to watch, for when a bully is defeated he becomes a craven coward. So when John's domineering ways and bullying tricks fail him, he turns 180 degrees upside-down and becomes an abject and defeated man.

In this state of mind John contemplates suicide. Unwilling to grow, and his previous egocentric pattern of life no longer possible, he sees no way to continue his life. His suicide threat is also the final trump card he can play. Surely Mary will be cowed by this, unable to stand the guilt reactions it would produce, and will once more resume her appointed role as his whipping post.

This will be a real test for Mary. She may begin to doubt her decision to leave her husband; other people tell her that poor John is suffering so much she should go back to him. The thought that he might kill himself may make her feel that his death would be her responsibility. It will take all of Mary's growing strength and wisdom to understand that what her husband does with his life is between him and God. Indeed, if she rescues him from his egocentric despair because of her own egocentric reasons, she is depriving John of what might be his last opportunity to change.

The Affair

No presentation of masculine relationships would be complete without a discussion of that love relationship a man may have with a woman outside of marriage known as "the affair." First, we will consider the effect the affair is likely to have on the man and his marriage. Second, we will consider some of the reasons a man may have for entering into an affair.

It is almost needless to point out that an affair will complicate a man's married life considerably. It will also pose a problem for the man: whether to tell his wife of his extramarital relationship or keep it a secret. No matter which choice the man makes there is a price to be paid.

If, for instance, a man tells his wife of the other woman in his life, his relationship with his wife is disrupted. There may be stormy scenes, arguments, tears, and angry threats. His wife may in retaliation go out and have an affair of her own. In fact, if there aren't such reactions, if his wife is able to accept his affair with equanimity, it is a sign that she doesn't care very much about him. There are few women who can share their man in sex and love with another woman if they love and want him for themselves.

In order to avoid these stormy and distressing scenes, many men who have an affair will keep it a secret from their wives, but this only adds other complications. For one thing, it takes an effort to keep such a secret. Love affairs send out a kind of psychological fragrance—or odor as the case may be—and other people who are sensitive to such things "sniff" out an erotic involvement between two people. Moreover, a woman who is tuned in to her husband, especially a woman who is close to the unconscious, can pick up her husband's errancy in love in spite of his best efforts to keep it secret. It is by no means unusual for such a woman to have dreams about her husband's love affair, and I have known cases in which the woman dreamt of the actual other woman who was involved. In addition, there is an attempt on the part of the unconscious to bring the matter into the open. Eventually some mistake is made that gives away the secret: the man leaves his mistress' phone number around, or a letter from her is found in the pocket of his coat when his wife takes it to the cleaner. In all sorts of sometimes ridiculous and unlikely ways the unconscious plays a trick and the affair is brought into the open.

When the wife finds out about her husband's love affair in this way, naturally she feels hurt and betrayed. She would feel hurt and betrayed anyway, but when her husband doesn't tell her openly and she has to find out on her own, these feelings are markedly greater. If a man is open and honest with his wife about his love relationship outside of marriage, she probably will be angry and terribly upset, but she gives him credit for his honesty.

The betrayal aspect of an affair threatens the existence of the marriage. There is a spoken or unspoken contract to marriage and it seldom includes the possibility of other love relationships. When the marriage contract is violated in this way the marriage is in danger. The antidote for the injury to the marriage usually involves a great deal of discussion and interchange between the man and his wife, but sometimes nothing will heal the wound if the man was not honest with his wife. Once humpty-dumpty has been broken it is not easy to put him back together again, and this is also true about trust.

Nevertheless many men choose to keep the affair a secret. They may do this because they see the affair as short-lived and they don't want to give up or threaten their marriage. Or they may tell themselves that they don't want to hurt their wives. They may be honest when they tell themselves this, but the truth may also be that the man who chooses the secret way may simply not want to go through the tears, anger, or quarreling that divulging the love affair would bring about.

Of course the shoe may fit the other foot and it may be the wife

who has a love relationship outside of the marriage. It is often said that
men tend to be polygamous and women monogamous. Men certainly
are likely to have a polygamous streak, but it is not so clear that women
are monogamous. It may be that social circumstances reinforce a woman's attachment to the marriage more than they do a man's. For instance, the woman may have a greater need to preserve the marriage
because it is the container in which she raises the children, while this
may not be so important to the man. But how a woman looks at love
relationships outside of marriage is a subject for another book since this
one is devoted to masculine psychology.

As for the reasons underlying the affair the following will include
some of the most common.

1. LONELINESS

If a man is separated from his wife for a long period of time, loneliness for the comfort a woman can give may lead him to an affair which
he sees as purely temporary. In fact, he may not even regard this as an
affair, especially if it takes place a long distance from home. One man
came for counseling because of his wife's extramarital relationship. He
was terribly angry with her and felt deeply betrayed. In the course of
one conversation, however, he told his therapist of a long-standing relationship he had with a woman in a country overseas that he often visited on business. The therapist asked him how he could be so angry with
his wife when he had an affair of his own. He looked surprised and
announced that this had nothing to do with his relationship with the
woman overseas. Japan was a long way away and therefore wasn't an
affair. There was nothing the therapist could do to change the man's
"logic," and his anger at his wife persisted, leading to the breakup of
their marriage.

2. PROJECTION OF THE ANIMA

We have already noted that the anima projection seldom survives
prolonged everyday intimacy with a woman. For this reason even
though a marriage may have been initiated because the woman carried
the anima projection of the man, in the course of time this projection
will fall away from the wife. It will then quite likely fall on another,
relatively unknown woman. The man now feels the same attraction,

fascination, and erotic desire toward the other woman that he originally felt for his wife. If he has an unsophisticated consciousness he may suppose that this means he no longer loves his wife, and probably never did, and that he loves the other woman instead. Hoping to find "it," that is, the ultimate love relationship, which he once thought would be in the marriage but which has since eluded him, he may have an affair with the new woman who now carries the fascinating projection. Some men may go through a series of such relationships. Every time the projected image falls away from a woman and falls on another woman, they may, if they have not learned anything about themselves in the interim, run after her, always in pursuit of that beckoning but elusive image of the feminine which they hope to have for themselves forever.

A special instance of the projection of the anima is the problem of the "double anima." In such a case, two anima images are projected; one woman carries one image and another woman carries the second. Typically the wife carries the anima images associated with Demeter and Hera, and another woman carries the image of Aphrodite. It is as though his adoration is being claimed by two or more goddesses. The more unconscious the man is of his own psychology and the archetypal nature of the unconscious, the more compulsively enslaved he will be to his erotic fantasies and to the two or more women who carry his varying projected anima images. The affairs that can develop out of such a psychological structure have at their heart the urge from the unconscious for the greater consciousness and individuation of the man's personality.

3. THE NEED FOR EXPERIENCE

Sometimes a man is drawn into extramarital relationships because he has to find out something. This may particularly be the case with a young man who marries before he has had enough experiences with women. It is natural for a young man to want personal experiences with women, to "play the field" before tying himself down to the single relationship of marriage. If this need has not been fulfilled, there is an unlived life in him that still clamors to be expressed. Affairs may be the result.

One young man came for marriage counseling because he found himself a prey to erotic fantasies about several women other than his wife. He was not a psychologically sophisticated person and could only conclude that he didn't love his wife as much as a man should. He saw his wife as an intelligent and capable woman whom he liked a great deal, but couldn't understand if this were so why his erotic imagination was going elsewhere.

This young man had a kind of rugged honesty about himself, so he told his wife about what was going on inside his mind, left her, got an apartment and proceeded to make relationships with the women who were the objects of his fantasies. He made love to several women, but after each encounter he was left with a feeling of disappointment. Somehow the reality didn't measure up to the fantasy. His last such experience ended miserably for both himself and the unfortunate young lady who got involved with him. She came to his apartment and they made love and fell asleep. He woke first in the morning, looked at the woman in the bed beside him, and asked himself, "What is that woman doing here?" He had her out of there before breakfast, which must have been quite a shock to her. Not long after this he returned home and told his wife he wanted to return. She took him back and these many years later they are still married.

4. THE NEED FOR PERSONAL PSYCHOLOGICAL DIFFERENTIATION

Sometimes the extramarital relationship takes place because a man and his wife are too identified with each other. If a man becomes too absorbed in his wife and vice versa, the individual personality of each partner may be stifled. They become so much of a psychological unit that their personal identities are obscured. In such a situation, the creative forces of the unconscious, which seek to impel a person toward individuation, may find ways to bring about a more personal differentiation of personality. As long as this process is not made conscious it may have disturbing effects on both the individual and the marriage with disastrous results. One way this differentiation is sometimes brought about is through an affair. In such a case the anima will rise up, as it were, and project herself on another woman. The undifferentiated man will be drawn into a relationship with this new woman. Out of the resulting difficulties, emotional confusion, and disruption of the marriage relationship, there is the possibility that greater individual psychological awareness may emerge. In this case, the man may not really want to leave his wife, and the end result can be a better marriage relationship than before because the relationship now lives between a man and woman who have become more conscious and differentiated.

5. WHEN A MAN IS MARRIED TO THE WRONG WOMAN

Sometimes a man seeks out an extramarital relationship because he married a woman who is unsuitable for him. For this reason, one question to ask in the event of an affair is how the man feels about his wife. He may become involved with another woman because he has feelings of dislike for his wife that he has never faced.

One man came for therapy because he had been impotent with his wife for ten years. Naturally he was distressed about this, felt inferior, thought there must be something wrong with him, and all those feelings that a man would have under these conditions. Asked about his marriage he protested that it was quite good, other than the lack of sexual life, and that his wife was an exemplary person, whom of course he loved. However, the word love is often bandied about in a careless fashion; we are apt to say we love someone when we think this is expected of us. So the therapist asked him, "Do you *like* her?" This brought a much more thoughtful response. Eventually the man realized that no, he didn't like her, in fact he really wanted to get away from her. About this time another woman came into his life and he had an affair. He had no trouble at all with his potency and enjoyed the sexual side of the extramarital relationship greatly. Not long after, he divorced his wife and married the other woman. In this case the man was unaware of his negative feelings for his wife. He pretended to himself that he loved her and took all the blame on himself. However, his penis didn't lie; it refused to have anything to do with her, but was quite happy to make love to his new wife, whom he liked a great deal.

6. THE NEED TO DIFFERENTIATE EROS

Still another reason for the affair is the need a man may have to differentiate his Eros side. Some men have not honored that aspect of life that involves sex, love, woman, and relationship. The Greeks, as we have seen, regarded all this side of life as the province of Aphrodite, and they pointed out that every man must give appropriate attention to all of the goddesses. However there are certain men who may have devoted their energies exclusively to masculine pursuits. They may have followed Ares into war, or Apollo into science, or Zeus into a political career, and ignored Aphrodite. When they did marry it may have been under the aegis of Hera, that is, they married for social reasons, or political influence, or to further a business, and the personal love aspect may not have mattered. In the course of the individuation process of such a man, however, the goddess Aphrodite is almost certain to make her appearance. She will claim his attention by flooding his mind with erotic fantasies and urges, and, since Aphrodite is no respecter of marriage, these erotic desires will typically go out to other women, impelling him to extramarital adventures.

All of this will result in confusion, strife, arguing, and love-making. These are elements in Aphrodite's world, but out of such turmoil a new development may take place in the man, and his relationships with women may become real and differentiated.

7. THE AFFAIR AS AN EXPRESSION OF UNUSED CREATIVE ENERGY

Another reason for the affair is the example of the creative man who is not realizing his creativity. Sexual energy may not be sexual at all; it may simply be the place where an unrealized creative energy has gone. It is as though a certain quantity of creative energy that has not been made conscious and is not being fulfilled gets stuck in the body and turns up as sexuality. However, if such a man gets creatively involved, the energy for the affair may vanish. One man who was musically inclined found himself unemployed. Even his previous positions had been unsatisfactory from a creative point of view. He became enmeshed in an affair that he kept secret from his wife, and the whole matter drained him of a great deal of energy. But eventually a challenging opportunity came to him that fully engrossed his creative abilities. With this the sexual energy he had for the affair vanished almost overnight. He still liked the woman he had been making love with, but no longer wanted a love relationship with her. He lived monogamously with his wife and was frank to say that he really didn't have time nor interest for any other woman; one was quite enough. His new "mistress" was his music, and the goddess he was now serving was one of the Muses.

8. THE AFFAIR AS AN OUTLET
FOR SEXUAL FANTASIES

Men are prone to have highly charged sexual fantasies. These fantasies are extremely varied. While they can be placed in certain general categories, perhaps it is not too much to say that every man has his own particular variation. A man's sexual fantasies may seem strange to him. He may be embarrassed by them and feel shy about divulging them to anyone, even to his wife. If his wife is a fairly conventional person in matters of sex and has no instinct for relating to a man's sexuality, he may not share his fantasy life with her. Yet he is driven by these fantasies and wants to live them out with a woman. For this reason many men who have perfectly satisfactory marriages will still from time to time go to a prostitute, whom they will pay to live out their fantasies with them. But some men will find the idea of a prostitute too repelling and they may wind up instead relating sexually to another woman with whom they find they can live out their fantasy life. Because of their importance, we will discuss such sexual fantasies in more depth in a later chapter. But for now we will turn to other relationships in a man's life, particularly men as fathers, and men as sons.

Suggested Reading

Guggenbuhl-Craig, Adolph, *Marriage—Dead or Alive,* tr. Murray Stein. Zurich: Spring Publications, 1977.

Johnson, Robert A., *WE: Understanding the Psychology of Romantic Love.* San Francisco: Harper & Row, Publishers, 1983.

Lynch, James, M.D., *The Broken Heart.* New York: Basic Books, 1977.

Masters, Wm. H. and Johnson, Virginia E., *The Pleasure Bond.* New York: Bantam Books, 1975.

Myers, Isabel Briggs and Peter B., *Gifts Differing.* Palo Alto: Consulting Psychologists Press, Inc., 1980, pp. 127–135.

Sanford, John A., *The Invisible Partners: How the Male and Female in Each of Us Affects Our Relationships.* New York: Paulist Press, 1980.

Chapter 8

Masculine Relationships: Part Two
Men as Fathers and Sons

The Father-Son Relationship

The father-son relationship has a major impact on a man's psychological development. A positive father-son relationship, characterized by mutual love and respect, helps a boy develop a healthy masculinity. Healthy masculinity enables him to be forthright and assertive in the manner Robert Bly speaks of when he says that masculinity is "forceful action undertaken not without compassion, but with resolve."[1]

A father can assist the process of his son's acquiring masculinity by paying special attention to his son's accomplishments and validating them as signs of the boy's growing into manhood. Things like earning a good grade on an exam, getting a hit in a baseball game, or doing well on a work project can be celebrated and thereby become experiences that contribute to the boy's sense of self-worth.

Although, as pointed out in Chapter 2, by the time a boy reaches adolescence it is typically not the father's province to initiate him, during boyhood there are many experiences father and son can share that build masculinity and have an initiatory quality. If the father has the right attitude he can help his son feel good about himself and develop confidence that will last a lifetime. If the father is supportive and patient when he helps his son learn a sport or a skill, the son comes to feel that he is capable; he believes in himself because his father believes in him and lets him know it.

Play, if it is done right, can be a good way for father and son to relate. When a father plays with his son he needs to realize that play is supposed to be fun. If they throw a football to each other he doesn't have to try to make his son the best on the block. If the boy enjoys himself he'll be more likely to naturally use his full athletic potential. Play also provides a context for physical contact between father and son. In Chapter 1 we spoke of the need of the small child for physical

---

1. Keith Thompson, in "A New Age Interview with Robert Bly." *New Age Magazine,* May 1982, p. 35.

187

affection from the parent. Robert Bly says that boys have a "body-long-ing" for their fathers.[2]

Companionate play is an important part of a father's role with his son, but there are also other important aspects of a father's role, such as teacher, advisor, law-maker and policeman. These involve the father in being the disciplinarian who sets limits on inappropriate behavior. Children, by their nature, require the setting of limits because they are primarily concerned with getting their own needs met. It is up to the parents to teach them to be concerned with the needs and rights of others. Also, if there are no clear-cut limits, the son may feel anxious because he isn't sure he can control his own impulses; he needs that control from adults. However, the son is unaware of this need and so may complain about being disciplined. The role of disciplinarian will not make a father popular with his son, but he needs to perform it to help him get control of his impulses. There will be many times when a father must step in and say "No." If he is not harsh and if he disciplines with fairness, his son will respect his strength. The son will then have a good role model from whom to acquire his own masculine strength.

When a father acts as a good role model it helps his son see him as a hero. During this stage, in the son's view, his father can do no wrong, can accomplish anything and can protect him from all dangers; he may picture his father as a mythical figure, or as the greatest man alive. In reality the son is projecting the archetype of the hero onto his father. This is an important stage in his development of masculinity because once he can project the hero image he can see it more clearly and begin to incorporate it into his own personality. However, if he were to continue to see his father as a hero and to rely on his father's strength he would not be motivated to develop his own strength. Therefore he must eventually drop his hero projection in order to become his own man.

Life circumstances usually force the boy to give up his image of father-as-hero. Few fathers can match up to the archetype of the hero for long, simply because they are only fallible human beings, not heroes. Sigmund Freud's experience of seeing his father realistically is recounted by Freud's biographer:

> . . . his father never regained the place he had held in his esteem
> after the painful occasion when he told his twelve-year-old boy how

---

2. Ibid., p. 37.

a Gentile had knocked off his new fur cap into the mud and shouted at him: "Jew, get off the pavement." To the indignant boy's question: "And what did you do?" he calmly replied: "I stepped into the gutter and picked up my cap." This lack of heroism on the part of his model man shocked the youngster who at once contrasted it in his mind with the behavior of Hamilcar when he made his son Hannibal swear on the household altar to take vengeance on the Romans. Freud evidently identified himself with Hannibal, for he said that ever since then Hannibal had a place in his phantasies.[3]

Though a boy must ultimately find his own masculinity and become his own hero, he may need to go through a transition phase during which he shifts from reliance on his father to reliance on a spiritual father or mentor. In a mentor relationship a boy or young man forms an emotional attachment to an admired older man. He absorbs the knowledge of his chosen mentor and may even mimic his personality traits and mannerisms in an attempt to identify with him and incorporate the mentor's qualities into himself.

The mentor or spiritual father may be a teacher the boy particularly admires, or a coach, minister, school counselor, psychotherapist, relative, neighbor, or family friend. Around the time of adolescence a boy may seek out such an older man; he may choose a man who is of a similar psychological type* and with whom he therefore feels a natural rapport. The mentoring relationship may center around occupational interests, with the youth selecting a mentor who has succeeded in an occupation the youth is interested in. It can also happen that the youth becomes interested in a career because it is his mentor's career. The mentor may help him learn the skills required for the career and also instill in him the confidence to pursue it.

The process of spiritual fathering, or mentoring, is an old one. It existed in ancient Greece where boys' families allowed them to be taken from their homes by older men who would educate them, imbue them with culture, and help them acquire the skills to function as independent men in the society.

The American Indians' process of spiritual fathering involved the Vision Quest that was described in Chapter 2. This illustrated a special

---

3. Ernest Jones, *The Life and Work of Sigmund Freud*. New York: Basic Books, 1961, p. 19.

*See Appendix A for information about psychological types.

function of the spiritual father, which is to help the young man deal with the inner world. Certain young men have a need to get in touch with their inner processes, including their unconscious psychological world, their dreams, spontaneous fantasies and spiritual experiences. For a young man who is strongly impacted by his inner experiences a spiritual father may be a necessity; otherwise the young man may feel almost unbearably alone in the world. The spiritual father is someone he can share his inner depths with and so get to know them in the safe container of relationship with a guide who has "been there" himself.

Our own society lacks formalized ways of providing spiritual fathers. When a youth in our culture needs to turn for guidance to a man other than his father he must have the initiative to find this man. Part of the reason that a young man's father cannot be his mentor may be that the spiritual father provides a model that is less threatening to the youth's independence; the youth is thus more receptive to the mentor's guidance than he is to his own father's. To be his own man he must separate from reliance on his father, but he is not yet ready to rely on himself, so he looks to his mentor.

Another reason a youth chooses a mentor is if his father has been physically absent or emotionally unavailable. He may then try to get the masculine identification, both personal and professional, he could not get from his father. Such was the case in the mentor-mentee relationship between the famous journalist H. L. Mencken, who was the mentor, and novelist/screenwriter John Fante, who was the mentee. The two men never met but communicated through letters over a twenty-year period beginning when Fante was twenty-one and Mencken fifty. In one of his letters Fante said facetiously of his father, "My father was very happy at my birth. He was so happy that he got drunk and stayed that way for a week. On and off for the last twenty years he has continued to celebrate my coming."[4] Though he jokes about it, this gives an indication that his father had a drinking problem and was unavailable to him when he was a boy; his father deserted the family when Fante was in his late teens. Thus the young aspiring writer was motivated for both professional and personal reasons to seek out Mencken as his mentor. Professionally Mencken helped him when he published Fante's first short story. On the personal level Fante sought

---

4. Michael Moreau, "My Mentor, Mr. Mencken," *Los Angeles Times Magazine*, April 26, 1987, p. 25.

in Mencken the father/hero figure he lacked. In one of his letters to Mencken he says, ''I still hold you, and always shall, my ideal of a man, and measure myself to you. I've got to have a god, and you're he.''[5]

During the mentoring phase the youth depends on the mentor for his identity. He may adopt the Identity Foreclosed state we spoke about in Chapter 2. However, since his ultimate purpose in seeking a mentor is to help him find himself as a man, he may eventually go through an Identity Moratorium in which he questions and challenges even his mentor on his way to achieving his own identity. Ultimately, to withdraw from dependency on his mentor and reach independent manhood, a man will need to get in touch with his inner Center, the Self, and rely on that greater part of himself as his mentor as described by C. G. Jung with reference to his own inner mentor.[6]

We have just seen how a relationship with a spiritual father can help a man make up for an inadequate relationship with his biological father. Now we will explore some of the many factors that may cause a father-son relationship to be inadequate. The factors of particular importance that we will discuss are: the father's over-zealousness in the teaching/advising role, the father's negative feelings toward his son and about his role as a father, a father's hurt feelings from his own childhood; the son's rebelliousness, differences in psychological types, and the problem of egocentricity in father and son.

We will start with the father's over-zealousness as advice-giver. The father who tries to coach his son only with the intent of improving him may cause him to feel unloved and to see his father as a taskmaster whose teaching he wants to reject. A classic example of a father who went to the extreme in this area is found in the incredibly voluminous letters of Lord Chesterfield to his son. Lord Chesterfield was a British statesman who, in 1732 at the age of thirty-eight, had an illegitimate son, named Philip Stanhope, whom he attempted to educate academically and to train in the social graces by relentlessly advising him about proper conduct. Perhaps it was because his son was illegitimate that Lord Chesterfield was so concerned with making him acceptable to society. The following are excerpts from his letters to his son:

---

5. Ibid., p. 22.
6. C. G. Jung, *Memories, Dreams, Reflections*. New York: Pantheon Books, 1963, pp. 182–183.

> . . . Although I now love you dearly, if you continue [to do good school work], I shall love you still more tenderly; if you improve and grow learned, every one will be fond of you, and desirous of your company; whereas, ignorant people are shunned and despised.[7]

> . . . the only return I desire is . . . your invariable practice of virtue, and your indefatigable pursuit of knowledge. Adieu! and be persuaded that I shall love you extremely, while you deserve it; but not one moment longer.[8]

Although Lord Chesterfield's letters are indeed full of excellent advice for anyone who desires to become more cultured and socially adept, they are so concerned with teaching and training that they don't give enough space to feeling and relating person to person. Therefore, the kind of father-son relationship they reflect is too limited, and it might make a son feel he would be lovable only if he were the perfect gentleman. This may reduce a son's self-confidence and, ironically, make him a less capable man. This rational approach to being a father doesn't accept the son as he is with his own unique personality. In the case of Philip Stanhope all the advice-giving did not work because he did not " . . . play the superfine gentleman on the paternal model. . . . "[9]

The next factor we will discuss that can harm father-son relationships is the problem of the father's negative feelings toward his son. In addition to the usual feelings of pride and happiness, a man may also feel resentment, jealousy and competitiveness at the birth of a son. He may see the son as an intrusion into the dyadic relationship between himself and his wife; he may be afraid his wife will love the son more than she loves him. Because the son is also a male the father may feel an instinctual rivalry. Indeed, much of the time and energy he was getting from his wife does go to the baby now. The fact that the mother typically forms the earliest and strongest emotional bond with the infant may contribute to the father's feeling left out.

The change in the marital relationship after the birth of a son may

---

7. Earl of Chesterfield, *Letters to His Son*. New York: Willey Book Co., 1901, p. 344 of the Appendix Juvenile Section.

8. Ibid., Vol. 1, p. 6.

9. Chesterfield, op. cit., "Special Introduction" by Oliver Leigh.

be particularly painful for a man who wants a large amount of mothering from his wife. A cycle may occur in which the father resents the child and acts in a rejecting way toward it so that it shies away from him; this intensifies the mother-son bond and makes the father feel even more left out.

The recent movement toward getting fathers involved in parenting as early as possible has helped to prevent the father from having negative feelings toward his son. Being conscious of these feelings, if he has them, may keep him from taking them out on his son. If he shares his fears and feelings with his wife, they may act to maintain and safeguard their dyadic relationship as husband and wife in addition to participating in their joint care-taking venture as parents. It will also help the situation if the father realizes that his role as father is an opportunity for him to grow out of the child role himself, if he has been in it in relation to his wife, and to become a more individuated man.

The problem of the father's negative feelings is not limited to the time when the son is newborn; it may continue into boyhood. Currently in our culture an increased awareness exists about the need for fathers to spend quality time with their sons, yet sometimes the father doesn't feel like it. He may be aware of how crucial his role is and how much is expected of him, but this only makes him feel guilty and resentful. It is like the cartoon in which the father, who is dressed in a business suit sitting stiffly and formally in the living room with his son, looks at his watch and announces, "Oops! Quality time is almost up."[10]

A father may resent his role as father because it takes up too much of his time and gets in the way of things he wants to do. Some of this resentment may simply be selfishness, but other aspects of his personality also may be thwarted by the demands of being a parent. One father of two pre-school boys had negative feelings about his sons because it seemed he never had any time for himself. He worked all day, and when he came home at night he was tired and wanted time for himself. Of course his wife was also tired, and since she had been taking care of the kids all day, she wanted him to help her with them when he got home. By the time they went to bed he was exhausted and resentful. In therapy he worked out a way to meet his own needs: he made an agreement with his wife that two evenings he would come home an hour later, taking a long bike ride or working out at the gym. In turn he would have the

---

10. Jim Berry, "Berry's World." *Los Angeles Times*, September 15, 1987, Part V, p. 5.

boys by himself for half of the day on Saturdays, allowing the wife time to herself. He found that he enjoyed playing with the boys on Saturdays when he felt more rested and had gotten something for himself during the week.

A father needs to find a way to deal with his negative feelings not only because they produce unproductive guilt, but because they will further impede his ability to relate to his son. So these feelings must be faced and accepted as part of his shadow. This will enable him to accept his own needs as valid and to provide for their expression in his life, which will ease his resentment toward his son and make the demands of being a father more manageable.

Another factor that may keep a father from being close to his son is the father's unresolved hurt feelings from his own childhood. If a man had a poor relationship with his own father, the whole area of father-son relationships may be painful for him. This type of father lives with a hurt little boy within himself, one that is always ready to be rejected, and this makes the father over-sensitive to what he perceives as rejection. He may either (1) try to avoid relating to his son, or (2) go out of his way to be a good father, but then, when he feels the son doesn't properly appreciate him, he may feel hurt and retreat from relating.

One man of the second type found himself withdrawing from relating to his six year old son because the boy had hurt his feelings. He had put a lot of effort into getting the boy what the father thought was the perfect birthday gift: a "Dodgers" jacket. He knew his son would love the jacket because it was exactly the kind of thing he wanted, but never got, when he was a boy. When his son opened the present he looked disappointed and said, "I like the 'Angels' better."

The father's first impulse was to snatch the jacket away and give the boy nothing. He didn't do that, but he did decide never again to go out of his way to try to please his son with a gift.

As he talked out his feelings in therapy he realized that he experienced his son's rejection of the gift as a rejection of himself. He had unconsciously decided that if his son was going to reject him, he would return the favor, and he had started ignoring the boy, until his wife noticed it and asked him why.

He had to do psychological work to overcome his hurt feelings and to see that the boy was just being honest, without concern for social graces or his father's feelings. The father worked to understand how his emotional wound from his bad relationship with his father was affecting the way he dealt with his son. As the Bible says, "The fathers have eaten unripe grapes; the children's teeth are set on edge" (Jer 31:29; Ez 18:2). By working on himself in therapy he hoped to avoid passing the wound down the line to his own son. If a man cares about his son he will engage in this type of self-examination; he will muster the courage to delve into his own painful childhood wounds and thus strive to prevent these wounds from interfering with his relationship with his son.

If a man has had a wounding relationship with his father he may be crippled by emotional weakness and an unwillingness to face the pain of life. Such a father may try to protect his son from painful experiences because he can't deal with them himself. Though it may appear that he is helping his son, in fact his "help" may damage the son's ability to deal with life. For example, a ten year old boy's beloved cat was run over by a car. The boy was away at the time, and the father decided to bury it without telling him about it, hoping the boy might think the cat just ran away. In this way the father sought to avoid a painful scene. As luck would have it, just as he was patting down the last patch of dirt on the grave the boy came home and saw what he was doing. Of course the truth came out, and the boy's grief was compounded with anger at his father for deceiving him. It would have been better if he had been told the truth in the first place. When a boy goes through an experience like the death of a pet it is an archetypal experience, and in spite of the grief it can help his emotional growth. It may be painful for a father to watch this process, but his son may need to experience the pain and learn that he can tolerate it and grow from it as well.

The next factor that may interfere with a father-son relationship is the problem of the son's rebelliousness. There are times when a father may be confronted with his son's acting in an objectionable way. For no apparent reason the boy becomes defiant and oppositional, disobeying rules he formerly followed, arguing incessantly, or giving the "silent treatment" to his parents, and generally making life miserable for them by being uncooperative. The son's rebelliousness poses a dilemma for the father because if he comes down hard on his son he risks driving him into further and more serious rebellion or squelching his fledgling attempts to find his own way through rebelling. However, if the father ignores the obnoxious behavior, this may result in increased rebellion just to get the father's attention.

The answer to the dilemma is for the father to have the right attitude. The father needs to have the wisdom to see the rebellion as part of a developmental stage in which the youth attempts to gain his autonomy. This attitude helps the father be more objective and to take the rebellion not as a personal affront, but as a necessity of his son's psychological development.

Psychologist Haim Ginott, in his book *Between Parent and Teenager,* discusses the way parents can handle rebellious behavior without giving in to or suppressing the adolescent. He recommends that they permit a certain degree of rebellion while openly registering their feeling of dislike for it. For example, imagine that a son wants to wear an earring in his ear. One father who objects to this might still ignore it, hoping the son would come to his senses on his own. Another father who objects might threaten to yank the earring out of his son's ear. Though Ginott wrote his book before this particular example was relevant, it would be consistent with his theory for the father, if he strongly objected to the wearing of the earring, to state his objection to his son *in feeling terms.* He might say something like, "I think it is disgusting to see a male wearing an earring, but it's your ear and if you want to do it that's your business." In this way the father states his feeling of disagreement with the son's behavior but does not try to make him conform. This allows the son to accomplish the purpose of his rebellion, to be different from his parents and thus develop a separate identity from them as part of his necessary struggle for autonomy. It is a necessary part of the rebellion that others recognize it as rebellion; thus when the father states his disagreement, this shows the son that the rebellion has registered. If the father has the right attitude it is less likely that bad feelings will develop that would injure the father-son relationship.

Another factor that causes problems in father-son relationships is the difference in psychological types. In any relationship type differences may present problems because it is generally more difficult for people to understand and accept behaviors and attitudes that are different from their own. When father and son differ in type, misunderstandings are more likely. For example, take the case of an introverted-feeling son who had an extraverted-thinking father. The father was a real "go-getter," a man very active in the outer world, who wanted to change the world to fit his conception of it. He lived a highly disciplined life and wanted to be in charge like an army general; he was most comfortable with structure and rules. The son, however, was quiet and re- flective, more interested in contemplation of the deeper meaning of life than in outer action. He felt restricted by his father's adherence to im- personal rules that didn't take into account the individual's feelings and moods. The father felt that his son was irresponsible because he didn't always do things in a timely and organized fashion. The son liked to spend many hours reading novels, which his father regarded as a waste of time; he wondered why the boy didn't get out and *do* something. He had no patience with the son's interest in fantasy and discussion of phil- osophical issues that led to no practical outcome. To the son, the fa- ther's attitude seemed to be an attack on what he felt most deeply, a demeaning of his highest values. His father's lack of respect for his in- terests caused him to retreat further into himself, distancing himself from his father. The distance between them further increased when the son chose to be an English major in college with the hope of becoming a writer. The father wanted him to be an attorney. It was only many years later when the son became a successful writer that the father saw that those many hours spent reading were necessary preparation for a writing career.

In order to prevent psychological type differences from interfering with his relationship with his son a father may need to make an effort to show that he accepts their differences. Such was the case with one introverted intuitive father whose teenage son was an extraverted sens- ing type. The father loved nature and he especially enjoyed cross-coun- try skiing because he could experience the silent pristine beauty of the mountains as he glided through the fresh snow. However, his son was thrilled by downhill skiing because it was faster. When they went to the mountains, the father, at first trying to uphold an ideal of father-son togetherness, dragged his reluctant son along on cross-country skiing, but the boy was bored and that ruined it for the father too. The father decided that the best solution was for each of them to do what he most enjoyed. So they went their separate ways during the day and shared their fun over dinner afterward. The father respected his son's wishes while also meeting his own. In a compromise solution such as this no one's preferences are seen as right or wrong; each person is respected for his unique needs according to his type.

In Chapter 3 we presented Kunkel's forms of the egocentric ego: the Star, the Nero, the Turtle, and the Clinging Vine. We explained how these forms of egocentricity are produced by the interaction between environment and character. Now we'll explore how they can affect the father-son relationship.

Egocentricity makes one selfish, narcissistic and unconcerned with the needs and development of the other person, qualities that are basically incompatible with good relationship. Therefore, egocentricity can cause problems in father-son relationships regardless of whether father and son have similar or different forms of egocentricity. Problems that may occur when forms are similar are as follows: Two Neroes will battle each other for power and control. Two Stars will compete for the limelight. Two Turtles will create a situation of deference and passivity like the classic comic routine in which two men stand at the entrance to a building, each saying, "After you," so that neither enters. Two Clinging Vines will be frustrated in their attempts to be overly dependent on each other.

When a father's and a son's forms of egocentricity are different, other problems may occur. If the Nero or Star father has a Turtle or Clinging Vine son, the psychological situation is similar to that of the extraverted father and the introverted son. The Nero and Star fathers feel secure only when in the superior position. The danger is that the tougher father will overwhelm the softer son, and reinforce the son's lack of confidence and his tendency to hide in his shell or act dependent. However, if the son himself gets tougher, it may threaten the father, a pattern that is aptly portrayed in the popular movie "The Great Santini," starring Robert Duvall as the fighter pilot father who treated his children like boot camp recruits. His eldest son had become a Turtle in an effort to adapt to his Nero father's stern militaristic style. Over the years the father often enjoyed beating his son at one-on-one basketball. As the son grew up he became a fairly skilled basketball player. The development of this skill enabled him to free himself of his egocentricity so that while playing basketball he was no longer the Turtle he had been. The game, at least temporarily, cured him; during it he acted from his Real Self. He became so good at the game that he finally beat his father, with the whole family watching and cheering him on. Though the father ostensibly wanted a son who excelled at sports, he didn't want to be beaten by him; that was too much for the father's Nero egocentricity to take. After losing the game he retaliated by bouncing the basketball off his son's head and calling him a girl, to which the son retorted, "This little girl just beat your butt."

If the father is a Turtle or Clinging Vine and the son a Nero or Star, the situation is similar to the introverted-father, extraverted-son pattern discussed earlier. The father is likely to feel weak and insecure and he may resent his son's success in the outer world because the culture says the father is supposed to be the one who is more capable. This type of father will need to be big-hearted about validating his son's superior capabilities in the outer world.

When father and son interact with each other from their egocentric positions, they try to use each other to meet their own needs. If the father can be the first to transcend his egocentricity he may be able to break this pattern and thereby enhance his relationship with his son.

In addition to these factors we have considered, there is another underlying factor that may damage the father-son relationship. This is the archetype of the negative father. This archetype is ruled by the primitive emotions of fear and jealousy and sees the son as an enemy to be conquered or eliminated. In its most extreme form the negative father archetype is represented by the father who seeks to destroy his son.

The negative father archetype is gruesomely depicted in Greek mythology. Uranus, god of the sky, felt so threatened of having his place usurped by his children that he stuffed them back into his wife Gaia, the earth. However, one of them, the son Cronus, obtained a sickle from his mother, ambushed his father Uranus, and castrated him. When it was time for Cronus himself to become a father, he too became fearful because he had been told that a powerful son would overthrow him. So Cronus devoured each of his children as they left their mother's womb. His wife, Rhea, deceived Cronus by wrapping a stone in swaddling clothes and substituting it for his son Zeus. Cronus ate the stone instead of eating Zeus. Zeus thereby survived and grew up to overthrow Cronus and force him to give back all the swallowed children.

These myths portray the dangerous energies that may sometimes erupt into human father-son relationships. As an archetype in the unconscious the negative father energy can dramatically affect the father's ego personality and turn him into a bad father. Just as the Greek myths depict, men who have had negative fathers, and who thus may have been contaminated by this archetype, may be more likely to become bad fathers themselves. For example, in the instance of child abuse, those fathers who have been abused as children tend to abuse their own children.

When a father is severely abusive the results can be tragic, as in

the following case in which the son took revenge on his physically abusive father. Richard Jahnke was a Cheyenne, Wyoming teenager who
hid in the garage with an arsenal of guns waiting for his father to return
home after a dinner out with Mrs. Jahnke.[11] When the father came home
the boy killed him with shotgun blasts. At the trial Richard's mother
testified that the father began hitting the boy when he was only two
years old and a pattern of physical and emotional abuse continued
throughout his childhood. Richard's father had even sneaked into his
room and whipped him while he was asleep. The father had also been
beaten as a child and he was giving his son the same treatment he had
received. Mrs. Jahnke also said that Mr. Jahnke had told her he loved
her, but, he had said, " . . . it's just that the children . . . [are] in the
way."[12] On one occasion when Richard argued with his mother his father had threatened to get rid of him. In his courtroom explanation of
why he killed his father, sixteen year old Richard said, "If someone's
torturing you all your life, you will plot ways to kill him."[13] Richard
had thought about killing his father for years before he did it. When he
finally committed the act he was following the violent example he had
learned from years of abuse by his father. The Jahnke case demonstrates
the destructive effects of the father who is possessed by the negative
father archetype and whose uncontrolled jealousy and cruelty create a
deadly anger and need for revenge in the son.

   The negative father archetype also appears in less drastic, but still
damaging forms, in ordinary father-son interactions. One man related
the following incident: he was jogging around a track while a father and
his son, who appeared to be about ten years old, were playing baseball
on the field inside of the grass oval made by the track. The father hit
fly balls to the boy and the boy deftly caught almost all of them. As
long as he caught them his father was silent, but on the rare occasions
when he missed one the father yelled brutally things like, "That was
terrible! Can't you play any better than that?" The father's harsh tone
of voice caused the boy's little shoulders to hunch over and his head to
bend down until his chin rested on his chest. After each scolding the
boy was more tentative playing the next ball. His errors began to increase and the father yelled more. The father may not even have been

---

11. Alan Prendergast, *Rolling Stone,* "It's You or Me, Dad." May 26, 1983, pp. 41ff.
12. Ibid., p. 42.
13. Ibid., p. 41.

aware of how critical he sounded, or of how he was decreasing the boy's confidence and actually impairing his natural ability to play the game. This father was acting like a modern-day Cronus, swallowing his son's ability with criticism.

If a man who has been abused by his father wants to avoid doing the same to his son, it is often not enough for him merely to be aware that he has been abused and to make a conscious decision not to do it. The anger from his abused childhood will need to come out somewhere, and his son is a vulnerable target. One physically abused man decided he would never treat his son this way; he never hit him, but he never had much to do with him either. Perhaps he feared that if he ever got into a deep relationship with him, his emotions would be touched and his anger might come out. His son felt he didn't love him, and in the end the result was almost as bad as if he had abused him. This shows that a father does not need to be actively negative to have a negative effect on his son. If the father is physically or emotionally absent and uninvolved, it may also have detrimental effects on the boy's character and impair his development of masculinity. The pattern of abuse or neglect may continue down through the generations until one father makes the effort to overcome it through self-examination and personal counseling.

In addition to appearing in the family, the negative father archetype also shows up in the culture. If a scientist gets a new idea, for example, the scientific establishment may actually try to destroy him and his new idea. This is what happened in the sad case of Dr. Semmelweiss.[14]

Dr. Ignaz Philipp Semmelweis was a Hungarian obstetrician in Vienna who, during the nineteenth century, discovered that large numbers of women were dying of puerperal fever after childbirth because their doctors were not washing their hands before giving them pelvic examinations and delivering their babies. Semmelweis first reasoned out that the disease was communicated via the physician's unwashed hands. He then empirically demonstrated this by physically barring physicians from entering his wards until they washed their hands and noting that the deaths stopped in his hospital, while in other hospitals the deaths continued. The medical establishment of his time was like a

---

14. Ronald J. Glasser, M.D., *The Body Is the Hero*. New York: Random House, 1976, pp. 32–41.

pompous negative father and refused to believe, even after it had been proved, that something as simple as hand-washing could have anything to do with the deadly disease. His colleagues ridiculed him and would not accept his proof. He finally went insane because he could not bear the torment of watching mothers die when it could easily have been prevented. Dr. Semmelweis died of an infection he got from rubbing against his restraints after he had gone insane. Though it was too late to save all those many lives that were lost to the disease, time eventually proved Dr. Semmelweis right and he was " . . . later to be considered one of the greatest benefactors of humanity. . . . "[15]

We have discussed both the beneficial and the harmful effects of the father-son relationship on a man's development. Now we will discuss the father-daughter relationship before concluding with a section on the healing of father-son wounds.

The Father-Daughter Relationship

Some of the factors that affect the father-son relationship also play a part in the father-daughter relationship, but there are also special problems in the latter. We can divide these relationship factors into ego issues, problems of typology, and emotional (or affective) issues. We will begin with a discussion of how ego problems may intrude into the father-daughter relationship in an unfortunate way.

Many of the problems in father-daughter relationships have to do with the father's thoughts, feelings, and attitudes toward women in general. There is a long-standing devaluation of women in our culture that has shaped the attitudes of most men. Our patriarchally-oriented culture sees women and feminine values as less important than men and masculine values. In order for a father to properly respect and love his daughter he will need to overcome this negative cultural conditioning. He may have to challenge a deeply ingrained attitude that his daughter is not as valuable as a son would be.

A man with a negative attitude toward feminine values may not be able to overcome his disappointment if he has a daughter instead of a son. Such a father may put down his daughter's creative animus when it begins to manifest itself. This may wound her spiritual and intellectual development and create in her a lack of confidence in her abilities

15. Ibid., p. 32.

in these areas. Or he may simply ignore his daughter, and, if he has a son also, devote his attention to him. This will wound the daughter on the emotional side. She may believe that she is unlovable to a man, because when a child is not loved the child makes the assumption that it is because he or she is unlovable.

In one case, a woman with a father who ignored her had powerful erotic fantasies of being completely loved by a man, but her first relationships with men were the exact opposite: encounters with men who devalued her and left her more wounded than ever. While she aspired for a man's love, she found herself increasingly resentful of men, and was drawn to repeat in her relationships with men the same kind of rejection she experienced as a child with her father.

In another instance, a daughter whose father devalued feminine values and over-valued masculine ones showed his daughter a great deal of attention, but it was all intended to force her into a one-sidedly masculine form of development. Her father perceived that she was a bright child and tried to mold her intellectual capacity into his image of what she should be like. The woman could recall her father forcing her to memorize long lists of facts, and compelling her to read books in areas where he felt she should excel. So anxious was he that she be a super-achiever in school that, even though he himself was a teacher, he encouraged her to cheat in examinations. However, he was not interested in her emotional development, which he discouraged as unimportant. Since he was a more impressive personality than her shy and retiring mother, he influenced her a great deal. Because she could never satisfy his demands for achievement, and sensed that she was not loved for herself but only won his favor when she satisfied his ambitions for her, she grew up feeling she was a failure and was not the kind of person a man could love. She also developed a "demon animus," that is, there was within her a driving masculine side that criticized her constantly and could never be satisfied. It was as though her father lived on within her in the form of a critical, never-to-be-satisfied voice.

In the case of this woman, the problem was not only that the father devalued the feminine, it was also that he projected his own ego ambitions on her. As with the son, so with the daughter, if a father sees his child in the light of his unresolved ego ambitions it brings a negative, destructive twist into the relationship. Such a father may resent his daughter because he cannot vicariously participate in her accomplishments as he could in those of a son. He finds it hard to identify with his daughter, and since he tends to see his children, not as persons in their own right, but as extensions of his own ego, he may lose interest in her. If the father himself has not had a successful life, and wants his children to live out his own unrealized ambitions, he may be disappointed in a daughter who is not able to do this for him. He may also resent his daughter because she is not as likely to carry on the family name as a son would, even though the daughter has as many of the family genes to pass on as does a son. When a father ignores, rejects, or criticizes his daughter because she does not fulfill his ego needs, it is, of course, terribly wounding to her.

The ego problem between a father and his daughter may be further exacerbated by personality type differences. Let us say, for instance, that the father is a thinking type and the daughter a feeling type. In such a combination there is a constant risk of misunderstanding: the daughter feels that her values are not understood or respected, and the father is frustrated by what he takes as his daughter's lack of logic. The thinking type father, like Mr. Spock in "Star Trek," is interested only in the impersonal analysis of problems. The feeling type daughter focuses on interpersonal relationships and personal values. Their opposite perspectives may keep them at odds with each other. The best solution is toleration and understanding for each other's viewpoint. Since the father is, supposedly, the more mature one, he may be the one to broaden himself in order to incorporate the feeling perspective of his daughter.

For example, one man liked to go deer hunting, but his teenage daughter objected to it. In tears she told him she felt as though he was killing "Bambi." Her father tried to overcome her objections with rational arguments, such as the idea that it is not harmful to shoot some of the deer because if they were not hunted the deer population would increase so much that many of them would starve. The daughter was not persuaded by his logic; she was so moved by her feelings for the tragic fate of the one unfortunate animal her father was going to shoot that she could not take into consideration his rational approach. Furthermore, her feelings in the matter were so strong that they interfered with their relationship, for she could hardly bear to think of her father killing a helpless creature.

There are no easy answers to such conflicts. If the father liked deer hunting a great deal he would not be likely to give it up out of deference to his daughter's feelings, and if he did he might resent her for it. In this particular case the man stopped trying to convince his daughter with his rational arguments. Instead he told her that even though he did not feel the same way she did, he could understand and respect her feelings. The same strong feeling function in the daughter that led her to object to her father's deer hunting also led her to respect his openness and understanding. In this way, though they might never agree about deer hunting, the relationship was kept intact, as both of them came to understand and honor the standpoint of the other.

A father may have difficulties with the emotional side of his relationship with his daughter as well as with ego issues. For instance, a man who is out of touch with his feminine side may feel awkward in his relationship with his daughter. She is an unknown quantity to him, and he may not be sure what to do with her. If he has a boy he waits until the boy is old enough and then tosses him a football or a crescent wrench, but what is he to do with a little girl? He is in a dilemma. If he plays with her as he would with a boy, he may fear that he is over-developing her tomboy side, and there is always the danger that in an effort to please her father such a girl might overly identify with her masculine side. However, if her natural inclinations lead her to sports and mechanical things, her father may be able to relate to her much as he would to a son. But if her interests are in more traditionally feminine things, the father may be at a loss to know what to do with her. Not to play with her at all is unsatisfactory because then he is ignoring her.

He could, of course, relate to her by sharing some of his own thoughts and feelings, but if he has not developed this capacity in himself he will be unable to share with her. This is especially likely to be the case with the kind of man we discussed in Chapter 1 who has not broken free of his mother complex and therefore finds it difficult to share intimately with a woman. Such a man will be too passive when it comes to close relationships, and this will carry over into his relationship with his daughter too. Indeed, he may even expect her to initiate the relationship and feel rejected if she doesn't.

If it doesn't come naturally to a man to relate to his daughter, he will need to work on the problem. If he finds it difficult to learn how to play with her, he can nevertheless usually find ways to share activities with her. When she is small he can read her stories; when she is older he can go horseback riding with her or bicycle riding. Sometimes the most important thing is not what is done but just spending time together. One young woman reports that when she was growing up she spent a great deal of time just riding in the car with her father when he was going about his business or on family errands. He liked to take her with him, and she, being a contemplative child, was happy to read her books when he was busy with other things. Relating then sprang up in an easy, natural way. They enjoyed each other's company, and the girl grew up secure in the feeling that her father loved her.

A daughter needs a certain amount of her father's eros. She needs to know he loves her, and she is nourished by his feelings for her, his playing with her, even his flirtatiousness with her. This enriches her own eros nature, increases her confidence in herself, and prepares her for creative relationships with men later in life.

However, there are dangers in the emotional relationship between a father and a daughter as well as helpful factors, for a problem develops if the growing girl begins to carry the emotional, eros side of her father that properly belongs to a woman of his own age. If, for instance, the man has not worked out his emotional relationship with his wife, he may put an excessive and overly incestuous emotional burden on his relationship with his daughter. The daughter should never become a love substitute for the wife, nor should his intimacy with her become a substitute for intimacy with an adult woman.

Such a situation may be further complicated by the projection of the anima of the father onto the daughter. It is not at all unusual for the daughter to carry the projected anima image of the father. This in itself is not necessarily a bad thing. It may simply enliven the father-daughter relationship, provided that the man has an adult love relationship with his wife. In some cases, however, the projection may be so strong, and the man's adult relationships with women so incomplete, that the normal father-daughter eros may turn into sexual energy and constellate sexual fantasies in the father. The possibility then arises that sexual abuse of the growing girl may come about because of the father's incestuous sexual interest in her.

In such a case it is imperative that the father face his feelings of attraction to his daughter and realize that just because he feels them does not mean he has to act on them; he needs the moral capacity to realize that to act on such feelings in a sexual way would be harmful to all parties concerned. To a certain extent such feelings are natural, but if they are excessive or compulsive the father will want to seek professional help, for the effects of sexual experiences between the father and the growing little girl are disastrous for her. She will feel a crippling sense of guilt and shame that will haunt her into adult life, and will feel defiled by his sexual interest in her.

So a father walks a narrow way with regard to his emotional relationship with his daughter. If he withholds his affections and ignores her natural need for his nourishing eros side, he wounds her, but if he makes her a substitute for an eros life that should be lived out with an adult woman, he injures her too. However, if the father pursues his own individuation he will be able to find the middle way. He can then discover that he and his daughter are different but real people who need each other.

Healing Father-Son Wounds[16]

The father-son relationship has far-reaching effects on the son's psychological development. As we said at the beginning of this chapter a good father-son relationship can help the son acquire healthy masculinity. By the same token, a man who has had a poor relationship with his father may carry with him for his whole life the emotional baggage of low self-confidence and insecurity about his masculinity. This may cause him either to over-compensate by acting "macho," or to be passive and unable to be assertive when life requires it of him. A man who has these problems needs to learn how to heal himself so he can function more effectively as a man.

Before a man can begin to heal himself of his father-son wound, he first must become aware he has such a wound. He might discover it in any number of ways. One man realized it when he had recurring dreams of fighting with his father. In these dreams he repeatedly struck his father with his fists, but his father just kept bouncing back up like a "bo-bo" doll; no matter how hard he hit him he couldn't keep him down. In a counseling session the man recalled the long-forgotten memory that his father had frequently whipped him with a belt when he was a boy. He came to see that he unconsciously hated his father and had never forgiven him for his cruel treatment. He made a conscious effort not to forget the negative experiences that had become an important part of his personal history. He had to mourn the loss of the good father he

---

16. For a treatment of the father-daughter wound, the reader may be interested in Linda Leonard's book *The Wounded Woman*. Boulder: Shambhala, 1983.

had never had, and then he was able to forgive his own father. Whereas
before he had forgotten and not forgiven, now he forgave but did not
forget.

Another man became embarrassingly aware of the negative effects
of his poor relationship with his father when he caught himself saying
to his own son the same criticisms, in the same harsh tone of voice, that
his father had said to him. It wasn't pleasant for him to see himself
imitating these negative aspects of his father, but by being conscious of
them he was able to get control of himself and treat his son more kindly.
Once a man has the courage to face his wound, he can act to heal himself. He can't change the past, but he can attempt to understand it, work
through his unresolved feelings about it, and avoid repeating it with his
own son.

Working through feelings in order to heal oneself may involve
doing some sort of ritual to make the realization concrete. One man who
had a hypercritical father, and lacked self-confidence as a result, found
a way of healing himself. As a boy he loved to play baseball, and he
was fairly good at it when just playing for fun in a sandlot. However,
when the Little League tryouts came he became nervous and could not
perform up to his potential. For this reason he wasn't chosen for the
teams and never satisfied his desire to play competitively. When he was
in his mid-thirties, however, he started to play softball. He found that
he was no longer nervous; he wasn't inhibited by the old anxieties and
could use his full athletic potential. He discovered that he was a better
player than he had thought. He joined a team and had many heroic adventures in games, hitting a game-winning home run in a league championship and making sparkling plays in the field. This was a
tremendously healing experience for him. It gave him self-confidence
which generalized into other areas of his life, and helped heal the boyhood wounds and the feeling of failure he had carried for so long. By
going back to the beloved sport of his boyhood he was able to live out
a lost part of himself, the athlete-hero, and this nourished his sense of
masculinity and self-worth. For him it was like a delayed initiation into
manhood.

Another man who was in his early forties came to recognize that
many of his bad experiences with his father were probably caused by
differences in their psychological types: he was an intuitive type and his
father was a sensing type. He recalled their fishing trips and how his
father, who was naturally skilled at such things as tying hooks on lines,

would become impatient and criticize him for being so inept and hope-lessly tangling the line. The man felt a horrible sense of failure when he thought of these experiences, probably because they were repre-sentative of other aspects of his relationship with his father. As a grown man he suddenly became interested in fishing again. At first his critical inner voice told him he couldn't do it, that he would be a failure and make a fool of himself in front of the other fishermen. Indeed, the first time he went to a lake he tangled his line on a rock, and, in trying to undo it, slipped and fell into the water. He persisted, though, and watched, read about fishing and eventually mastered the knots, casting, and other fishing skills he never could do as a boy under his father's critical scrutiny. He found that going out alone in the morning to fish was like recapturing his lost boyhood and redeeming it. It was true play for him in a way it had never been with his father. After he became a more skilled fisherman he asked his aging father to go fishing; his father had mellowed with time and they actually enjoyed themselves. Some-times real healing takes place in seemingly small areas of one's life.

The steps a man takes to heal himself of a father-son wound may vary according to his individual personality, but there are also some specific things that may be helpful. These include a man's doing the following:

(1) Undergoing personal psychotherapy to uncover and share his emotional wounds, to gain insight and understanding, and to get help to change ineffective behaviors and self-critical attitudes that hinder the expression of his creative life potential. The therapist may play the role of spiritual father or mentor, helping to make up for the lack in the man's relationship with his father.

(2) Engaging in inner work, including working with his dreams, doing active imagination, and journaling to get in touch with the inner hurt little boy and the inner critical father. Two books that are helpful in this regard are Robert Johnson's *Inner Work,* and Morton Kelsey's *Adventure Inward.* (See the suggested readings.)

(3) Working on his relationships with his son(s) and with men friends so he does not repeat the negative kind of masculine relationship he had with his father.

(4) Honestly and fully recognizing his own hurt and anger that stem from his bad father-son relationship, and grieving the loss of a good father when he was a boy and desperately needed one.

(5) Forgiving his father. Forgiveness comes more easily after the

realization that the big bad negative father was really a hurt little boy himself who was only repeating the bad fathering he had.

An inadequate father-son relationship cannot be relived, but with psychological work it can be redeemed on the inner level, resulting in the healing of the hurt little boy in the grown man and a consequent strengthening of his masculinity and effectiveness in the world. A bad father-son relationship can sometimes be healed on the outer level too, if father and son can make a reconciliation with each other. These things take moral courage, but if a man can do them he may heal himself and develop his masculinity in the process.

Suggested Reading

Bly, Robert, "What Men Really Want: A *New Age* Interview with Robert Bly" by Keith Thompson, *New Age,* May 1982, pp. 30ff.

Fleming, Don, *How To Stop the Battle with Your Child.* West Covina, Cal.: Don Fleming Seminars Publishing Co., 1982.

Ginott, Haim, *Between Parent and Teenager.* New York: Avon Books, 1971.

Johnson, Robert A., *Inner Work: Using Dreams and Active Imagination for Personal Growth.* San Francisco: Harper & Row Publishers, 1986.

Kelsey, Morton, *Caring: How Can We Love One Another?* New York: Paulist Press, 1981.

———. *Adventure Inward.* Minneapolis: Augsburg Pub. House, 1980.

Stein, Murray, "The Devouring Father," in *Fathers and Mothers.* Zurich: Spring Publications, 1977. Additional authors are August Vitale, Erich Neumann, James Hillman, and Vera von der Heydt.

Chapter 9

Masculine Sexual Fantasies

Chapter 7

Masculine Sexual Fantasies

Sexual fantasies make their appearance early in a man's adolescence, and continue throughout his lifetime. They come and go autonomously, beguile his imagination, captivate his consciousness, and often become obsessive. They are partly related to his physiological processes (for instance, if physiologically he needs to release semen, fantasies will be more prominent), but they also have a markedly psychological character and content. One way or the other they will play a large role in his life.

Sexual fantasies qualify roughly as normal or abnormal. As far as I know, no authority has ever decided what constitutes a normal sexual fantasy, but plenty of authorities seem to know what constitutes an abnormal one, since several common sexual fantasies qualify for admission in the "bible" of psychiatric diagnosis, *The Diagnostic and Statistical Manual of Mental Disorders*. We will look at some of them in more detail shortly. Whether regarded as normal or abnormal, sexual fantasies can be obsessive. For this reason, one problem men face is that they frequently feel driven to act out their sexual fantasies with a woman, or, in the case of a homosexual male, with another man. The strength of this drive to express his sexual fantasies concretely can easily lead to social problems, or disrupt personal relationships. The situation is complicated by the fact that few men find the acting out of their sexual fantasies fulfilling. Somehow the reality seldom meets up to the expectations of the fantasies. In any case, even when sexual satisfaction has been achieved, the fantasies return later on. For this reason a man may be driven to seek out one sexual experience after another in an attempt to satisfy and fulfill his fantasy life. If in addition to this a man feels uneasy about his sexual fantasy life because he is afraid it falls into the abnormal category, then his difficulties will increase.

Considering the prevalence and importance of a man's sexual fantasies it is remarkable how little serious thought has been given to their inner meaning. Not even C. G. Jung had a great deal to say on the subject, which is surprising since sexual fantasies are highly symbolic. Only in recent times have a few Jungian analysts begun to explore the psychological content of sexual fantasies. This lack of knowledge is unfortunate, for the less a man understands the psychological meaning

213

of his sexual fantasies the harder it will be for him to come into the correct relationship with them and avoid the social and personal relationship disturbances they can bring.

The attitude of the Christian Church has, at least in times past, been partly responsible for the difficulty men experience with their sexual fantasies. If psychiatry takes the position that many sexual fantasies are pathological, the church has taken the position that sexual fantasies are sinful. St. Augustine, for instance, in his *Confessions,* laments that in spite of all his efforts the devil torments him in his dreams by coming to him in the form of a beautiful and seductive woman. Of course, in his view this takes his thoughts away from God.

With the church saying that sexual fantasies are sinful, and psychiatry saying that many of them are pathological, it is no wonder that many men keep their sexual fantasy life hidden, hardly daring to look at it themselves. James Hillman once said that the trouble with Christianity is that "it doesn't ever let you just look at things."[1] The depreciatory attitude of the church and psychiatry toward the variety of masculine sexual fantasies certainly keeps many men from "just looking at" them in an objective way to see what they are saying. In this chapter we will do some "just looking at" masculine sexual fantasies with an eye out for the psychological meaning represented in their highly symbolic content. We are not directly concerned with the issue of sexual morality.[2]

Making Sense of Sexual Fantasies

Let's begin by comparing a man's sexual fantasies with those of a woman. Of course women have their sexual fantasies too, and they can become as obsessive as a man's. Like men, women are shy to reveal their secret sexual fantasy life, but occasionally one does. Etty Hillesum, in her diaries,[3] tells of her difficulty in settling down to "real work" because of her intense erotic fantasy life. As with men, so with women, the fantasies do not always jibe well with reality. She writes,

1. James Hillman and Laura Pozzo, *Inter Views.* New York: Harper Colophon Books, 1983, p. 87.

2. Morton and Barbara Kelsey, *The Sacrament of Sexuality.* Warwick, New York: Amity House, 1986.

3. *An Interrupted Life: The Diaries of Etty Hillesum 1941–1943.* New York: Pantheon Books, 1983, pp 5 and 6. German copyright, 1981.

And that is something I have to learn and for which I must fight to the death: all fantasies and dreams shall be ejected by force from my brain and I shall sweep myself clean from within, to make space for real studies, large and small. To tell the truth, I have never worked properly. It's the same with sex. If someone makes an impression on me, I can revel in erotic fantasies for days and nights on end. I don't think I ever realised how much energy that consumes, and how much it is bound to detract from any real contact. Reality does not chime with my imagination, because my imagination tends to run riot.

She goes on to describe a sexual encounter with a man who had been at the center of her fantasy life for a long time:

There was an immediate and mighty collision of my extravagant fantasy life with the sober reality: an embarrassed and sweating man tucking a crumpled shirt into his trousers when it was all over.

It remains for a woman analyst to explore a woman's sexual fantasies more deeply, but it can be noted that generally speaking a woman's sexual fantasies are more personal and romantic than those of a man. In Etty Hillesum's account of her sexual fantasies she says, "If someone makes an impression on me. . . . " This is often the genesis of a woman's sexual fantasies: some particular man makes an impression on her and then off goes her erotic imagination with romantic fantasies about that man. The most usual theme of such fantasies, though this theme finds innumerable individual expressions, is that the man in question appears in her imagination as the ultimate lover. She will be loved and desired by him completely. If she lives these fantasies out with the man who touched her erotic nature she will want him to be that kind of lover to her. Herein, of course, lies the possibility for disappointment since few men, if any, are capable of living up to the image of the lover that plays through the woman's imagination, especially if their sexual fantasies and those of their women lovers do not coincide.

The disparity between the erotic figure in a woman's imagination and the actual man who becomes her lover is like the difference between the god Eros and an ordinary mortal man. Author Oscar Wilde describes the love of his character, Sibyl Vane, an actress from the lower classes, for Dorian Gray, an aristocrat. Sibyl Vane says to her mother, "Mother, Mother, why does he love me so much? I know why I love him. I love him because he is like what love himself should be. But what does he see in me?"[4]

In Oscar Wilde's story things turn out badly for the unfortunate woman who loved Dorian Gray, a man who turned out to be considerably less than love himself. (When Dorian Gray found it no longer to his advantage to have a relationship with Sibyl Vane he ruthlessly rejected her, which led to her suicide.) It is a sad fact that ordinary men cannot be the god Eros to a woman, but fortunately men can sometimes approximate Eros to the extent that they have genuine feelings of love and affection for the women in their lives, and are sensitive lovers.

Another interesting difference between the sexual fantasies of women and those of men is the different roles played by *hearing* and by *seeing*. When a man meets a woman it is what he sees that arouses his first sexual response. He is likely to say, "She was beautiful . . . She had such a well-formed body . . . Her hair was so wonderfully long and flowing . . . " In pornographic magazines, the important element is the pictorial representation of the many beautiful women. It can be said that men are moved to make love by their eyes. On the other hand, women can be quite taken with a man who is by many standards homely, and are generally less erotically aroused by how a man looks because it is what he says that counts with them. For them, their erotic passion is aroused by a man's words.

In Rossini's opera "The Barber of Seville," the love-struck Rosina sings a song about Count Almaviva in which she declares that his words have captured her heart. As she reflects on the voice of the Count calling to her from below her bedroom window she is filled with the passion to be united with its owner. Oscar Wilde, who seems to know a lot about these things, says much the same thing when he has his feminine protagonist assert, "We women, as someone says, love with our ears, just as you men love with your eyes, if you ever love at all."[5] No doubt this is one of the reasons why pornographic literature has never been sought after by women as it has by men.

If many women like to believe their men are like love himself, many men like to see in their woman the ultimate seductress. In fact, men often long to be seduced, and a common fantasy is that a beautiful

---

4. Oscar Wilde, *The Picture of Dorian Gray*. Garden City, New York: International Collectors Library, p. 56.

5. Ibid., p. 184.

and seductive woman will lure them into love. Behind this image of the ultimate seductress is the image of the anima in her most beguiling and soul-like form. In Oscar Wilde's story Dorian Gray tells his friend, the artist Basil, the reason for his affection for Sibyl Vane. The young girl was an actress, in a cheap and common theater, but she played her part with such depth and charm that the young man was deeply moved. Basil replies:

> If this girl can give a soul to those who have lived without one, if she can create a sense of beauty in people whose lives have been sordid and ugly, if she can strip them of their selfishness and lend them tears for sorrows that are not their own, she is worthy of all your adoration, worthy of the adoration of the world.[6]

Plutarch noted that the "soul of a lover lives in someone else's body."[7] When a man projects an anima image, such as the one Basil describes, into a woman, that woman carries his soul for him and he longs for her sexually as if that would connect him with his soul. Unfortunately when a man brings such expectations into his love relationship with a woman he is making more of her than her earthly, human nature can fulfill. When the disparity between the numinous image of the anima, and the human reality of the woman becomes apparent, the fantasies the man has built around her will collapse, as quickly, sometimes, as a balloon that is pricked by a pin. If a man's development as a human being is lacking, or if there is no real basis for a relationship between the man and woman, the relationship will quickly come to an end.

Masculine sexual fantasies have a certain impersonal aspect to them. A man's sexual imagery can be like a wild, erotic drama that appears spontaneously on the screen of his consciousness and carries him away into a quasi-fantastic world. When gripped by the power of such fantasies a man is, so to speak, just a little bit mad. Under the impetus of the fantasies, as we have noted, he will often want to act them out with a woman as a partner, but this may be difficult to do. If he is married, his wife may not want to play out his fantasy with him.

---

6. Ibid., p. 76.
7. *Plutarch's Lives*, chapter on Mark Antony. The Harvard Classics edition, translated by Dryden, corrected and revised by Clough. New York: P. F. Collier and Son Co., 1909, p. 387.

She may even be repelled by it, or she may not even know of it since he may be too embarrassed to reveal it to her. One reason prostitution thrives is because a man can go to a prostitute and she will act out with her customer whatever fantasy he chooses.

Most men are uncomfortable about this situation. They may feel guilty about their sexual behavior and unsatisfied with its results. They may blame their wives or lovers for their failure to participate in and satisfy their sexual fantasies with the requisite enthusiasm. When they make love, they may find themselves fantasying about some other woman, or some particular sexual scene known only to them, and this may make them feel guilty. In fact, the proper measure of a man's love for his wife or sweetheart is his sensitivity to her emotional and sexual needs.

The content of masculine sexual fantasies varies enormously; they are almost always more untamed and fantastic than the man's actual sexual life. Even in what might be called a normal sexual fantasy a man will usually have some particular element about the woman that arouses his erotic desire, or will see himself making love in some particular way. And even in the normal fantasies, the woman he sees himself making love with may not be his wife or lover. Any woman who has caught his eye, and therefore received the projection of his anima, may turn up as the sexual partner in his fantasies. And, just as often, the figure of his imagination is no one he knows at all in his waking life, but is the image of woman as his imagination presents it to him directly.

The sexual nature of men shows up in their dreams. One study showed that a man's dreams involve more sexual activity than a woman's dreams. The sexual activity was also more direct and obvious. In contrast, women's dreams are more filled with relationships, but not necessarily with sexual relationships. Researchers James Wagenvoord and Petyon Bailey write:

> Women dream about being indoors or in familiar settings. Their dreams are peopled with more women than men, and the interactions are friendly, with little overt sex. The faces that appear are recognizable. Men, on the other hand, confront strangers in dream scenes that are highlighted by physical violence. In their dreams, male figures outnumber female figures by two to one, but when a woman enters the dream, the physical activity may turn sexual.[8]

---

8. James Wagenvoord and Petyon Bailey, *Women: A Book for Men*. New York: Avon Books, 1979, p. 100.

Behind such sexual fantasies lie powerful psychic images and forces. If a man is able to examine the content of his fantasies objectively he may reach a new understanding of himself. This means that he must resist using his fantasies just for auto-erotic pleasure. He must also resist giving in to guilt feelings about them, condemning them because he supposes some moral or medical authority would do so. They just are what they are, and they have their own meaning, nor can a man change them to suit his wishes. To examine sexual fantasies in this way is not to encourage them or give way to them in a socially destructive way. To the contrary, the more understanding a man can acquire about the meaning of his sexual fantasies the freer he will be of their compulsive quality. He will be helped in this endeavor if he can share them with a therapist, or some other suitable person who can help him understand their underlying meaning. It also helps if he writes out his fantasies in all the detail with which they present themselves to his imagination. It seems to satisfy something in the fantasies to be acknowledged and expressed in this way, and it brings the man into a more constructive relationship with them.

As we have seen, the most basic underlying element in a man's sexual fantasies is the need for him to contact the anima and her world of the inner realm, and for many men the anima is contacted primarily through sexual intercourse. In that brief moment of sexual orgasm a man and his anima are at one with each other. If, however, a man's psychological development is lacking, the sense of union with his feminine self will be fleeting, and the man will be driven to repeat his sexual experience again and again. His lover will sooner or later realize that something is amiss. She will sense that she is not loved for herself. She may find his sexual demands unrelated to her needs and desires, and feel that she is more an object to him than anything else. She will feel this in spite of the fact that the man, during intercourse with her, may protest his love for her. During his moment of sexual fulfillment he does indeed feel flooded with love, but it is an experience of archetypal love and not of human love and therefore is not related to the actual woman in his life. Should she refuse him sex for one reason or another he may become sullen and peevish and punish her with passive-aggressive behavior. Such a man needs to learn the distinction between his anima and his lover and how to relate properly to each one.

Types of Sex Fantasies

We will now examine some different masculine sexual fantasies and see if we can discern their inner, symbolic meaning. Because so little work has been done in this area of a man's psychology our examples will be limited and our explanations of their symbolic meaning will be hypotheses that need to stand the test of time.

Analyst Edward C. Whitmont in his book *The Symbolic Quest*[9] tells of a male patient who was unable to have intercourse with a woman without first kissing her foot. This sexual fantasy struck the man as highly unusual and he was convinced that he must be perverted in some way. Analysis revealed that the man was predominantly identified with his masculine intellect, and regarded himself as superior to women because of his good mind, which he fancied women could not have. His feminine side and the feminine values of life were devalued, and his ego was characterized by an arrogant masculinity. When we look at this man's sexual fantasy in the light of his one-sidedly masculine and ego-centric attitude we can see its meaning: It is necessary for this man's individuation that he humble himself, lower his head, and properly value the feminine. His sexual fantasies and desires forced him to do symbolically what he had to accomplish psychologically in order to become a whole person; his intellect had to be sacrificed, and he had to learn to value what he had hitherto devalued. All of this was thrust upon him with the inner necessity that sexual fantasies in a man can arouse. Looked at in this way his sexual fantasy was not an illness but an attempt at a cure.

Mythology offers a paradigm of the serving of the feminine by the masculine in the story of Hercules. Hercules incurred the wrath of Apollo, who condemned him to slavery for a year. When he was sold as a nameless slave he was purchased by Omphale, queen of Lydia. For a year Hercules served his queen, humbled and unknown. He is represented in Greek art sitting at the feet of his mistress spinning wool and dressed in a long flowing oriental robe. Thus the great masculine hero became quasi-feminine himself in the service of the feminine power, a fitting compensation for a man whose development had become too one-sided and exaggerated in an exclusively masculine direc-

---

9. Edward C. Whitmont, *The Symbolic Quest*. Princeton, N.J.: Princeton University Press, 1978, p. 20.

tion. This part of the Hercules myth also touches on the themes of masochism and transvestitism, which we will look at in more detail later on.

Whitmont also cites an example given by Zurich analyst Adolph Guggenbuhl-Craig[10] of a client who suffered from a compulsion to steal women's underwear. Driven by the urgency of this fantasy, the man got into difficulties with the police that finally sent him to the analyst. In this case it was the man himself who unearthed the symbolic meaning of his sexual fantasy; he found the key when he read Goethe's dramatic poem *Faust*. In part two of Goethe's drama, Professor Faust, after a long search, finally found Helen, the most beautiful woman in the world, and the object of his greatest longings and desires. For some time Faust and Helen enjoy each other's company in the heavenly world but ultimately the time comes when she must leave. Faust reaches out to hold her back, but she wrests herself away from his grasp and departs—leaving in his hands her garment and veil.

The man saw a connection between Faust and himself. He concluded that he too had once seen a heavenly vision of the feminine, then lost it, but was left with a symbol of it, in this case a woman's underwear. As he grasped more and more what the image of the eternal feminine meant to him his sexual fantasies became less compulsive, his conscious personality expanded, and his relationship to the feminine became more complete.

Such experiences led Guggenbuhl to hypothesize that sexual fantasies are "individuation fantasies." He writes, "Sexuality, with all its variations, can be understood as an individuation fantasy, a fantasy whose symbols are so alive and so effective that they even influence our physiology" (p. 82).

This story brings up another important aspect of a man's erotic life. As we observed in Chapter 2, it often happens that when a man is young there appears to him spontaneously a glorious vision of a feminine figure that is so numinous it never leaves him. Such an experience may come to him in a particularly striking dream, the effect of which lingers on for some time, or it may have struck him when he beheld a particular young woman. After such an experience the man may recall having felt incredibly whole for many days. Then alas! with the passage of time, the incursion of the world into his thoughts, his growing ego-

10. Guggenbuhl-Craig, *Marriage: Dead or Alive*, p. 84.

centricity, and the darkening of his soul as he loses his original innocence and naiveté, all but the dim memory of the experience fades from
his consciousness. Yet, deep in his heart the vision lives on, leaving
within him a profound longing for fulfillment through union with the
feminine that he once had such a glorious vision of. It may well be that
many sexual fantasies in men were originally formed from such experiences.

The power of masculine sexual fantasies demonstrates vividly the
reality of the anima. One therapist reports a case in which a young married man came to him because he was a transvestite. His client explained that from time to time he would feel an uncontrollable urge to
wear women's clothing, and this urge was accompanied by strong erotic
arousal. The young man explained that it was as if there was a woman
inside of him demanding that he wear women's clothing. The therapist
suggested to him that he talk with this woman within and explain to her
that while he appreciated her he had to maintain his masculine identity.
His client never engaged in such a dialogue, and the therapist had the
feeling that the woman within him thwarted it. The therapy did not last
long, and the therapist lost track of his client. However, two years later
the therapist met the woman who had been his client's wife, and he
learned from her that his erstwhile client had undergone a sex change
operation and was now living as a woman. In this man's case it could
be said that while he had a man's body the woman soul within him was
stronger than his masculine soul, and that his urge to wear women's
clothing was a symbolic expression of the desire of his feminine side
to make her appearance in his outer life.

Another group of masculine sexual fantasies centers around young
girls, and can have tragic results when the man is so unconscious and
morally undifferentiated that he cannot keep from acting them out. But
they too have their symbolic meaning. It can be suspected that when
sexual fantasies involve a child the ego structure of the man is too old
and rigid. To compensate and heal this atrophied ego, the unconscious
produces the symbol of the child, and the erotic attraction this symbol
has for him seeks to bind him to the eternal youthfulness of the unconscious. In such a case, the importance of making the symbolic content
of the fantasies conscious so they will not be compulsively acted out is
clear.

Other compensatory fantasies involve an erotic attraction to ''inferior'' women. In such a case a man may be compelled to seek out prostitutes, even though he is married and has other means of sexual satisfaction. Men with such fantasies are in too high a position in life. They have gotten above themselves too much, perhaps by seeking too much power, being too intellectual, or trying to be too spiritual or morally elevated. One case concerned a man who was a clergyman. Even though he knew that discovery could ruin his career he was compelled periodically to seek out a woman of the streets. The power of the sexual fantasy can be understood as an attempt of the unconscious to bring about a more whole person by adopting a compensatory position to that of an ego which, in trying to be too superior and morally elevated, has gotten too far off the ground.

The earth itself may have an erotic attraction to a man who has become too separated from his chthonic nature. For example, a man might be erotically attracted to masculine footwear of various sorts, symbolizing his need to walk firmly on the earth of reality in order to become whole. Or a man may have an urge to have intercourse on the earth, or even to roll on the earth as a prelude to intercourse. In such cases we are reminded of the Greek myth of the wrestler Antaeus, a bandit who compelled all travelers to wrestle with him. Antaeus could never be defeated because he was a son of Gaia, Mother Earth herself, and whenever he touched the earth with his feet his strength was renewed. (Hercules finally overcame him by lifting him in the air and strangling him.) So some men may need to ''touch the earth'' in order to make contact with their sexual potency.

In some cases married men who have intense erotic attractions to other women may be ''too married.'' We have already seen that there are many reasons why a man's anima may go to a woman other than the wife. In addition to the reasons already mentioned, a man may be prey to sexual fantasies about a variety of women because his life is too tied down. When a man marries he does not just marry his wife. He may also be married to his work or business, to feelings of obligation of all sorts, to fixed ideas that he has to make so much money or live in some specific way. There are all kinds of things in life that a man ''marries,'' and if no room is left for the unexpected, the varied, the unusual, the anima image may take the form of the kind of woman who offers him fantasies of an illegitimate sexual relationship. Behind this is the need for a man to divorce himself from some obligations, ideas, and commitments that he has become too involved in, so that he may acquire a new kind of consciousness that is capable of more freedom of action in life.

By far the best treatment of the symbolic meaning of sexual fantasies is found in a book by Jungian analyst Lynn Cowan entitled *Masochism: A Jungian View.*[11] Cowan writes with such subtlety, depth, and nuances of meaning that no summary of her point of view will do her book justice. Nevertheless, her book is so important for the subject of the symbolic meaning of masculine sexual fantasies that no treatment of the topic would be complete without a comment on it.

Cowan notes that masochism sometimes refers to a general life posture and sometimes to a specific kind of sexual fantasy. In both cases, the masochist is a person who is both repelled by and yearns for a posture or situation in which he or she suffers, is humiliated, or is mistreated. In sexual masochism, powerful erotic fantasies are associated with being in certain specific, humiliating situations. While Cowan herself did not say so, I suspect that women are more prone to be drawn to masochistic life situations, and men more prone to masochistic sexual fantasies, though there are certainly plenty of examples of each in both sexes.

With regard to masochistic sexual fantasies, Cowan begins by noting that they are regarded by society and psychiatry as pathological. Freud referred to masochism as a perversion, and the Psychiatric Diagnostic Manual lists it under item 302.83 as an example of a psychosexual disorder. Cowan agrees that masochism has a bad reputation, and that in fact it is part of masochism itself to *want* a bad reputation. She agrees that masochistic sexual fantasies become pathological when they are only a surface phenomenon, that is, when there is no relationship to their deeper meaning. When masochistic fantasies are acted out literally and unconsciously they lose their contact with the gods and goddesses who give them their life, and thus lose the symbolic content that gives them their meaning. The resulting low level of consciousness drags the fantasies into a purely auto-erotic expression, and this constitutes their pathology.

Having said all this, Cowan goes on to note that masochism is a religious as well as sexual phenomenon. She observes that religions require and endorse the humbled posture of the masochist. Every time the

---

11. Lynn Cowan, *Masochism: A Jungian View*. Dallas: Spring Publications, Inc., 1982.

worshiper bows his head or kneels he is adopting physically the masochistic posture. In times past, the religious masochistic attitude called for the infliction of pain as well. For instance, the Flagellants of the early eleventh century roamed through Europe whipping and lashing themselves in order to be purified before God. They were seized with a frenzied desire to find and express penance by submitting themselves to painful torture. Such a longing for penance, she notes, "is not to be taken lightly, nor profaned by personalistic causal explanations. Psychiatric terms, and even psychoanalytic theory, do not do justice to this desire, which is essentially religious, rather than symptomatic of personal pathology" (p. 20). For, "Before science regarded masochism as a disease, religion regarded it as a cure" (p. 19). In Christian language, masochism is a way of staying with the "down-and-under side of Christianity" (p. 27). Thus masochism swims strongly against the religious current of our times, when what passes for religion turns out to be ways of offering the ego what it wants, which is always to stay on top.

Cowan tries to place masochism in a total setting and see its inner values. She points out that it comes not from the ego, but from the soul, which requires a certain amount of suffering. We are reminded of the statement by Meister Eckhart, "Suffering is the swiftest steed that bears you to perfection."[12] It is the soul that craves suffering, even when the ego wants to avoid it at all costs. So masochistic fantasies are sometimes forced on an unwilling ego by a willing soul, mingling together repulsion and enjoyment. In this way the soul creates its own reality of pathos, suffering, and meaning, and in so doing finds true humility. For the masochistic yearning of the soul is not to be seduced into auto-erotic tailspins, but to find and express a genuine submission to the Self.

Part of the meaning of masochism is to compensate for a life that is too structured, too ordered, too correct, too successful, too ordinary, and too normal. At the same time that the ego seeks to build up exactly such a life, the soul rejects it, and hungers for a life filled with pathos and emotion, creative disorder, and a life-giving dose of the fantastic. This is why sexual masochists, she notes, tend to be successful people by social standards. Professionally, sexually, maritally they have achieved success. Their egos are strong and able to cope with life, and they have a keen, often exaggerated, sense of responsibility. It is for

---

12. An untraced quotation from Meister Eckhart.

exactly this reason that their masochism is necessary: it offers the cure for a one-sidedly ego-dominated striving, conforming, controlled, and successful way of life.

Thus, in a strange way, masochism is not only subjection, it is also release. The soul welcomes its masochistic bondage in order to become free from another kind of bondage: the bondage to the tyranny of normalcy, the straight-jacket of correctness, the confinement of rationality, and the servitude to collective social standards.

The masochist, through his pain, subjection, and humiliation, serves other gods than the gods of the ego. In so doing, the masochist lets go of old ego constructs. In masochistic fantasies, the old structured ego is dissolved and mortified. The masochist is turned inside out, opened up to the shadowy realm of the unconscious where one does not get off so lightly, lowered to a deeper ground than that provided by the world of conventional values and aspirations, and placed in contact with a number of gods and goddesses, that is, archetypal powers, that are banished from the conscious world.

This is not done willingly, but out of a deep inner necessity. Indeed, one of the deities whom the masochist serves is the Greek goddess Ananke, whose name means "necessity." The necessity whom Ananke calls on a man to serve, however, is not outer necessity, but inner necessity, the necessities of his own soul.

To be sure, one wishes that the path the soul lays out would be straighter, more conventional, more socially acceptable. But here too another deity appears who must be served: Hermes, the trickster god, the god of travelers, the god of cleverness and theft. The treasure hidden in masochism must be stolen carefully, under cover of night. This is all Hermes' business, and "Hermes will be served, no matter how respectable, straight, and up-front we wish to be."[13]

Of course all of this is shameful, and the masochist experiences shame; indeed, without being forced into a shameful position he would not experience the excitement of erotic arousal. Here we see the Greek goddess Aidos, whose name means shame. It is she who underlies all painfully shameful erotic experience, from the simple act of involuntarily blushing at the name of one's lover, to the wildest of masochistic fantasies.

Aidos, however, was not a separate goddess in herself, but was

---

13. Lynn Cowan, *Masochism,* p. 42.

part of the retinue of Aphrodite, goddess of love. Wherever beautiful Aphrodite went she was accompanied by her companion goddesses, which included Ananke, Aidos, and many others. The masochist serves Aphrodite. He achieves freedom from the conventional by plunging himself into the service of the great goddess herself, she whose power was so irresistible that not even Zeus was immune from it. Indeed, the language in which Aphrodite is described is the language of masochism. For Aphrodite was said to "ensnare" people's hearts, to inflict people with the "lashes of longing," and to "chain" people with her charms. She herself was often pictured in Greek art as Aphrodite in chains. For hers is the power that binds; she binds the soul to her, people to themselves, lovers to each other.

For this reason, masochism also serves the feminine. Its strange power, its delight in the darkness, its irrationality, its appeal to the soul, its circuitous route, its erotic arousal, its passion, its stirring to love— all of these emanate from the great feminine archetype that Aphrodite is a part of. And all of this compensates in many men an ego development that has gotten too far away from its roots in the world of the feminine. Cowan observes that thus "masochism disallows the devaluation of both archetypal femininity and madness" (p. 110).

Wherever Aphrodite goes, her son Eros is not far away, and so Eros also emerges in the phenomenon of masochism. Eros, god of love: whoever he shot with his arrow was fated to love the next person he met. So there is thrust on the masochist the necessity to experience the power of Eros over him. Eros is a hard, driving, relentless god, who both blesses and tortures those on whom he inflicts his power. In masochistic fantasies one experiences both a blessing and a torture: "gifts" of the god Eros.

Cowan might also have mentioned the connection between Eros and the symbolism of binding. Marie-Louise von Franz points out that Greek art showed the goddess Psyche (soul) tied by Eros with her hands behind her back to a column on top of which is a sphere.[14] She says the image represents how we must be bound by love and passion to the individuation process, represented in this case by the pole and the sphere. The binding represents the fact that we cannot escape, that it is a matter of necessity.

---

14. Marie-Louise von Franz, *Apuleius' Golden Ass*. Zurich: Spring Publications, 1970, p. V-6.

The connection between binding and love as an unavoidable necessity is also brought out in the symbolism of love charms. In Brazil, for instance, there is a form of magic known as "Amarrar," a word that means "to tie up." A woman can avail herself of Amarrar in order to magically "tie up" to her the man whom she wishes to have as her lover.[15]

Such symbolism might appear in the erotic fantasies of men who would like to escape from the world of love, passion, and suffering, but are not allowed to by the unconscious powers that have the individuation of that man as their goal.

But underlying all of these deities is the most powerful and strangest of them all: the god Dionysus. Dionysus was represented as a feminine-man. He appeared most characteristically in the form of a beautiful but somewhat effeminate youth, and was widely worshiped by women. He was the god of ecstasy, of the abandonment of rational consciousness to the wildness of nature and divinity. To be a worshiper of Dionysus was to abandon oneself to ecstatic union with him. We are reminded of Plato's belief that God could only be known through "divine madness." Dionysus appeared with such wildness and such power, and brought forth such unheard-of responses in human beings, that he seemed to mock all human order. Therefore in Greek mythology Dionysus often had to overcome the hearts of men before they could do him proper homage, and those who resisted him he destroyed. The masochist, in his experience of sexual "madness," is forced to acknowledge those powers that the god Dionysus represents. The god literally overcomes him, breaking down the confining order of his consciousness, and compelling the man to acknowledge his divinity.

Thus, through a forced submission to Dionysus and all that he represents, the soul finds its way to God. One becomes bound to the divine world in order to escape another kind of bondage. The bondage of the masochist becomes a kind of freedom in itself. One becomes free from contemporary religious forms that have become so ordered they have become sterile, from the self-serving ego, from the collective demand for normalcy and correctness, not by casting them aside but by serving the other powers of life. Cowan writes, " 'To burst the bonds' is the purpose of both Dionysian and masochistic experience. Both break out

---

15. Pedro McGregor, *The Moon and Two Mountains*. London: Souvenir Press, p. 195. Informally published and no date given.

of a style of consciousness which has become a bondage. It is indeed strange that this is done through another form of bondage, through servitude to this madness which is the god himself. Yet the stronger the bonds of law, duty, and custom, the more urgent the claim of Dionysus in the opposite direction'' (p. 111).

In our culture Dionysus and the powers he personifies are greatly repressed. The god himself, however, cannot be destroyed; he still stirs the human soul. Poet Diana Azar has put it this way:

DIONYSUS GOES TO SCHOOL

The Academy's a civilizing influence.
It teaches Dionysus to shut his maw when he eats
wipe the blood off his chin and
not talk with his mouth full of the
raw lamb of God.

It makes him move to town where he
receives the full moon of communion
thinly on his tongue
enrolls in Origins of Greek Civilization
burns his Pan pipes and takes up the lute
trades his goatskins for a pair of Calvin Kleins
invites the maenads to his house to sip
Chateau Mouton Rothschild while
listening reverently to the Rite of Spring
on a state of the art stereo made in Japan.

It reminds him people perspire
satyrs, centaurs, sweat.
It reasons with him to comb burrs out of his beard
bathe often in a clean well lighted place where
no mud
oozes in
on Hippocratically uncloven toes.

He learns how to distinguish lie from lay
and, on sheets as clean as conscience,
to take intransitive loves one at a time
after sponges jellies spermicides shields foams
are squirted and/or duly
inserted in place.

But sometimes when the moon is full
and stalks the woods like a white wolf
he hears the drum beating the heart of darkness out
and, leaving his husk on the bed,
rises howling
to suck blood from the moon's neck
and smear it all over his loins and mouth.

Come morning he Socratically deduces that the pillow
slip's dark stain is
test correcting ink.
The Academy's a civilizing influence.
Next time he'll score 100%.*

We have noted the importance of binding as a symbol in certain
sexual fantasies. It is hard to say whether that which binds—a rope,
thread, or cord—is more of a sexual or religious symbol. In the church,
for example, the cincture worn by priests in the Roman Catholic and
Anglican Churches is usually a rope and symbolizes the doctrine of the
church that binds the priest to Christ. In her book, *Individuation in
Fairy Tales,* Marie-Louise von Franz also refers to the Islamic image
of the rope as a symbol of the laws of Mohammed, "Those who hold
to the rope of his laws" (p. 55). And in Stewart Farrar's *What Witches
Do,* he notes that in the ancient rites of Wicca, initiates were bound in
a kneeling position and scourged, the binding representing their religious bond to the goddess whom they served, and the scourging being
a symbol of purification.

The rope is a frequent symbol in shamanism. Mircea Eliade says
that there is a rope which connects heaven (the world of the gods) and
the earth (the world of mortals). The shaman has found this rope and
holds it, which symbolizes his connection to the spiritual world from
which comes the power to heal.** Other shamanistic traditions tell how
a medicine man can climb at night by means of a rope, invisible to ordinary mortals, into the sky, where he can hold converse with the star
people.[16] The cord also connects the shaman not only to the spirits, but

---

*From the "South Coast Poetry Journal," No. 2, p. 48.
**There are innumerable references to the symbolism of the rope in shamanistic lore, col-
lected by Eliade in his two books *Mephistopheles and the Androgyne* and *Shamanism,* published
by Sheed and Ward and Princeton University Press.

16. Mircea Eliade, *Shamanism.* Princeton, N.J.: Princeton University Press, 1964, p. 50.

also to his spirit wife, from whom he gets his shamanic inspiration, and with whom he has sexual relations (pp. 72–76). Von Franz also points out the importance of this symbolism, adding that it represents the connection with the collective unconscious.[17]

There is also a curious Nez Perce Indian tale entitled "Coyote His Son He Caused to be Lost."[18] In this tale, Coyote's son climbs a tree to reach a cache where a deer has been placed. He climbs and climbs until he reaches the sky-world of the spider people. He is kindly received and stays with the spider people for some time. The spider people spin and spin and spin. They are like the Greek goddess Lachesis, one of the Three Fates, who spins out the thread of fate for a person at that individual's birth. Finally it comes time for Coyote's son to return, and the spider people lower him back to earth on the thread they have been spinning. Coyote's son goes on in the story to perform various exploits on behalf of his people. Like a shaman, he finds the way to the sky-world, stays there and learns from the spirits (that is, the spider people), then descends. In this case his ascent was made via a tree, and his descent by means of a thread.

Leo Tolstoy in his *My Confessions* reports a dream that closely parallels shamanistic symbolism of the rope. In this dream he finds himself suspended high in the air on a network of cords. Only the cords keep him from falling into an abyss. He marvels that he does not plunge down, but finally realizes that he is held by one particular cord, which passes around the middle of his body, and is evidently suspended from some invisible point above him, keeping him in a perfect state of balance.

One of the most complete descriptions of binding as a religious symbol is given us by the Sioux Indian shaman Lame Deer in his description of the Yuwipi ceremony. In this ceremony the medicine man is tightly wrapped with cords in a darkened room while the assembled people wait in silence. In due time the spirits fill the room with their energy and power. The medicine man, whose binding creates and symbolizes his connection to the spirit world, is then able to talk with them for the benefit and healing of the people. Afterward the Yuwipi man (shaman) stands up, remarkably freed from his bonds, and therefore

---

17. Marie-Louise von Franz, *Niklaus Von Der Flue*. An unpublished lecture; #4, pp. 3–4.
18. Archie Phinney, *Nez Perce Texts*. New York: Columbia University Press, 1934, p. 360ff.

restored to his ordinary human condition.[19] Eliade reports much the same ceremony among the Samoyed shamans: "They let themselves be tied up, then invoke the spirits, and at the end of the seances they are found freed from their bonds."[20]

All of these images point to the same thing: that the rope or cord can symbolize a connection between the ego and the collective unconscious. What in shamanic lore is called the world of the spirits we would call the archetypal world of the collective unconscious. The archetypes are exceedingly numinous. This means that they have the power to grip us emotionally. Their energy can be constellated in us either sexually or spiritually. If the energy hits "the sexual center" it will constellate erotic imagery.

The image of bonding symbolizes the inescapability of this connection in the case of certain people who are, as it were, fated to undergo the individuation process. One is bound to the world of the unconscious and cannot escape from it, in much the way that Ixion, in Greek mythology, was bound to the wheel, and Christ was bound, and then nailed to the cross.

It remains to consider masculine homosexual fantasies. The subject of homosexuality was briefly considered in Chapter 8; now we will explore the subject further. To begin with, to refer to homosexuality as though it is a uniform phenomenon is misleading, for there are many expressions of male sexuality that we call homosexual that actually differ markedly. In general we refer to homosexuality whenever a man has a sexual erotic desire for another male, or for the phallus, or some other masculine symbol. Yet such desires may take quite varied forms. Some men are exclusively homosexual and have intimate relationships only with other men. But others marry, have children, and develop a heterosexual life, yet are overwhelmed from time to time with what appears to be a desire for a homosexual experience. For purposes of clarification, I am going to describe these varied experiences under three categories: the homosexual fantasies of a man with an incomplete masculine development, bisexual, homoerotic fantasies, and the sexual fantasies of a man who can be called a true homosexual.

Homosexuality is a common phenomenon not only in our culture

---

19. John Fire/Lame Deer and Richard Erdoes, *Lame Deer: Seeker of Visions.*
20. Eliade, *Shamanism*, p. 228.

but, as far as can be determined, in diverse cultures throughout history. There are ample examples of it in Graeco-Roman culture. The Bible refers to it a number of times, so it must have existed among the ancient Hebrews and Canaanites. It occurred among the American Indians. Homosexuality appears to have occurred in men in all cultures and in all times. Yet its cause is uncertain and a matter of dispute.

Homoerotic and Homosexual Fantasies

Most psychologists would say that homosexuality is due to environmental factors that involve too much mother and not enough father. For instance, if the mother is overwhelmingly powerful, the boy's nascent masculine strivings may be overpowered. The mother's animus, if it is in control, may effectively wound the boy's tender masculinity. But the mother may also wound the boy's sexuality by being overly seductive. Especially if her erotic needs are not satisfied with her husband or some other man, they may be directed to her son. Through overt or subtle erotic seduction the boy may be drawn too far into her world, filling him later in life with a fear of feminine sexuality which effectively keeps him from sexual life with a woman. It can be mentioned in passing that the mother's erotic seduction of the son can be as destructive a form of sexual abuse as the more overt sexual activities a father forces on a daughter.

When the relationship with the father is inadequate the difficulties for the boy are compounded. We have already seen in the chapter on father-son relationships how complex and important this relationship is. Here we need only remind ourselves that if the father is too strong for the son, rejects him, is missing from the home, or is too weak a man to be a fitting masculine role model, the masculine development of the boy may be impaired.

Such conditions are said to be the breeding ground for homosexuality and, indeed, they are certainly factors to be taken into account. On the other hand, many boys have found themselves growing up under such circumstances and have developed heterosexually. One gets the feeling from some robust boys that even if they were raised by ten overwhelming mothers with no father in the home they would still wind up as heterosexuals. In fact, in Greek myths, heroes such as Parsifal and Perseus typically grew up only with a mother's influence, the father being dead or unknown, and yet they went on to become virile masculine heroes. The fact is that the exact causes of homosexuality are unknown. They may be a combination of psychological factors and genetic predisposition. There may also be an archetypal factor at work, which we will consider later.

If a man is destined by natural disposition to be heterosexual, but his masculinity has been injured in the ways we have described, he may have an incomplete masculine development. Such men may be married and have a family, yet from time to time a homosexual fantasy may intrude into consciousness that produces a secret sexual life. This fantasy may involve homoerotic thoughts about some virile or unusually attractive man, or there may be homosexual fantasies centering around the phallus. Such fantasies represent symbolically a need to become reconnected with masculinity. The masculine side of such a man is not strong enough. It needs to be reinforced. His missing masculinity becomes projected onto another man or onto the phallus, and his sexual cravings contain the craving of his soul to ingest the missing masculinity so he can complete himself.

He may have such fantasies especially when he feels exhausted or when his ego has become fragmented; then he needs the healing and synthesis of his fragmented masculine ego. The fantasies may also come as a compensation for too much exposure to women. If such a man has lived with a woman or women for a long period of time his masculinity may become eroded; he needs to reconnect with the wellspring of masculine power that he has projected outside of himself onto a fitting object. A great many men may find from time to time that they have such a sexual fantasy flitting through their consciousness, but in men whose masculinity is robust and well established these fantasies are not likely to be very strong. Men with fantasies such as these are not to be regarded as true homosexuals. It is more accurate to say they are men whose basic inclination is heterosexual but whose masculine development has been aborted or weakened because of the conditions they have grown up in and are now living in.

A bisexual man may also have a heterosexual family life with concurrent homosexual fantasies. Typically he will have as the object of his fantasies a real or imagined youth. It is often a middle-aged or older man who falls in love with a younger man who has the attributes of a young Adonis. If we were to examine the dreams of this man we would see that an Adonis-like young man is a prominent figure in his dream life. It seems that he projects the inner image of a divine youth onto the outer young man, with the result that he is sexually attracted to the young man. Both the image of the young man in his psyche, and the outer young man who receives the projection of the image, typically embody both masculine and feminine virtues. The young man has a strong, virile body, a youthful and vigorous masculinity, yet he also has certain feminine attributes and graces that lend to his appearance a youthful beauty and subtle gentleness. The image is that of a virile young man who also embodies a distinctly androgynous quality. This image is like a young Adonis, and can be understood to be one of the many images of the Self.

The longing for such a young man may become particularly strong as a man grows older. A good example of this kind of homoerotic desire is found in Thomas Mann's novelette *Death in Venice*. Author Mann says of his protagonist, the aging Aschenbach, who has fallen in love with the youthful Tadzio, "His eyes took in the proud bearing of that figure there at the blue water's edge; with an outburst of rapture he told himself that what he saw was beauty's very essence; form as divine thought, the single and pure perfection which resides in the mind, of which an image and likeness, rare and holy, was here raised up for adoration."[21] In the case of a man like the aging Aschenbach, the appearance of the youthful Adonis can be understood partly as a compensation for the aging of the ego. The ego and the body age; the unconscious remains both eternally old and eternally youthful. Out of the unconscious come youthful images to compensate and attempt to heal a man whose conscious adaptation has become too old too fast. The sexual fantasies are an attempt to reconnect the man with the sources of life within himself. So the image of the Self becomes that of a divine youth. Nevertheless, the images remain those of the Self and the man's Self-image is carried by a masculine-feminine image and figure. This gives this man a bisexual character. In a heterosexual man, it is the feminine element that is missing from his consciousness and becomes projected onto a woman. The masculinity lies in the ego, the feminine side in the image of the unconscious being projected onto a woman. The two together make up a totality of masculine and feminine. But in the bisexual man it is as though a one-sidedly masculine sexuality identity has been refused, and the Self-image is contained in the single figure of the divine androgynous youth.

---

21. Thomas Mann, *Death in Venice*. New York: Random House, 1936, p. 44.

I mentioned that the unconscious is both young and old at the same time. As a consequence, the image of the Self in a man may be carried either by a youth or by an older man. Sometimes a young man and an older man enter into a homoerotic relationship in which the young man projects onto the older man an image of the Self as a wise, old man, and the older man projects onto the young man the image of the Self as the divine youth. In the case of the young man, such a relationship is often a compensation for a missing or inadequate father figure. Or it may be a calling forth from the young man of the urge to maturation and wisdom. In most such cases, the young man, if he develops properly, eventually leaves his homoerotic attachments to older men behind him.

In the case of the older man, it cannot be said that the origin of his homosexual inclinations is to be found exclusively in his personal psychological history. The impression one gets of such a man is that he is born to be this way, and that his bisexuality has an archetypal basis to it. Thus his bisexuality becomes part of his fate, and his psychological task is to realize what it means on the symbolic level. As long as the image of the divine youth is only projected outside of himself, the man lives out his longings on too low a level of consciousness. The Self then is not realized, and his sexual fantasies become obsessive. But if he can relate to the inner image in his psyche of the divine youth as Self, he can transcend the purely sexual longings and find their spiritual and psychological meaning as well.

Finally we turn to those cases of what I call true homosexuality. A certain number of males are born to be homosexuals. They differ from heterosexual males because of their relationship to the anima. In a heterosexual man, the anima, as we have seen, is more or less distinct from his masculine ego. In the true homosexual the anima is, as it were, homogenized with the ego. One becomes aware in such a man of the distinctly feminine quality of his consciousness, but it is so blended throughout the ego that one cannot make a distinction between ego and anima. As a consequence, his ego has a certain hermaphroditic structure. Under such conditions, heterosexual relationships are out of the question, for the opposites of masculine and feminine cannot relate and unite until they have first been separated and distinguished from each other. Homosexual relationships of various sorts, in which the homosexual man often plays first the masculine, then the feminine role, are therefore the norm.

These men may have many positive qualities. They can be quite sensitive, are often easy to talk with, frequently have a gentle, healing quality, and are given to artistic inclinations. In primitive communities, many shamans were homosexual, and in our own day there are certain individuals with healing gifts who have such a homosexual disposition. On the negative side, the predominance of the anima quality can make such men tend to be peevish, fickle in relationships, and over-sensitive. These qualities make long-lasting, intimate relationships difficult.

The American Indians had an explanation for this kind of homo-sexuality that is as good as any I know, even though it is couched in mythological rather than scientific terms. Among different western tribes it was believed that during puberty the moon appeared to a boy offering him a bow and arrow in one hand, and a woman's pack strap in the other. If the boy hesitated when reaching for the bow and arrow, the moon handed him the pack strap. These young men became "ber-daches," or homosexuals. They wore a special kind of dress and per-formed special functions in the tribe. For instance, they often served as matchmakers, and while they did not go to war, as did the other young men, they might accompany the war party to care for the wounded. Ber-daches were naturally accepted in the Indian community. They were not ridiculed or despised, but simply regarded as a special sort of man.[22] To put this in psychological language, it is a way of saying that some men instinctually, that is, for archetypal reasons, do not reach out and grasp a masculine identification. Therefore they fall partially under the spell of the anima who shapes their ego development in a different way.

Throughout this discussion of masculine sexuality we have seen the importance of the anima. We will come back to her in Chapter 11 when we discuss images of the masculine psyche in fairy tales, myths, and dreams. But now we need to round out our picture of masculine individuation with a look at the meaning for men of old age.

---

22. Cf. *Indians*. Alexandria, Va.: Time-Life Books, 1973, p. 129.

Suggested Reading

Cowan, Lynn, *Masochism: A Jungian View*. Dallas: Spring Publications, 1982.

Kelsey, Morton and Barbara, *The Sacrament of Sexuality: The Spirituality and Psychology of Sex*. Warwick, New York: Amity House, 1986.

Monick, Eugene, *Phallos: Sacred Image of the Maculine*. Toronto: Inner City Books, 1987.

Chapter 10

Individuation and Old Age

We have frequently had occasion to mention the individuation process as it takes place in men. Now is the time to draw together some of our conclusions in order that we may contemplate more deeply the meaning of individuation for an elderly man.

Jung once said that individuation was the task of the second half of life. However, if we understand by individuation the unfolding and making conscious of the Self, then it is best to see the process beginning at the very inception of life. For this reason we noted that boyhood is not merely preparation for life, it *is* life already, and the experiences that a man has as a child become an indelible part of his soul. Childhood is also a time when what the Greeks called fate is particularly visible. Fate, as we noted, consists of the conditioned, unalterable facts of our existence. We are born into this world to certain parents, in certain parts of the world, and at certain times of history. We have inherited certain genes that give us a fundamental physical and psychological structure which, for better or worse, we must live within. Fate is like being dealt a hand of cards with which we must play the game of life. We may play our cards well or poorly, but the cards are something we cannot avoid. Many of these cards turn their faces to us in boyhood. Childhood is thus a time in which we discover the fundamental fate we must live with as creatively as possible in order for our individuation to take place.

Of course the idea of fate does not nullify the idea of free will. Without free will there can be no individuation in any meaningful sense of the word. We cannot alter the fundamental circumstances of our life, but we can alter our attitude toward these circumstances, and we can become conscious of the goal and purpose of our lives toward which the unconscious strives. For life is not only fate, it is also destiny. Destiny can be understood in terms of destination. If fate consists of the unalterable circumstances of our lives, destiny refers to our proper life goal toward which we are meant to move. Fate cannot be avoided, but our destiny may be fulfilled or unfulfilled. Fulfilling our proper destiny requires the living of a conscious life, and is the task of individuation.

As noted, in adolescence a vital aspect of our development takes place at an accelerated rate: the establishment of an ego mature enough to forge ahead into adult life and make a place for ourselves in the world. The task of finding one's place in the world, which includes finding a work to do, making a relationship to the opposite sex, and separating ourselves from our parents and our infantile longings, is so vitally important that the spiritual dimension of adolescence has often been obscured. The fact is, however, that adolescence also has a spiritual or psychological dimension to it that hinges around the establishment of a meaningful connection between the ego and the unconscious, consciousness and the Self. The importance of this spiritual dimension to the adolescent, as we noted in Chapter 2, is indicated by the initiation rites of primitive cultures that included initiation into the realm of masculine spirituality. We also noted that in the American Indian Vision Quest the young man's initiation ordeal was intended to bring about a connection with what we would call the Self. In today's culture this spiritual task of adolescence goes begging, and our youths suffer as a consequence. As a result most men enter into adult life without a spiritual or psychological foundation. They lack any connection to the masculine mysteries that once were shown to them in initiation rites. Jung once remarked that the mysteries were at one time a man's business, but in our present culture they are a woman's business.[1] Men suffer and are held back in their psychological development because they have abdicated their ancient spiritual role and function.

Individuation among men may begin with a conscious realization that there is a task to perform, or it may take place unconsciously as a man proceeds to live life to its fullest. If, for instance, a man has become an alcoholic, and then realizes that he must free himself from his compulsion to drink, joins Alcoholics Anonymous, and tries to increase his psychological and spiritual understanding, we could say that at this time in his life he began to undertake the process of individuation in a conscious way. Other men, however, may have been maturing through the kinds of life they were leading, since life itself demands it of us.

"Red-Blooded" and "Pale-Blooded" Men

Kunkel used to speak of the red-blooded men and the pale-blooded men, and how they matured in different ways. His reflections, I am sure, stemmed from his experience in World War I. Kunkel is the only

---

    1. C. G. Jung, *The Visions Seminars*. Zurich, Switzerland: Spring Publications, 1976, Book One, p. 25.

major psychologist I know of who was involved in the fighting of one of the two World Wars. He graduated from medical school in Germany just when World War I began and was immediately taken into the medical corps of the German army. Since he was one of the youngest doctors, he was assigned to the front lines; he was the first doctor a wounded soldier would see, and he spent many months in the trenches during the heavy fighting. Eventually, Kunkel himself was wounded— he lost an arm as a consequence—and this ended his career as a soldier, but by then the war and what he saw happening around him had made a deep impression on him. One of the ideas he was left with as a result of his experiences was that some men matured by living dangerously and some by living reflectively, and these he termed the red-blooded men and the pale-blooded men.

Because red-blooded men mature by facing death and risking themselves there is a great thirst in them for adventure. For this reason they may welcome war, for on the battlefield they may, in their own way, meet their God. A good example of such red-blooded men and their delight in war is found in the American Indian warrior of the plains riding into battle with his customary cry, "This is a good day to die." War for them was the way to prove themselves and to demonstrate their courage. In fact, they were more interested in proving their courage than in killing the enemy since it was better to "count coup" on an opponent than to actually kill him. ("Counting coup" meant to make some physical contact with your enemy without killing him; such a feat brought special renown.) One author wrote: "I have talked with old warriors and seen the reminiscent gleam come into their eyes when describing old encounters. They spoke with undisguised admiration of their foes' appearance as they galloped past. Brilliant uniforms and martial music of bygone European armies never glamorized warfare more than the feathers, paint, and war cries of the Plains Indians."[2]

Writing from his own experiences in war Kunkel once said, "I was a doctor in the war and used to notice the lieutenants there. On the average they were killed after half a year, but in that half year the expression on their faces changed very much. They found something on the battlefield and this imminent danger of death did something to them. Not since the Middle Ages has life been so dangerous—completely insecure and completely in the hands of God. This experience of being

2. *Indians of the Americas.* Washington, D.C.; National Geographic Society, 1955, p. 79.

completely in the hands of God from day to day cannot be duplicated except on expeditions and in a shipwreck."[3]

In our present time, unfortunately, another major war would be a complete disaster. Even if it was fought it might not provide the arena for courage that wars in the past provided since it would very likely be fought electronically and at such a distance that the face of the enemy would never be seen. The winner would be the side with the best technology, not the side with the most courageous soldiers, and of course the losers would be civilians and civilization itself. As a friend of mine once remarked, "They've gone and ruined war." Of course there are other adventures to seek besides war, such as mountain climbing or a solo sea voyage, but the fact is that the world today is not such an adventurous place for red-blooded men as it was in the past. This may cause a problem, and may account for some of the wild and reckless behavior that we witness in many young men today, such as riding on fast motorcycles. The opportunities for meaningful adventures are fewer, but the psychological need is just as great.

The pale-blooded men are the Hamlets of this world. Their virtue is their reflectiveness, their defect is their reluctance to live dangerously and decisively. As Shakespeare's Hamlet said:

> Thus conscience makes cowards of us all,
> And thus the native hue of resolution is
> Sicklied o'er with the pale cast of thought.
> And enterprises of great pith and moment
> With this regard, their currents go awry,
> And lose the name of action.
>   (Act III, Scene 1, Line 83)

The differences between the two types of men are not easy to account for. It is tempting to say that the red-blooded men are extraverts and the pale-blooded men are introverts, and probably on the average this is likely to be true. Nevertheless, many introverted men have been men of war. (Even General Patton paid attention to his dreams.) If the pale-blooded man has a bit of the red-blooded man in him he will be able to understand his masculine counterpart, but if he is almost totally

---

3. From an unpublished lecture entitled "Christianity and Psychology," Part II, p. 92.

lacking in red-bloodedness he will only be critical. The fact is that red-blooded men need a pale-blooded ingredient and vice versa, for the opposite quality is the pathway to the third type of man whom Kunkel calls the gold-blooded man. With a touch of pale-bloodedness in him, the red-blooded man becomes reflective enough to undergo conscious development, and with a touch of red-bloodedness in him the pale-blooded man can risk himself enough in life to develop certain essential masculine virtues that can only be acquired by facing danger. The result is the gold-blooded man who, while he would not want to kill others, is not afraid to be killed himself if life requires it of him. The three types are exemplified in the Bible, says Kunkel, by Joshua (the red-blooded man), David (who adds to his red-bloodedness the reflectiveness of the pale-blooded man), and the author of the Fourth Gospel whose gold-bloodedness enabled him to present so vividly both the inner dimension of his Lord and also his Lord's red-blooded courage in facing the crucifixion. In fact, Kunkel says the gold-blooded man is the true Christian.

Another description of the different ways men have of individuating can be found in the Old Testament story of Jonah. It will be remembered that Jonah was called by God to go to the wicked city of Nineveh and tell the people to repent, but Jonah didn't want to do this, so he boarded a ship in order to get away from God. God retaliated by sending a terrible storm. The sailors did their best to save the ship but things only got worse. Then it was discovered that Jonah was the problem, and Jonah told the sailors the only thing that would save them and their ship was for them to throw him overboard. The honest sailors didn't want to do this and kept trying everything they knew to save the ship from the ravages of the storm, but when nothing worked they reluctantly cast Jonah into the sea, where he was promptly swallowed by a great fish. Jonah, repentant at last, prayed to God to spare him, and after three days the fish vomited Jonah onto the shore. The reluctant prophet now did as God commanded him to do: he went to Nineveh and told the people that God would destroy them for their evil deeds. To the prophet's chagrin, the Ninevites repented to a man, and God forgave them their sins.

There are only three "characters" in the cast of this whimsical but profound story: Jonah, the sailors, and the Ninevites (other than God himself, of course). Each of them illustrates a different path taken toward individuation. Let's begin with the sailors. As we read of their attempts to save the ship from sinking in the terrible storm, and their efforts to save Jonah once they discover he is the cause of their misfortune, we cannot help but like them. The sailors typify those men who are called on to find what they are meant to do in life, and to work at it diligently and honestly, honoring God as they do. It would seem that men who are meant to live this way, and do so, have gained credits toward salvation. The Ninevites, on the other hand, live life the wrong way, but at the crucial moment they achieve enough self-honesty to see the error of their ways and change their lives around. They achieve a certain kind of consciousness because they see and acknowledge their shadow. And God reckons that to them for salvation too. Then there is Jonah. Jonah is the least likeable person in the story. He is the one singled out by God for a special task, and is the one who has the direct relationship with God. We would say that he is the one with the closest and most conscious relationship with the unconscious. He is also, therefore, the one who has to undergo the greatest psychological development and live out a life in which he serves others by relating them to the word of God for their lives. He would correspond to the shamans, healers, and men of the inward spirit of our time. He stands in contrast to the sailors and the Ninevites. The red-blooded sailors need just a touch of what Jonah is all about, and the Ninevites need enough to enable them to become conscious enough to find their way back to the true path in life. But Jonah must live with and for a conscious relationship to the process of individuation and all that it means. Men such as Kunkel, Jung, and others who have had to face and live with the reality of the unconscious are the Jonahs of our century.

Individuation and the Dark Crisis

Whether a man is confronted with outer crises, like the red-blooded men, or inner crises, like Jonahs, or a combination of both, life will sooner or later constellate a dark situation that must be endured. If our individuation is to proceed, a man must pass through that dark crisis. As we saw in Chapter 3, only this can purge away his egocentricity, but, in addition, only in this way can a certain kind of enlightenment or conscious realization of the shadow come about. Jung once remarked that the unconscious always tries to bring about as impossible a situation as it can in order to bring out the best in us. Kunkel would agree that the "archangels" (as he fancifully put it) arrange life situations and inner, psychological situations that require us to respond from our creative centers. Failure to meet these crises with courage and consciousness results in a regression that blocks our further development.

Sometimes these crises center around or include choices. Life, of course, involves a series of choices that we make consciously or unconsciously, but sometimes the element of choice looms large. While Jung never used the term, I like to speak of the "archetype of choice." An archetype of choice springs from a moral order that includes the polarities of good and evil. The good and evil from which we must choose are not of our human making but are archetypal, that is, there is a moral order that is fundamental to life. The kind of choices we make will profoundly influence our innermost souls. For instance, a businessman may see an easy but illegal or immoral way in which to make a "killing." The choice he makes when confronted with this dilemma will profoundly influence the course of his inner life. A married man may find himself in love with another woman; how he deals with this situation, what choices he makes, and how he relates to the two women in his life will profoundly affect him. The importance of choice adds to the process of individuation a moral and spiritual quality. It is not only a psychological process; it is also a religious process in the deepest sense of that word.

A touching example of choice was told to a therapist by his Jewish client. The therapist was asking about his client's family and learned that he had parents, but no extended family except for one aunt. When the therapist inquired about the extended family he was told that they were all killed in the holocaust, except for one aunt. Why was the aunt not killed? The story was told: She was led out to face a firing squad of German soldiers. When she passed the soldier who was to shoot her he whispered, "When I shoot, run." He shot in the air, and she ran and escaped.

This unknown German soldier chose not to shoot. If one had asked the other soldiers in the firing squad why they shot they probably would have said, "We had no choice. We had to follow orders." Nevertheless, this one soldier *did* choose. We don't know what happened to him. His action may have been noticed and he himself may have been executed. Whether he lived or died, his soul would have been clean, and this too is individuation. Novelist Oscar Wilde wrote of the soul: "The soul is a terrible reality. It can be bought and sold, and bartered away. It can be poisoned, or made perfect. There is a soul in each of us. I know it.''[4]

So individuation cannot avoid a confrontation with evil. Evil has an inner and outer reality. The inner reality is our tendency to do evil; the outer reality is the evil that we are forced to confront in our outer life. In a confrontation with evil, choice is essential, as the American Indian knew. Writes Brad Steiger: ''Indians were always confused by the Christian idea of a devil as a separate entity, for they understood that there was no such thing as a devil, that good and evil are both present in man himself. It is the choice that brings out the influence of one or the other.''[5]

Work, Relationships, and Dreams

For most men, individuation is also closely connected to their work. We are meant to do something in this world. Each man has a particular quality to his personality that suits him for a certain kind of work. It is important, as we saw in Chapter 4, that he find his proper life-work, whether this means he is to be an artist, a carpenter, a teacher, or whatever it might be. Beethoven would hardly have been Beethoven had he not composed music; Picasso would not have been Picasso had he not painted; Jung would have missed the point of his life had he not devoted himself to the study of the psyche. Sometimes, as we saw, it is not possible in our culture for a man to find and do a work that is suitable for him. His basic inclinations for work may have to be satisfied in an avocation, or, at the least, he must consciously realize what he is all about even if he can find no viable activity in the work place of our day to fulfill it in.

But relationships are equally essential, for without them most men will become too narrow. It is in the nature of masculine consciousness to focus on something and move toward it as though he had blinders on to everything else in his life and personality. A man's relationships draw him away from his one-sided, focused tendencies, and enable him to see life's broader aspects. They introduce him to the realm of Eros, make him vulnerable to his feeling and emotional side, and help him

---

4. Wilde, *The Picture of Dorian Gray,* p. 201.
5. Brad Steiger, *Medicine Power.* New York: Doubleday & Co., 1974, p. 124.

see the reality of other people. Some men who have unusually strong creative gifts become so engrossed in their creative activities that the relationship side of their lives is neglected. As a result they may become geniuses but not whole men, and often their lives suffer tragically as a result. Beethoven, for instance, was brilliant as a composer but unbearable as a person. Van Gogh was an enormously original artist, but when his interest in and fascination for art unexpectedly left him in the middle of his life he had little else to fall back on and committed suicide.

Men need a lot of help if they are to develop properly. As a rule, they are less gifted than women when it comes to psychological matters. Fortunately they do not go through life unaided. For one thing, their dreams are a faithful guide to the state of their souls. Among some American Indians it was said that the Great Spirit knew the human soul would wander in error and darkness, and so sent dreams to guide it on its way.[6] As we have seen, even our sexual fantasies can give us guidance about the direction in which our individuation lies. The Epistle to the Hebrews tells us that God sent angels to help lead human beings to salvation, and the fact is that we do have spiritual guiding powers within us. In order to avail ourselves of their help, however, a man must separate himself from the collective rejection of the inner life and boldly accept the reality of his unconscious, spiritual dimension.

The spiritual dimension is of the greatest importance to elderly men, for the inner meaning to old age is the completion of our lives and personalities, the "rounding out" of life that can only take place when there is time and inclination for reflection.

The Primary Task of Old Age

Kunkel once said that in the first half of life psychological work is most important and in the second half of life spiritual work is most important.* Of course one cannot draw a hard and fast line between what is psychological work and what is spiritual work, nor can we overlook the fact that the spiritual side of individuation is important in our youth as well as the psychological work, and vice versa. Nevertheless

---

6. David Villasenor, *Tapestries in Sand.* Happy Camp, Cal.: Naturegraph Publishing Co., 1963. See chapter entitled "Death and Dreams."

*From a private conversation with Fritz Kunkel.

there is some truth to what Kunkel said. A young man in his twenties, for instance, may need to analyze his childhood, deal with his mother and father complexes, understand the dynamics of his relationships with women, employers, and peers, and grasp the way his ego and shadow work. All of this can be regarded as psychological work, and, of course, if not accomplished earlier, may have to be done in a man's old age. But the primary task of old age is to understand the overall meaning of one's life, to shift the focus from ego to Self, to prepare oneself for death, and to reflect on matters of human existence and God. It is also the time when a man will need to learn how to live meaningfully and courageously under the difficulties that old age often brings: diminution of physical strength, loss of position and influence in the world, the loss of close friends and relatives through death, and, of course, the challenge posed to the ego by the imminence of one's own death. It is a time that calls for a shift in the focus of consciousness, a shift that brings about the kind of wisdom that only can come to a person who has lived for a long time.

While sorting through some family archives I once ran across a comment by my great-great-grandfather when he was an old man. Grandfather White had lived a long and difficult life capped by the Civil War. A pastor in a Presbyterian church in the Shenandoah Valley during the dreadful conflict, he had suffered many things, including the occupation of his church by the Union army, the death of his friend and parishioner, Stonewall Jackson, the death of one of his four sons at the Second Battle of Manassass, and the wounding of a second son later in the war. Prematurely aged by these hardships and by illness he reflected, "For myself, now at age sixty-five years, with many physical infirmities, there remains but little, very little, of earthly ills to fear or of earthly good to expect."[7] This comment expresses nicely the difference between the spirit of an old man and that of a young man. His attitude is not one of pessimism, or of resignation, but simply a shift in the nature and focus of consciousness.

This shift in a man's ego can be likened to the passage of the sun through the sky. In the morning, the sun rises newborn with the dawn, climbs steadily into the sky during the morning, reaches its zenith at noon and seems to linger there during the mid-day hours; then it begins slowly to descend; by evening its light is dimmed, and then at last it

---

7. H. M. White, D.D., *William S. White and His Times*. Richmond, 1891, p. 198.

sinks below the horizon and disappears. So it is with a man's ego: it arises fresh and new at birth, surges upward into life during youth, reaches its height of power and effectiveness in middle years, and then begins a slow descent into the twilight of old age until it finally disappears into the unknown at death.

The task of the rounding out of life is made easier if the foundation for it has been laid in our younger years. If the individuation process has already been taking place, then in our old age it may near a stage of completion, but if a man has persisted in living unconsciously and has failed to develop in his earlier years it is unlikely that he will achieve growth in his final years. In old age we see the psychological fruits of a man's life in an exaggerated form. For this reason, as they grow older, people seem either to become more difficult, boring, and helpless, or more related, wise, and interesting. It is as though everything about the person that was always there is now seen in bold relief.

The twilight years of a man's life can be said to begin with retirement, and retirement poses a great challenge to men. Retirement can be either voluntary or forced, but in either case it means for a man a radical change of life. The problem posed is that most men do not get along well with nothing to do. Even when a man complains about his work, he is usually better off having somewhere he must go and something he must do. The adage, "If you don't use it, you lose it," is never more true than when a man retires. At this advanced time of his life, if he does not continue to use his mind, his body, and his faculties, he may lose them quickly and sink into a speedy demise or senility. The best retirement for this reason is one in which a man has things to do. This often requires that a man plan carefully for his retirement long before the day comes upon him. This means not simply financial planning, but planning on what he will do with his time and his energy.

When a man retires, the "games" he may have played earlier in life are usually over. He's no longer the important executive in the corporation or the greatly needed doctor. He no longer can amass large amounts of money but is forced to live on what he has already earned. He is "on the shelf" and will likely find himself not needed or wanted by a world made up of men far more youthful and vigorous than he is now. Of course he may find it a great relief to give up the life he once lived with such vigor but which has now become stale and old to him. Nevertheless, his task is to find new activities, and new self-designed work and play that are meaningful to him.

If a man can solve this problem, the years of retirement may be rich ones for him. A host of possibilities may now emerge—possibilities that have had to be suppressed for all these years because his life was so filled with obligations. An avocation he once toyed with may now become a new work in itself. One man I know, who was an executive in a big company for many years, became a book-binder when he retired. Book-binding was an art that had long fascinated him but he had never had time to develop it. He set up a book-binding shop in his house and became skilled at this new work, which he did more for pleasure than for profit; the books that he bound testified to his love of books as well as his love for the work.

The body becomes especially important during a man's twilight years. Rather, the body has always been important to a man but now it becomes clear just how important it is. It is said that as a woman ages she fears the loss of her beauty, and as a man ages he fears the loss of his strength. It is true that a man's body does lose its strength, elasticity, and staying power as he grows older. But it is also true that if a man is healthy it is amazing what his body can continue to do for him if he treats it correctly.

Part of the individuation process has to do with the body, for the body, in this lifetime at least, is also a part of the whole Self. When we begin to individuate, what we put into our body becomes important. Our diet needs to be a healthy one. Also we need to find that form of vigorous exercise that is suitable for the age of our body and our psychological nature. If during the years prior to retirement we have put into our body things that are healthy for it, and have used it correctly, the chances are that we will continue to have a healthy body through much of our old age. For instance, men who run find that as they grow older they lose a certain amount of speed each year, but they do not lose a corresponding amount of endurance. It may take longer to run ten miles after a man is sixty than it did when he was thirty but he can still do it, and derive as much satisfaction from it as before.

The lives of many men show that retirement and old age can be productive years. In his *Letters,* Jung frequently complained of his fatigue after the age of seventy, but the fact is that between the age of seventy and his death at the age of eighty-six, Jung wrote many of his major books. Famous composers and artists also have often remained productive and active right up to and throughout their old age.

So when a man retires and enters old age it can go either way for him. Life can slip away, or it can bloom again in a new way. It is best, however, if a man approaches these years with the idea that they can be years in which he does a new work and not years of idleness and play. The new work will not be forced on him from outside as an obligation but will emerge from inside of himself. It can be a work free of the demanding, compulsive quality that hounds the work of most men during their middle years; it can be a new career. If a man has such a work to do it will also probably come as a relief to his wife, for a man's retirement also poses a challenge to her. Retirement may give the two of them a long-awaited chance for travel and a sharing of life together that has long been denied them, but it may also weigh the relationship down with too much togetherness. As one woman once remarked, "I married him for better-or-for-worse but not for lunch."

The Emergence of the Anima in Old Age

Old age is inevitably a kind of defeat for the male ego, but the compensation for a man can be the emergence of the anima. At this time of his life a man's feminine side comes more to the surface. This is why it is often said of an old man, who once was abrasive and difficult to get along with, that he has "mellowed." As the anima becomes increasingly important in a man's psychology, however, it is important that he find the right relationship to her. If he does not, he will become a feminized man. Then he will lose his masculine psychological virility and independence and become passive, increasingly dependent, and ineffectual, as though the anima has absorbed his ego.

When this happens his ego changes—the wrong way. In an older married couple, we often find that the woman, who once was the more retiring and shy spirit, now becomes aggressive and bold, and the man, who once took charge of things, now becomes passive and timid. The woman's animus has taken her over and the man's anima has taken him over and the result is a confusion of sexual roles that is unsatisfactory to both. On the other hand, if a man finds a positive relationship with his feminine side she adds a great deal to his old age. Now he is able to be more related, to appreciate finer and more subtle values in life, to find, perhaps, a new relationship with things of the earth, to find the colorful side of life, and to broaden the scope of his interests and imagination. He also becomes increasingly reflective, in a positive and creative way.

Author William Least Heat Moon lost his wife and his job on the same day. His response was to get into his old Ford van and begin to roam around the country; his only rule was that he would travel only on the "blue highways," that is, the country roads rather than the freeways. One evening, he tells us in his book, *Blue Highways,*[8] he pulled into a campground. Next to him was an old couple who were traveling in their motor home. William Moon struck up a conversation with the gentleman, who described his wife as an officious woman with lots of opinions who spent a good deal of time complaining about him. The old man said, "She was complaining today about me spending my sunshine years just driving around and doing nothing constructive." Then he added, "She doesn't know that's what old men are supposed to do—stand and look."

The Collective Significance of the Tasks of Old Age

The rounding out of his consciousness and personality that is the task of old age has meaning not only for the man himself but also for the whole world. That may sound like a strange and exaggerated statement, but there is reason to believe that it is the development of the wholeness and consciousness of individuals that holds this shaky world of ours more or less together. When a person develops psychologically he or she adds a small but vital increment of spiritual development and psychological wholeness to humanity, and such a person's act of becoming conscious is known, and registers, in the collective unconscious. A woman who was having difficulty finding any meaning in her old age because she didn't feel she was important to anyone anymore had a dream. In this dream she descended with six scientists to the bottom of the sea in order to explore the depths of the ocean. The dream concluded, "and what they discovered became known throughout the whole world." This dream showed the woman that her life was important, and that its importance lay in her ability to go to the depths of the unconscious in order to become conscious of what it contained, and that this psychological work mattered not only for her but for the development of humanity as a whole.

Through creative contemplation a man can become conscious of the overall pattern at work in his life. In the Book of Genesis, Joseph

---

8. William Least Heat Moon, *Blue Highways.* Boston: Little Brown & Co., 1982.

has become the prime minister of Egypt. When he was a young man Joseph's jealous brothers had abducted him, thrown him into a well, and planned to murder him. When some slave traders came by they sold him as a slave instead, certain that he would soon die in Egypt and they would not be directly responsible for his death. But Joseph survived, eventually became the prime minister, and saved the realm from famine. When the famine spread to the land of Canaan, Joseph's father and brothers came to Egypt for food and there they met Joseph, their erstwhile victim. Joseph forgave them and the family stayed in Egypt, living in peace until the old father, Jacob, died. Then the brothers were afraid. They said to themselves: Now Joseph will surely revenge himself on us; he has only held back for the sake of our father. Joseph, knowing their thoughts, brought them before him and reassured them of his forgiveness and that they should have no fear. For, Joseph added, in reference to the way they had treated him as a youth,

> Do not be afraid; is it for me to put myself in God's place? The evil you planned to do me has by God's design been turned to good, that he might bring about, as indeed he has, the deliverance of a numerous people (Gen 50:20).

Joseph has seen "God's design," that is, the work of the Self in his life. He certainly did not see God's design when as a callow youth he was sold as a slave; then he experienced what was happening to him only from an egocentric point of view. But from the perspective of his later years he saw the overall pattern woven throughout the events of his life, both good and bad. This is an important way of becoming conscious, and awakening to the reality and meaning of the Self.

Old Age in Fairy Tales

With our culture's fascination for youth and dread of old age there is relatively little written about a man's final years. However, one psychiatrist, Allen B. Chinen of San Francisco, has found in fairy tales an interesting source of psychological information about old age.[9] In an article entitled "Fairy Tales and Transpersonal Development in Later

---

9. Allan B. Chinen, "Fairy Tales and Transpersonal Development in Later Life." *The Journal of Transpersonal Psychology,* 1985, Vol. 17, No. 2.

Life,'' Dr. Chinen brings out some important points about the problems, possibilities, and psychological tasks that await an old man.

Chinen begins by noting that most fairy tales have youthful protagonists, but nevertheless there are a number of fairy tales in which the
protagonists are elderly, especially those from the Orient, where the
bias against old age is not as great as it is in Western culture. The fairy
tales in which the leading figures are old reflect the concerns of a mature
ego, in contrast to fairy tales in which youthful figures predominate and
which reflect the concerns of an emerging ego. Chinen points out that
most of the older-person fairy tales begin with a scene in which the old
person lives in great poverty, barrenness, and isolation. Of course it is
a fact that in old age we are relatively impoverished in terms of energy,
at least relative to the energy we had as a youth, that our lives are barren
compared to the many possibilities it once had when we were young,
that we may be financially destitute, and that we may be isolated because so many of our friends and relatives have died. But Chinen notes
that the fairy tales soon leave the image of poverty and develop a story
that leads ultimately to what he calls a ''transcendent event.''

In one way or another, often by miraculous means, more as a gift
than through the direct efforts of the old man or woman, the protagonist
is given the gift of an insight into a transcendent order over and beyond
that of the ego. As a result of this experience with the transcendent, the
old person goes through a process of transformation. Such psychological changes are never shown in the fairy tales of youthful figures that
remain essentially the same throughout the tale no matter what high adventures take place. In this way the fairy tales stress that old age is a
time for inner change, for the reforming of one's attitudes and personalities, and for the increase of consciousness and spiritual development.

This is surprising, for we are often led to believe that when we are
youthful we are malleable and ready to change, but that in old age we
are rigid. This may be the case when a person has not laid the foun-
dations for individuation, but it may also be that it is precisely in old
age that the great personality changes take place. Youth, in fact, has its
own form of rigidity, which comes from the entrenched egocentricity
that we noted in Chapter 3, but which, by the time a man reaches old
age, has now been considerably softened and lessened.

As a consequence of the experience with the transcendent, the focus of the personality of the old people in the fairy tale shifts from ego
to another Center. One consequence of this change is that the old man

or woman enters into a unique state of innocence. Personal evil is faced, private ambitions are abandoned, and the old person lives free of guilt as well as free of illusions about himself. He has achieved what Chinen calls the state of "emancipated maturity," which can be taken as a synonym for what we have called individuation.

So important are these themes in fairy tales that Chinen concludes that fairy tales that feature older people as the main protagonists represent the development of consciousness and experience of enlightenment as the proper goals for the final part of a person's life. The final goal of such fairy tales, however, is perhaps the most interesting: the illumination thus attained by the older person is represented as important not for the person's private development, but for the salvation and freeing of the world! We are taken back to our earlier point that when an old person develops his or her consciousness it has an effect far beyond that individual's own personality.*

Death and After Life

And finally, like the period at the end of a sentence, comes death. When we are young it seems as though life will go on forever; when we are old we may be so gripped by the fact of our mortality that we live with a sense of its imminence. One man once declared that a day did not go by in which he did not think about his impending death. This was not a product of his morbid imagination, but evidence of a healthy awareness that his earthly life would come to an end. The subject of death is a vast one and it would take us beyond the scope of this book to explore it,** but it is appropriate to conclude our discussion of old age with at least a comment on the matter of how a person is to live correctly with the knowledge that his death is not far away.

It is an interesting fact that though the ego and the body age, the unconscious, as death approaches, acts as though it were going to go on forever. The unconscious is aware of death, sometimes even predicts it, and yet it presents itself as a stream of life that will not be interrupted by the death of the body. For this reason, Jung once said that, while we cannot be certain, it looks as though life on earth is only part of a long story, and for this reason one should hang on to life and live as though

---

*In Chapter 11 we will discuss two fairy tales of older people in more detail.

**The interested reader is referred to the suggested reading.

it were going to continue.[10] This brings up the interesting possibility that what we call individuation may also continue in some way we cannot visualize once we leave this space-time continuum in which we must live while in this earthly, bodily existence.

That there is life after death is hinted at both in the wisdom of developed personalities throughout the ages, and in contemporary dreams. The American Indian, Chief Seattle, once spoke about his people, so many of whom had died. He concluded with this thought: "Dead, I say? There is no death. Only a change of worlds."[11]

A clergyman, who had been ill for many years, had a dream shortly before his death that strongly pointed to the existence of another life opening up for him. His dream was reported by his wife, to whom he told it, as follows:

> . . . he sees the clock on the mantelpiece; the hands have been moving, but now they stop; as they stop, a window opens behind the mantelpiece clock and a bright light shines through. The opening widens into a door and the light becomes a brilliant path. He walks out on the path of light and disappears.[12]

A week later this man died peacefully. The meaning of his old age, and his life, was complete.

Suggested Reading

Jung, C. G., *Memories, Dreams, Reflections*. New York: Pantheon Books, 1961.

Kelsey, Morton T., *Afterlife: The Other Side of Dying*. New York: Paulist Press, 1979.

Moody, Raymond A., Jr., *Life After Life*. Atlanta: Mockingbird Books, 1975.

---

10. C. G. Jung, *Letters 2*. Princeton, N.J.: Princeton University Press, 1975, p. 279.

11. McLuhan, *Touch the Earth*, p. 30.

12. John A. Sanford, *Dreams: God's Forgotten Language*. New York: Crossroad Publishing Co., 1968, p. 60.

Pelgrin, Mark, *And a Time to Die*. London: Routledge and Kegan Paul, 1961.

Phillips, Dorothy, *The Choice Is Always Ours*. New York: Harper and Row, 1960.

von Franz, Marie-Louise, *On Dreams and Death*. Boston: Shambhala, 1986.

Chapter 11

The Anima
and Masculine Development
in Dreams, Fairy Tales, and Myths

A mong the few books on masculine psychology available today is a book I mentioned earlier, Robert Johnson's book *HE!* It is a masterful book, a "must" for anyone interested in masculine development. Johnson based his study of masculine psychology on the legend of the Holy Grail and the story of Parsifal, the knightly hero who went in search of it. He showed through the eyes of this myth many of the complexities of a man's psychology and development.

Myths and fairy tales have the power to illuminate us about psychology because they are archetypal. They emerge straight out of the collective unconscious and in their own peculiar, archetypal language represent the typical and salient features of a person's psychology and development. While fairy tales are regarded by the rationalist of our day as old tales fit only for children, and myths as childish ways in which humanity tried to explain the world before science came into the picture, analysts see in these stories a treasure house of psychological information and insight.

Dreams likewise have been commonly despised in recent centuries, although there is currently, in certain circles, a resurgence of interest in them. Dreams are more individual than fairy tales and myths. They are products of one person's psyche and, like a tailor-made suit of clothes, are made to fit the individual dreamer's life and circumstances. But many dreams often contain archetypal symbols and motifs, and when they do they are instructive for all of us.

It is only fitting, then, that we conclude this treatment of masculine psychology by examining a few dreams, a fairy tale, and a myth. In this way we can gain a glimpse of how the unconscious sees masculine development. However, it will be only a glimpse. To give a thorough treatment of masculine psychology in dreams, fairy tales, and myths would be an exhaustive task. The intent in this chapter is only to introduce the reader to a vast field of rich information which can be pursued further for oneself, with the help of the related suggested readings.

The Anima in Dreams

We will begin with some examples of the anima as she appears in a man's dreams. The dream examples that have been chosen illustrate different facets of this mysterious feminine being. They cannot, however, be said to be typical, because there is no typical anima dream. Each dream is a unique product of the imagination of the unconscious. Therefore the following dreams are given as examples to show the way a man's dream life can bring into focus the anima, but they by no means exhaust the subject.

Our first example came to a young man about thirty years of age:

> I was being held a prisoner in my garage by a young woman (his girlfriend, G.). My hands were tied behind my back. The girl was also B., my sister. Then I managed to get free. She saw and grabbed a pair of scissors, as I also had a pair. I grabbed her and we wrestled. The odd thing about all this is that we loved each other—it was a matter of power. I was wrestling with her and begged her to stop or I would have to stab her. But she wouldn't stop, so I stabbed her partway into her right side. She collapsed and I nearly panicked. I pulled her outside. I was in tears and begging her not to die. I pulled open her blouse and sucked for a minute on her wound. Then I could see that she would live, and after that she stopped trying to make me a prisoner, but I kept a razor blade in my wallet anyway in case she ever tied me up again.

When we are told in this dream that the dreamer was held prisoner by G., his girlfriend, we might wonder if the dream was referring to the personal relationship between the young man and G. The dream, however, as though to make it clear that it is not referring to the dreamer's relationship with his human girlfriend, notes that G. is also B., his sister. The woman with whom the dreamer must contend is thus no human figure, but the archetypal figure of the anima, who can be seen in projection now as G. and now as B. Very often in a man's dreams a significant woman in his waking life may be used by the dream to represent the anima, although dreams may also represent the anima as an unknown woman. In the former case, only the context of the dream can tell us if we should take the dream on the personal or the archetypal level.

As the dream makes clear, it is a power struggle between the dreamer and the anima. As the dream begins it is the anima who has gained power. As we observed earlier, the anima gains power over a man by possessing him, through moods, fantasies, or by appearing in projected form. If a man does not see beyond these moods, fantasies, and projections to the inner image of the feminine, he becomes possessed by them—one could say, imprisoned. At first it appears that the young man is helpless in the hands of the anima figure, but then he manages to get free, though not without a struggle. Through his efforts to understand his situation he can free himself from the imprisonment of the anima. Then the power struggle ensues as the two wrestle together, a struggle that culminates in the wounding of the anima by the dreamer. As the dream makes clear, however, the young man desperately loves this woman at the same time that he must free himself from her. Well he might, for dangerous though she is, she is his soul to him and life would be unbearable without her. It is with a feeling of relief therefore that we find that the wound he gave her is not fatal, and she will live, but no longer have him as her prisoner.

Just to be on the safe side, the dreamer carries a razor blade in case she ever ties him up again. Because the razor is a sharp instrument it may symbolize his logos, or intellectual function of discrimination. We use much the same language to describe a knife, for example, as we do to describe the logos function of the mind. For instance, we might say of a man that "he has a sharp mind" or is a "keen thinker" or "cuts right to the heart of a matter." The dream motif of the anima as a dangerous figure who is nevertheless highly prized will reappear in the fairy tale that we will examine later.

The following dream came to a married man in his early thirties:

I am walking near the end of a runway to a small airport. I am walking with a younger woman. We have romantic feelings for each other. We are walking hand-in-hand as lovers do. She is someone I met years ago and has come from far away.

We soon lie down in the grass near the end of the runway and begin to kiss each other. We are startled by the closeness of the small planes that are landing on the runways. We have warm, loving feelings toward each other.

Shortly, another couple with their two children walk by us. The woman of this couple says hello and soon the man does also but with a puzzled look. As they leave we see that she is talking with him. This couple is one that we had met years earlier in school.

She has recognized us and knows that we are not married to each other. We get up and walk back home.

Later we correspond, but in secret.

Very much later my wife informs me that my son is having trouble in school. His teacher has called and said that while painting a picture of me, he was painting my right hand when he began to paint it as though it was bleeding and lots of blood was flowing. From that blood flow he drew a second right hand.

We will not analyze all of the details of this dream but will focus on the figure of the unknown woman as the anima. The opening scene of the dream describes the dreamer and the unknown woman as lovers. The atmosphere is romantic, loving, and tender, and in fact a positive contact with the anima rouses in a man all of these feelings. The dream says that the dreamer met her ''years ago.'' As we have seen, the anima image is often awakened in a man early in his youth. She has also come from ''far away,'' that is, from the collective unconscious, which can be described as far away from a man's waking world. Such language is also frequently found in fairy tales. A prince, for instance, in a fairy tale, might be led to the beautiful woman who is to be his princess but lives in a far away country.

The dreamer and his lover are enjoying each other when they are discovered by the other couple walking by. The second woman notes that the dreamer and his lover are not married; she also recognizes the man. The feeling is that they are ''caught'' and, like illegitimate lovers, they have a feeling of guilt about this. It is a beautiful but illegitimate relationship, and the end result is that they no longer see each other directly but only relate through correspondence.

It is this image of the anima that a married man often projects onto a woman outside of the marriage. If he becomes involved with the woman it leads to inner and/or outer conflict. Properly understood, the conflict is between the demands of his inner world and those of his outer world. The anima as the desirable but unmarried woman from afar personifies, among other things, the pull that the unconscious exerts on a man to enter into his inner world. This in itself can be felt as something illegitimate in our age which so values extraversion, and typically so involves a man in many commitments.

As the unmarried woman in his life, the anima also personifies everything to which the man is not ''married.'' His wife in his dream, on the other hand, may personify not the wife as such but everything to which the man *is* married, which is usually a great deal. As mentioned earlier, a man is married not only to his actual wife but to his work, to a feeling of obligation to support the family, to helping out at the church, to serving on this board or that, to making a certain amount of money, and so on. When a man is "very married" in this sense of the word the anima may appear as the enticing, illegitimate, unmarried woman. Psychologically she offers the man release from a way of life and psychological state that is too circumscribed and, as a result, has become sterile. In this way she is the bringer of conflict, but also the bringer of new possibilities.

We have said that the anima is like a man's soul. The word "soul" is an undefinable but essential word with many nuances of meaning. As we noted earlier, Oscar Wilde said of the soul: "The soul is a terrible reality. It can be bought and sold, and bartered away. It can be poisoned, or made perfect." We also noted that Jesus said of the soul, "What does it profit a man if he gains the whole world but loses his own soul?" The truth is that if a man goes against his own innermost Self, it damages this mysterious reality called the soul that is so aptly represented in his dreams as a woman. This seems clear in the following dream that came to a man in his early middle years who habitually smoked heavy doses of marijuana:

> I am with two other friends on weed. There is a nightmarish experience: a descending scale of notes is heard with broken thirds. Hands appear. I am fascinated by the music. Then there comes an eery presence of a "spirit." I feel intense panic, a sensation of the devil being there, and of a succubus. I try to suck at certain bottles. . . . A woman lives in a tacky house. She is fleshy, a slut, cheap, nude. She lies down waiting for me to make love to her, and I am going to do so when I notice green pus coming out of her vagina. I am repelled when I think of putting my penis into her and I turn and leave.

Since the dream begins with the picture of the dreamer and his two friends on weed, it is reasonable to assume that the dream is giving the view of the unconscious about his drug habit. The fascination of which the dreamer speaks is no doubt part of the experience of the use of marijuana, which can grip the ego by exerting a certain fascination upon it. Marijuana is often pictured in our language as feminine; in fact it is sometimes called "Mary Jane." It appears that the use of drugs in a man may be related to his longing for, but inadequate relationship to, the anima. Another young man on heroin referred, for instance, to "lady heroin."

The dream goes on to mention a "spirit." We could hazard the guess that it is the spirit of or in the marijuana. Alcohol, for instance, is often referred to as "spirits" because of its capacity to transform our conscious mood and evoke the unconscious. It appears very quickly, however, that this spirit is evil since the devil is now mentioned. The appearance of the devil in the dream may be taken as a compensation for the dreamer's tendency to treat his use of marijuana too lightly. He fails to see its evil and destructive influence on him. The dream then goes on to the plight of the woman within him. She is described in the most repelling language: a slut, cheap, and filled with some kind of disease or corruption. The dream thus shows what has happened to his soul. As he does something evil he also destroys his soul. This, of course, is the theme of Wilde's novel *The Picture of Dorian Gray*. As Dorian Gray lives a life of evil his soul, represented in the picture of himself that he keeps in a secret place, becomes increasingly ugly and distorted.

The final dream example shows the importance of the feminine in a man for his inner development. She appears in this dream under the symbols of initiation through the feminine. The dream represents the feminine not so much in the image of a woman as it does in what can be called images of "Yin." The dream, which came to a middle-aged man, is as follows:

> I am in a strange setting standing on a hill. There are several people with me but I don't know them. I am aware that there is a large cavern underground and I want to get into it. I notice a boy or young man going through a hole in the ground that leads to the cavern. I look at the hole and notice it is too small for me and I would get stuck. I want to get into the cavern so I look around for another entrance and find one on the other side of the hill. I go into the chamber. It is very large and complex. It is moist and has an ominous feeling. I notice a river running through the chamber. I walk along the river bed and as I do so I notice that the river bed is much larger than the current of the river, and that the river must become much larger at times. As I walk, I know I must be alert since the river may enlarge and fill the river bed at any time.

Caverns, holes, the earth, that which is dark, moist, and mysterious, pertain to the nature of "Yin." The dream is filled with these
symbols and so is a dream of the anima taken in its broadest sense. The
cave is like a great underground uterus, a place in which life may be
nourished and reborn. In ancient times, the women's mysteries were
often celebrated in caves. The hole that leads into the cave is like a
symbolic vagina through which the dreamer must penetrate in order to
reach the innermost feminine mysteries. There is danger here: the waters rise and fall, ebb and flow, like an underground tide that is mys-
teriously influenced by the moon. The dreamer is drawn into this
fascinating underground chamber which he proceeds to explore with
great interest.

We saw in our chapter on adolescence that when a man is on the
threshold of mature life he needs to be initiated into the masculine mysteries; but later in life he may also need to be initiated into something
of the feminine mysteries in order that his aging life may be reborn. It
is the boy in him that leads the way and shows the dreamer how to penetrate into the heart of this dark feminine realm within himself. There
he may make the discovery that his soul is within him, and through her
he may find new and larger life.

The Anima In Fairy Tales

Turning now from dreams to fairy tales, we will look at a good
example of the anima in the fairy tale related by Grimm entitled "The
Riddle." The fairy tale is as follows:

THE RIDDLE

There was once a King's son who was seized with a desire to
travel about the world, and took no one with him but a faithful servant. One day he came to a great forest, and when darkness over-
took him he could find no shelter, and knew not where to pass the
night. Then he saw a girl who was going toward a small house, and
when he came nearer, he saw that the maiden was young and beautiful. He spoke to her, and said: "Dear child, can I and my servant
find shelter for the night in the little house?" "Oh, yes," said the
girl, in a sad voice, "that you certainly can, but I do not advise you
to venture it. Do not go in." "Why not?" asked the King's son.
The maiden sighed and said: "My stepmother practises wicked arts;

she is ill-disposed toward strangers.'' Then he saw very well that he had come to the house of a witch, but as it was dark, and he could not go farther, and also was not afraid, he entered. The old woman was sitting in an armchair by the fire, and looked at the stranger with her red eyes. ''Good evening,'' growled she, and pretended to be quite friendly. ''Take a seat and rest your-selves.'' She fanned the fire on which she was cooking something in a small pot. The daughter warned the two to be prudent, to eat nothing, and drink nothing, for the old woman brewed evil drinks. They slept quietly until early morning. When they were making ready for their departure, and the King's son was already seated on his horse, the old woman said: ''Stop a moment. I will first hand you a parting draught.'' Whilst she fetched it, the King's son rode away, and the servant, who had to buckle his saddle tight, was the only one present when the wicked witch came with the drink. ''Take that to your master,'' said she; but at that instant the glass broke and the poison spurted on the horse, and it was so strong that the animal immediately fell down dead. The servant ran after his master and told him what had happened, but as he did not want to leave his saddle behind, he ran back to fetch it. When he came to the dead horse, however, a raven was already sitting on it devouring it. ''Who knows whether we shall find anything better today?'' said the servant; so he killed the raven, and took it with him. And now they journeyed onward into the forest the whole day, but could not get out of it. By nightfall they found an inn and entered it. The servant gave the raven to the innkeeper to prepare for supper. They had stumbled, however, on a den of murderers, and during the darkness twelve of these came, intending to kill the strangers and rob them. But before they set about this work, they sat down to supper, and the innkeeper and the witch sat down with them, and together they ate a dish of soup in which was cut up the flesh of the raven. Hardly had they swallowed a couple of mouthfuls, before they all fell down dead, for the raven had communicated to them the poison from the horse-flesh. There was now no one else left in the house but the innkeeper's daughter, who was honest, and had taken no part in their godless deeds. She opened all doors to the stranger and showed him the store of treasures. But the King's son said she might keep everything, he would have none of it, and rode onward with his servant.

After they had traveled about for a long time, they came to a town in which was a beautiful but proud princess, who had made it known that whosoever should set her a riddle which she could not guess, that man should be her husband; but if she guessed it, his head must be cut off. She had three days to guess it in, but was so clever that she always found the answer to the riddle given her before the appointed time. Nine suitors had already perished in this manner, when the King's son arrived, and, blinded by her great beauty, was willing to stake his life for it. Then he went to her and laid his riddle before her. "What is this?" said he: "One slew none, and yet slew twelve." She did not know what that was; she thought and thought, but she could not solve it. She opened her riddle-books, but it was not in them—in short, her wisdom was at an end. As she did not know how to help herself, she ordered her maid to creep into the lord's sleeping-chamber, and listen to his dreams, and thought that he would perhaps speak in his sleep and reveal the riddle. But the clever servant had placed himself in the bed instead of his master, and when the maid came there, he tore off from her the mantle in which she had wrapped herself, and chased her out with rods. The second night the King's daughter sent her maid-in-waiting, who was to see if she could succeed better in listening, but the servant took her mantle also away from her, and hunted her out with rods. Now the master believed himself safe for the third night, and lay down in his own bed. Then came the princess herself, and she had put on a misty-grey mantle, and she seated herself near him. And when she thought that he was asleep and dreaming, she spoke to him, and hoped that he would answer in his sleep, as many do, but he was awake, and understood and heard everything quite well. Then she asked: "One slew none, what is that?" He replied: "A raven, which ate of a dead and poisoned horse, and died of it." She inquired further: "And yet slew twelve, what is that?" He answered: "That means twelve murderers, who ate the raven and died of it."

When she knew the answer to the riddle she wanted to steal away, but he held her mantle so fast that she was forced to leave it behind her. Next morning, the King's daughter announced that she had guessed the riddle, and sent for the twelve judges and expounded it before them. But the youth begged for a hearing, and said: "She stole into my room in the night and questioned me; otherwise she could not have discovered it." The judges said: "Bring us a proof of this." Then were the three mantles brought thither by the servant, and when the judges saw the misty-grey one which the

King's daughter usually wore, they said: "Let the mantle be embroidered with gold and silver, and then it will be your wedding-mantle."

In Chapter 6 we noted that the figure of the anima often appears in fairy tales. "The Riddle" gives us a good example of this. It would lead us far afield to analyze all of the elements in this complicated and intriguing fairy tale. We will content ourselves with focusing on the negative and positive feminine images as they relate to the hero of our story, the King's son. The King's son himself can be taken as a personification of the heroic masculine impulses within a man. These impulses emerge from the Self, but are experienced by the ego and help the ego live heroically. For practical purposes therefore we will view the King's son as a man's ego as it first becomes entangled with the dangerous aspect of the feminine and finally wins a contest of wits.

The fairy tale is noteworthy because it shows so vividly the two sides of the feminine: the positive, helpful, and desirable side, and the dangerous and destructive side. The first duality appears in the opening scene when the King's son and his faithful squire encounter the sad but helpful girl on the one hand, and the evil witch on the other. The sadness of the girl reminds us of the damsel in the Holy Grail legend who had not smiled or laughed for six years. Her sadness might be a symbol of her neglect, or of her subservience to the negative figure of the witch. The witch personifies the dangerous aspect of the anima, which we have already described. She works her evil in subtle ways, that is, through poison. For instance, it often happens that the witch-anima poisons a man by injecting into him paralyzing thoughts. Men who begin to do something creative, for instance, who step out of the usual middle-of-the-road way in life, are bound to encounter the witch in the form of subtle but devastating thoughts which are something like, "But it has been done before . . . it wouldn't be worth your while . . . you could never get it accepted . . . no one would care . . . you don't have time." If they give in to these poisonous thoughts, that is the end of their creativity.

The King's son is able to avoid these negative effects because he is forewarned. In other words, he enters into the house of the witch with a certain amount of consciousness, and this winds up making the difference between a disaster and a successful outcome.

The tale continues to the scene in the inn, which culminates in the destruction of the witch, brought about by the help of the humble but faithful squire, who also wins the struggle because he is aware of the dangers. After the witch is destroyed, the innkeeper's daughter appears and reveals her treasures. That is, the positive side of the anima can now be seen, and she is the key to the inner treasures of the unconscious. However, our high-minded hero declines the treasures and rides away to further adventures. This is a mysterious part of the story. Many a fairy tale might end right here, with the giving of a treasure to the hero. But this hero is determined to go the whole way. He isn't satisfied with treasures for the ego, but wants to find his soul, his innermost life.

These adventures culminate in the riddle-guessing contest with the beautiful but proud princess, who is the witch revived and appearing again in another form. The beautiful but proud princess is the object of desire of many men, but she refuses to give herself in marriage unless a man can ask her a riddle that she is not able to answer. She has three days in which to come up with the answer. The number three is the fairy tale number and represents the completion of a process (like the "three strikes and you're out" in baseball). In spite of the fact that men lose their heads right and left in this riddle-guessing contest, that doesn't keep them from trying, and our hero is no exception. Only he wins.

He wins for two reasons. First, he has a superior riddle, which cannot be answered "by the book" but only by life experience. This riddle came through his earlier encounter with the witch. One might say that he brings into the contest some considerable experience with the negative anima, and this helps him. Second, he wins because of his wakefulness. When the princess slips into the room at night to steal his secret, the King's son is awake. This wakefulness is a symbol of his superior consciousness. In short, because he is conscious he is able to avoid losing his head and is able to win the princess as his bride.

Vanquished, the princess has to agree to marry the King's son. One wonders why he would want to marry such a dangerous woman, but he does because her dangerous side has now been overcome, and when this is overcome he has a beautiful and highly desirable bride. Translating the message of the riddle into practical experience, we could say that if a man is conscious of the anima, of her tricks, illusions, moods, and fantasies, then he can overcome her negative effects, and experience her as his own highly desirable soul. Where before she would have destroyed him, now she brings great beauty and psychological wealth into his life, for, as we saw in Chapter 6, when a man achieves a positive relationship to his feminine side his inner life is greatly broadened, his conscious life is made fertile, and he becomes fruitful and productive.

Masculine Development in Myths

During the late fourteenth century an unknown author wrote a long poem that had the archetypal quality of a myth. The poem, called *Sir Gawain and the Green Knight,* is set in the time of King Arthur and the Knights of the Round Table and tells the story of Sir Gawain's strange encounter with the Green Knight. We will first give a synopsis of the poem and then examine its meaning for masculine psychology.*

THE TALE OF SIR GAWAIN AND THE GREEN KNIGHT

It was the Christmas season and King Arthur and his knights and their lovely ladies were all gathered at Camelot for a great feast. King Arthur, however, as was his tradition, refused to eat a bite until some exciting event took place. He wanted a jousting challenge, a contest, or some wonder to occur before he would begin the feast.

Suddenly, as though to fulfill the King's wish, into the banquet hall burst a huge man on horseback. He was bright green; his skin, hair and clothes were all green. He was barefoot and he wore no armor. His horse was of the same green hue. When he dismounted it was apparent that he was probably the tallest man alive. And he was very muscular. In one hand he carried a bundle of green holly and in the other a huge green and gold razor-sharp axe.

The green man stood before the King and his knights who were seated at the banquet tables and told them he came in peace, which was why he wore no armor. He did not want war, and besides there was none there strong enough to match him in a fight anyway. Instead he wanted sport. He challenged any knight present to come forth and strike him one blow with the axe, and if any knight did so he would have to come to the Green Knight's abode in one year hence to receive a return blow.

King Arthur accepted the challenge. But Sir Gawain, perhaps the greatest knight in the realm, asked the King's permission to take the challenge himself, to which the King assented.

---

*This synopsis was constructed using J.R.R. Tolkien's translation of *Sir Gawain and the Green Knight.* Boston: Houghton Mifflin Co., 1978.

Sir Gawain stepped forth, took the axe and, as the Green Knight knelt down, delivered one swift and true blow to the green neck, severing the head. The neck spurted blood while the head rolled along the floor toward the seated knights who kicked at it to fend it off.

Then to everyone's surprise the Green Knight's body jumped up and nimbly retrieved the head. The body got on its horse and held its head by the hair. The head spoke to Sir Gawain and reminded him of his promise to come to the Green Chapel in one year to receive his return stroke from the axe.

Sir Gawain waited out the year at Camelot and then donned his armor and mounted his steed to go forth to meet the Green Knight.

On his journey he suffered the miseries of hard travel. He encountered many wild beasts which he had to kill. He slept out in the freezing cold and he finally became exhausted from the rigors of the journey. He worried that he would die and never reach his destination to fulfill his quest. He prayed to Christ and the Virgin Mary to lead him to a place where he could hear Mass. Just then he saw a castle before him.

When he got to the castle he was welcomed by Lord Bercilak, a tall, strong man with a reddish-brown beard. They had a feast and Sir Gawain ate, drank and rested. Lord Bercilak introduced Sir Gawain to his lovely wife Lady Bercilak. At the end of their dinner Lord Bercilak proposed that he and Sir Gawain make a bargain: he planned to go hunting the next three mornings while Sir Gawain rested and he said he would give Sir Gawain whatever he caught if Sir Gawain would give him in return whatever he got while he stayed at the castle. Sir Gawain agreed and gave his word to keep the bargain.

On the first morning Lord Bercilak got up early to hunt. He killed many deer. Meanwhile, at the castle Sir Gawain woke to find the lovely Lady Bercilak sitting on the end of his bed. She made it clear that she had amorous intentions, but Sir Gawain remained chaste with her and for hours they had pleasant conversation. Before she left she gave him one kiss.

When Lord Bercilak returned from the first day's hunt he presented Sir Gawain with the deer meat. Sir Gawain gave him the kiss, at which everyone laughed.

On the second morning Lord Bercilak hunted and killed a boar. Sir Gawain was again confronted with the seductive lady, but again he remained chaste and only accepted a kiss, which he again gave to the lord upon his return, and the lord gave him the meat of the boar.

On the third morning the lord hunted again but caught only one measly fox. The lady again came into Sir Gawain's room and this time she implored him ever more strongly to prove his reputation as a great lover and fulfill her desires. If he refused her he might insult her. But he remained chaste and was so polite that he did not offend her. She offered him her ring, but he refused. She then offered him a green belt which he at first refused, but then, after she told him it had life-saving properties, he consented to take the belt. She told him he must conceal it and not tell anyone he had it; he agreed. The lady also gave him three luscious kisses that day. When Lord Bercilak returned he gave Sir Gawain the fox; however Sir Gawain gave him only the kisses and not the belt.

The next day Sir Gawain set out on horseback for his meeting with the Green Knight at the Green Chapel. A guide was provided by Lord Bercilak. They got to the path that led down into a valley where the Green Chapel was. The guide warned Sir Gawain that those who take that path do not return because the Green Knight hews them to death. He told Gawain that he would not come through alive and suggested that Gawain not go to his meeting with the Green Knight. The guide promised never to tell anyone. But Sir Gawain said that if he were to turn away from the meeting he would be a coward. The guide galloped away and Sir Gawain spurred his horse down the path into the valley.

After he had ridden a while he heard the sound of steel being sharpened on a grindstone. He dismounted and tied his horse to a tree. He called out that he was there for his appointed meeting. The Green Knight appeared; he looked as he had at their first meeting, head on shoulders and axe in hand.

The Green Knight recounted their pact each to receive a blow from the axe. Gawain knelt in the snow to receive his blow. The Green Knight lifted the axe and brought it down, but stopped just before hitting Gawain. Gawain flinched and the Green Knight mocked him for being afraid, reminding him that he himself had not flinched even when his own head was lopped off. Gawain told him to deliver the blow and that he would not wince again. The Green Knight once again feigned a blow but this time Gawain did not flinch. The third time the Green Knight brought the axe down hard but made it miss so that it only barely nicked Gawain because Gawain had failed on the third day to give him the green belt. So Gawain saw that the Green Knight and Lord Bercilak were one and the same, and the Green Knight explained that he had been enchanted and turned green by Morgan le Fay, King Arthur's half sister and a famous witch, who had sent the Green Knight to Camelot to test the knights' pride, hoping that Guenivere would die of fright when she saw the Green Knight's head lopped off.

On having it revealed that he had taken the green belt and failed to keep his pact with his host, Sir Gawain was ashamed and blushed red. He confessed to the Green Knight. He threw the belt at the Green Knight's feet and berated himself for being so cowardly as to have taken the belt. The Green Knight told him that because he confessed and admitted his errors and because he had served penance by receiving the nick from the axe he was purged and made clean. He gave Gawain the green belt as a reminder of their encounter. Sir Gawain said he would wear the green belt as a reminder of his failure and that if he became too proud because of his prowess in arms one look at the belt would remind him of his imperfection.

The Green Knight who was also Lord Bercilak then invited Gawain back to his castle. But Sir Gawain would not accept the invitation. Sir Gawain then went into a tirade about all the women in history who had deceived men and said that men should not believe women.

Sir Gawain and the Green Knight then clasped and kissed and each went his way.

When Gawain returned to Camelot he showed them all the notch in his neck that he got for his dishonesty. He told them the truth about the green belt. And then all the knights laughed in good humor and each one donned a green belt.

Psychological Interpretation of Sir Gawain and the Green Knight

There are many literary and psychological interpretations of the tale of Sir Gawain and the Green Knight.* We will focus on the theme of a man's conscious involvement in his individuation, which includes the psychological tasks of becoming less identified with the persona, confronting the shadow, shedding egocentricity, dealing with the feminine, and connecting to the true masculinity within. Consciously engaging in his individuation is the next phase after a man has already proved his masculine ego strength in relation to the outer world by completing the tasks of developing his intellect and/or skills, attaining his

---

*See the list of suggested readings at the end of this chapter.

career, and forming a relationship with the opposite sex. First we will discuss the problem of the man who is overly-identified with the persona or mask that he wears to function effectively in society.

Sir Gawain is a good example of the kind of man who perfects his outer persona qualities. He adopted the masculine persona of his time and became a chivalrous knight, reflecting in himself the values of piety, loyalty, courtly manners and physical courage. In a wonderful metaphor the Green Knight compared Sir Gawain to average knights, calling him "a pearl among peas." Sir Gawain was seen as the epitome of what a man could be, as close to perfection as humanly possible. He was the late medieval equivalent of today's athletic superstar or successful corporate executive.

The perfecting of the persona is an important aspect of a man's psychological development. According to Jungian psychology, however, the persona is only one aspect of the total personality. Thus if a man is overly identified with his persona he is one-dimensional and he remains unaware of those other parts of himself that exist outside of his persona image; those parts then become his shadow. In the case of a bold knight like Sir Gawain, whose persona identification was one of manly courage and self-sacrifice for the values of chivalry, the unconscious shadow side would be deceit, fearfulness and self-interest. Thus, though Sir Gawain appeared outwardly perfect, from a psychological perspective he was not a whole person. He still needed to integrate his inner opposite sides, the unknown and even repugnant, parts of himself. His individuation required that he become conscious of his total personality with its faults as well as its virtues.

Modern men are in a situation similar to Sir Gawain's, that is, they are taught to be over-reliant on a masculine persona, and thus they need to move beyond this one-sided adaptation. Our culture's ideal is for them to develop rationality and physical prowess, but too often this occurs at the expense of the nurturing and feeling qualities of the personality. Today's man may be effective when the problem to be solved requires logic, technical expertise or brute strength, but when it involves human emotion and interpersonal relationship he is often at a loss.

Sir Gawain's shadow side was his fearfulness which was exposed when he took the green belt from Lady Bercilak in order to save his life and when he flinched at the Green Knight's first feigned blow with the axe. The shadow side of modern men and of our culture is the realm of feeling, the feminine, and intuition; these are the non-rational qualities that are the opposite of a rationality that puts all things in tight, logically distinct compartments. The more one is identified with one's rationality the more likely it is that the opposite will pop from the unconscious in unexpected ways; witness the irrational moodiness, irritability, and temper outbursts of some of the most rational of men. These raw feeling reactions compensate for their excessive rationality, but it would be better for them and their relationships if they integrated their emotional reactions into consciousness instead of splitting them off. Then the man will not be "perfect," just as Sir Gawain wasn't, but he will be working to be a more complete or whole person.

Sir Gawain's Egocentricity

Sir Gawain's form of egocentricity was the "Star." In fact, his symbol, which was emblazoned on his shield, was the pentangle or five-pointed golden star. In Chapters 3 and 10 we made the point that for each form of egocentricity there is a particular kind of life event that produces a crisis or a "dark night of the soul." As we noted, the crisis, if faced and lived through courageously, can be the thing that assists the individuation process. For the star form of egocentricity the crisis occurs when some embarrassing or humiliating thing happens to tarnish the Star's reputation.

Sir Gawain underwent the humiliation of having his shadow exposed by the Green Knight when he was discovered not only to have fearfully flinched at the feigned swing of the axe, but also to have concealed the green belt, which he did out of fear for his life. Since a knight is not supposed to allow fear to cause him to break his vows of chivalry, Sir Gawain was found wanting in the very area where he was supposed to be strongest. This is the ultimate humiliation for a man who is a "Star" knight. But in the Star's humiliating experience lies the potential for psychological growth. This experience may help him recognize that his identity (in Sir Gawain's case, as the perfect knight) has been a false self, and that indeed he is not superior but as human as the rest of humanity. This may bring him closer to people, deflating his superiority complex and making him a person with whom it is easier to relate. His humiliation may simply humble him, so he takes his true measure as a person, not seeing himself as perfect, but as having the good and bad qualities of everyman.

As we said in our last chapter, crises of the egocentric ego may center around choices. The most difficult choices occur when a man is caught in a moral dilemma. Then he is put in the position of having to make an individual decision that may be in conflict with the collective standards of society. Making such an individual choice may lead to further differentiation of the personality and understanding of one's true self.

Sir Gawain was put in a moral dilemma when the Lady Bercilak offered him the green belt and asked him not to tell anyone about it. If he refused the belt he ran the risk of offending a lady, a violation of chivalry's code; and if he accepted it and told, he would break his promise to her. But he had also made a promise to Lord Bercilak to give back to him anything he received at the castle. The code of chivalry could not help him decide what to do because according to the code Sir Gawain had to keep his bargain with his host while at the same time he was also enjoined not to displease a lady. The deciding factor for him was the belt's reputed life-saving properties. When caught between the horns of a dilemma he chose the course of action that would, one, preserve his life, and, two, not offend the lady, though it did violate his word to his host. Since he had refused the lady's sexual favors and her ring, he no doubt could also have refused the belt. But it was fear for his own life that caused him to take the belt.

His decision came straight from his instinctual need for survival, not from his respect for the code of chivalry. The part of the personality that is primarily concerned with self-interest and survival, even at the cost of violation of standards of conduct, is the shadow. Sir Gawain used his shadow to help him deal with his moral dilemma, but that he did so without admitting it to himself was shown when the Green Knight confronted him about the belt and Sir Gawain blushed in embarrassment. This was the key humbling experience he needed to help him shed his Star egocentricity and recognize his ordinary humanness, that is, his need to save his life. When he returned to Camelot he admitted his humanness and showed them the belt. Then when they all donned green belts he became more a part of the human community. This is what may happen when one sheds one's egocentricity. The Star is no longer the Star, but he may be more loved for himself.

Sir Gawain made his choice and it led to his humiliation and the ultimate recognition of his imperfection. If a man can accept parts of himself of which he is ashamed, he will be a more complete man. It can be a great relief to him to find that he does not have to be perfect. Since Sir Gawain was accepted by the community at Camelot, one would imagine that he would be more likely to accept himself as imperfect.

Sir Gawain's Relationship to the Feminine

As masculine a hero as Sir Gawain was, it is significant that the life-saving option was presented to him by the feminine in the form of the lady offering him the green belt. As we have said earlier in this book, part of a man's individuation involves his developing a relationship with the feminine aspect of his psyche.

Before Sir Gawain faced the Green Knight's axe he was confronted with the seductive wiles of Lady Bercilak at the castle.

The lady of the castle can be seen as an anima figure. It is important for a man to maintain his ego consciousness when dealing with the anima, and not to lose his head and allow himself to be seduced by her. Had Sir Gawain allowed himself to be seduced by her the axe blow he received would have been far worse than a slight nick. The Green Knight implied later that if Sir Gawain had "lost his head" with the lady, he would literally have lost his head to the axe. Because he controlled his passions he only "lost face" (embarrassment over concealing the belt) and not his head. The lady of the castle, like a man's anima, had the potential to be dangerous because of her power of seduction.

There are many ways a man's anima can seduce him. For example, he may be attracted to another woman upon whom his anima becomes projected, causing harm to his relationship with his wife, or he may be seduced by his anima into buying an overly expensive car with which his anima has fallen in love. The anima can bring a man's downfall, but she can also be a life-saver because, as we said earlier, she provides him with a connection to his own soul. Whether a man's anima works for ill or good depends to a large degree upon his relationship to her.

A man needs to learn to relate to both the inner and the outer woman; he does this by finding out how she feels about things and by sharing his feelings with her. To make his relationship with Lady Bercilak, Sir Gawain spent hours talking to her; he did not ignore her. He may have rejected her advances but he did not reject her as a person; he became friends with her. He treated her as a man should treat his anima. Since he had the strength to resist her seduction he was not afraid to relate to her; he did not have to close himself off from her to protect himself. An immature man is afraid to share his feelings with a woman because he has not yet attained his masculine strength. He fears that his honesty and openness may give her power over him. But when a man has acquired his own masculine strength, he need not be fearful of relating to a woman because he feels confident he can stand up to her and maintain his own position while listening to hers. Then he may share his vulnerability as a human being and his fears and needs, instead of projecting them onto a woman and expecting her to fulfill them while he remains in a one-sided rational adaptation, preoccupied, for example, only with his business concerns.

Sir Gawain related to Lady Bercilak with sensitivity and warmth, yet he did not allow her to convince him to do anything he did not want to do. When relating to her he combined sensitivity with strength; he cared if her feelings were hurt, but did not allow himself to be manipulated to violate his basic values to make her feel better. His chivalrous-knight persona was helpful to him because by using it he was polite yet strong at the same time.

Many men merely tolerate relating to women so that they can get them to fill their sexual needs. It is typical of a low level of masculine psychological development for a man to use a woman this way. It usually ends badly between them, with the woman being emotionally hurt because she believed the man really liked her as a person and not just as a piece of flesh for his pleasure. It also wounds the man in his relation to the feminine and he carries an unconscious guilt within himself that may contaminate all his relationships with women. The tale of Sir Gawain and the Green Knight is instructive for men's and women's relationships in pointing out that had Sir Gawain tried to use the lady for his own sensual pleasure disaster would have resulted.

In one of the final scenes of the poem, after Sir Gawain's sin of accepting and concealing the belt was exposed, he railed against all women as beguilers of men. This is a low moment for Sir Gawain because he is not able to take full responsibility for his own choice, but instead blames it on the woman. Understandably, Sir Gawain was angry when he discovered that he was tricked and that Lord Bercilak was actually the same person as the Green Knight and that he and the lady were working together. But his irrational reaction in blaming the woman is unworthy of a great knight and shows that he still has a patriarchal mentality with regard to women which requires that he do more work on the feminine element.[1]

Sir Gawain and Masculinity

As the tale of Sir Gawain and the Green Knight shows, there comes a time in life when a man must risk pulling back from his identification with the hard, strong, masculine persona, and not be tied to the mask of the fearless ever-confident masculine hero image. Then he becomes a more real human being who is paradoxically strong enough to admit his human weakness.

Sir Gawain has already shown persona masculinity as a famed knight and lover of ladies, but now his individuation process involves him in the development of true masculinity. This kind of masculinity involves moral courage and psychological honesty and the strength to individuate. True masculinity then becomes a blend of courtly manners, physical courage (but not macho bravado), and the capability for and interest in psychological insight into one's own character. When a man achieves a combination of these qualities in himself, he has found true masculinity. The new image of masculinity that emerges from the tale shows that the "Real Man" is the one who can admit his weakness, his vulnerability, his fear, his humanness and imperfection. Whereas the former masculine model extolled the virtues of physical courage, the new model also touts psychological and emotional honesty and moral courage.

Sir Gawain is a cultural representative of masculinity. Whatever changes in consciousness he underwent that affect his expression of his masculinity also affect the whole culture's image of what men are like. The tale tells us that even the best of men is a fallible human being whose real manliness comes not from perfect adherence to an outer code of stereotypic male behavior and attitudes, but from his ability to admit his humanness. Then he is not a perfect man, but a more complete one.

---

1. See Louis B. Hall, *The Knightly Tales of Sir Gawain.* Chicago: Nelson-Hall, 1976, pp. 153–175, the tale, "The Wedding of Sir Gawain and Dame Ragnell." Sir Gawain's character continued to individuate, as in this historically later tale Sir Gawain demonstrated a psychologically mature attitude toward the feminine.

Suggested Reading

Campbell, Joseph, *The Hero with a Thousand Faces*. Princeton, N.J.: Princeton University Press, 1968.

The Complete Grimm's Fairy Tales, Introduction by Padraic Colum; Commentary by Joseph Campbell. New York: Pantheon Books, 1944, 1972.

Hall, Louis B. (tr), *The Knightly Tales of Sir Gawain*. Chicago: Nelson-Hall, 1976.

Henderson, Joseph L., *Thresholds of Initiation*. Wesleyan University Press, 1969.

Hillman, James, *Anima: An Anatomy of a Personified Notion*. Dallas: Spring Pubs., 1985.

Howard, Donald R., and Zacher, Christian (eds.), *Critical Studies of Sir Gawain and the Green Knight*. Notre Dame: University of Notre Dame Press, second printing, 1970.

Jung, C. G., *Dreams*. R. F. C. Hull, tr., CW vols. 4, 8, 12, 16. Princeton, N.J.: Princeton University Press, 1974.

Jung, C. G., *Man and His Symbols*. New York: Dell Publishing Co., Inc., 1968.

Raffel, Burton (tr.), *Sir Gawain and the Green Knight*. New York: New American Library, Inc., 1970.

Sanford, John A., *Dreams and Healing: A Succinct and Lively Interpretation of Dreams*. New York: Paulist Press, 1978.

Tolkien, J. R. R. (tr.), *Sir Gawain and the Green Knight*. Boston: Houghton Mifflin Co., 1978.

Tuchman, Barbara, *A Distant Mirror: The Calamitous 14th Century*. New York: Ballantine Books, 1978.

von Franz, Marie-Louise, *The Feminine in Fairy Tales*. Zurich: Spring Pubs., 1972.

von Franz, Marie-Louise, *The Golden Ass*. Dallas: Spring Pubs., 1970.

Zimmer, Heinrich, ed. by Joseph Campbell, *The King and the Corpse*. First Princeton/Bollingen edition, second printing, 1973. Chapter 1, Part 1, is about Sir Gawain and the Green Knight.

Appendix A

Jungian Psychological Typology

The following brief summary does not pretend to do justice to the complexity of Jung's theory of psychological type. Our intention is merely to provide enough basic information so that the reader can see how types affect masculine psychology and relationships. For more detailed information on types the reader is referred to the Suggested Reading list at the end of this Appendix.

Jung's typology shows that people naturally fall into two major categories: extraverts and introverts, depending on whether their life energy is directed toward the outer world of people, objects and events (extraverts), or toward the inner world of their own subjective thoughts and feelings (introverts). These basic attitudinal differences in people are like left- and right-handedness in that they are innate and it is difficult to change one's natural inclination.

Generally speaking, extraverts like an active life and introverts prefer a contemplative one. Extraverts rarely tire of being with people; they are energized by people. But introverts need more time alone to process their experiences and will become exhausted if forced to continually relate to others. Introverts tend to be on the shy side and to wait for the world to affect them, while extraverts want to go out and affect the world.

A key point for our discussion of father-son type differences is that extraverts and introverts rarely understand each other. Introverts may experience extraverts as loud and pushy, and extraverts may see introverts as morose and passive.

Regardless of their skewed perceptions of each other, each attitude type has its unique gifts. Extraverts meet new people easily; they keep the world going. Introverts have depth of thought and feeling; they give the world meaning. A value of learning about typology is that it can give one an appreciation of the differences between people so that one does not automatically denigrate that which is different from oneself.

Jung's theory of types also contains four "functions": thinking, feeling, sensing, and intuition. Sensing and intuition, the perceptive functions, are used by the personality to perceive data. Which data are important to perceive is determined by whether the person is an extravert or an introvert. If an introvert, then data from the inner world of thoughts, feelings, and images will be important. If the person is an extravert, data from the external world will be of foremost concern. The sensing function provides data via the five senses, and the intuiting function gives information through hunches, subliminal perceptions, and unconscious processes. Intuitives, when asked how they know something, may say, "I don't know how or why I know it; I just do." Sensing tries to determine what a thing is, while intuition seeks to determine its meaning.

Thinking and feeling are the evaluative functions that help us come to conclusions about what we perceive. The thinking function uses logic to analyze data and experience; it tends to be impersonal and concerned only with the logical validity of a conclusion. Feeling operates quite differently, making evaluations based on personal values instead of logic. Regarding evaluations, thinking asks, "Does it make logical sense?" while feeling asks, "Do I like it?"

Picture a thinking and a feeling type going on a nature walk: the thinking type sees a bird and wants to know its name and what characteristics distinguish it from other birds. The feeling type is more interested in whether he or she likes that kind of bird, and in its value as one of God's creatures.

On this same walk a sensing type would be more tuned in to the colors, smells and textures of the experience. The intuitive type would be impressed with the grandeur of creation, the Great Chain of Being, or the like.

These different personalities naturally lead to different experiences of reality and differing values. To a person of one type the person of another type seems to be missing the point. Each person is caught in his or her own perspective like a person who has on red-lensed glasses so that the whole world looks red.

The type theory becomes more complicated when the two attitudes of extraversion and introversion are linked with the four functions to produce eight combinations. For example, combining extraversion with feeling produces an extraverted feeling type, a warm and outgoing person whose main interest is in people. A child of this type will, for instance, know every kid on the block and want to bring them all home for dinner.

Another example of one of the eight combinations is introversion paired with thinking to give the introverted thinking type (just the opposite from the extraverted feeling type). The introverted thinker is immersed in the world of ideas and may appear awkward and tactless with people, especially in social situations. This is the classic "ivory tower" thinker, the theorist who is concerned with ideas for their own sake and not with transforming them into practical reality.

Two other aspects of Jungian typology that are important to consider are judgment and perception. Judgment and perception are two separate ways of dealing with the outer world. Actually, we have already spoken of them in discussing the four functions: thinking and feeling are judging functions, that is, they are interested in coming to conclusions about data. And sensing and intuition are perceptive functions; they are interested in obtaining the data.

The type who uses judging to deal with the outer world prefers structure and organization; he or she likes to have things "nailed down." But the perceptive type likes to be more spontaneous and feels constricted by structure and planning. A judging type will have weekend plans, while a perceptive type prefers to wait to see how he or she feels before deciding what to do on the weekend. The negative side of the judging type is rigidity, and of the perceptive, unreliability.

In an extravert, because his or her main interest is in the outer world, the judging or perceptive function will also be the major characteristic of the personality. For example, an extraverted thinker, who is a judging type, will use his main function, thinking, on the outer world. But in an introvert the main function is used in relation to the inner world and so it is hidden. Thus, though the judging or perceptive function will still be used in relation to the outer world, it will not be the true indicator of the introvert's personality. For example, an introverted feeling person, who is a perceptive type, will be flexible in relation to the outer world, but in relation to the inner world will be judging; he or she will have firm, even inflexible, inner values arrived at by feeling.*

When extraversion or introversion and feeling or thinking, sensation or intuition, and judging or perception are combined, the result is sixteen possible type combinations. For example, a person can be an

---

*The interaction between introversion and extraversion and judging and perception is explained on p. 74 of Meyers, Isabel Briggs and Peter B., *Gifts Differing*. Palo Alto: Consulting Psychologists Press, 1980.

extravert with a thinking main function and a sensation auxiliary function and then would be a judging type because his main function, thinking, is a judging function.

A father who is an extraverted thinking type might come across like an army general. He is well-organized, likes a highly structured life, goes by the book and has little tolerance for those who go against convention. As we describe in Chapter 8, the introverted feeling son who has such a father will often find himself in conflict with and overwhelmed by the imposition on him of his father's extraverted values.

For further applications to the father-son relationship see Chapter 8, and for a description of how types affect a man's work, see Chapter 4. A familiarity with type theory is valuable because it is useful in understanding almost any human interaction.

Suggested Reading

Jung, C. G., *Psychological Types;* CW 6, Princeton, N.J.: Princeton University Press, 1971.

Myers, Isabel Briggs and Peter B., *Gifts Differing.* Palo Alto: Consulting Psychologists Press, Inc., 1980.

Appendix B

Adolescent Development as Illustrated by Alice in Wonderland*

---

*This article by George Lough appeared in a similar form in *The Journal of Adolescence,* 1983, 6, 305–315. It is included as an appendix to elaborate on cognitive development in adolescence which was touched on in Chapter 2. Though *Alice in Wonderland* is about a female, cognitive development is a concept that applies equally to males. The parenthetical phrases indicate the references listed on p. 304.

291

INTRODUCTION

The timeless and captivating story of Alice's journey into Wonderland offers excellent examples of some of the basic concepts of adolescent psychology. Alice's adventures can be viewed as symbolic representations of many of the more important aspects of adolescent development. The story's bizarre characters and strange incidents provide dramatic and humorous illustrations of such topics as adolescent initiation, identity formation, physical development, social and moral development and especially of cognitive or intellectual development, that is, the attainment of sophisticated adult logical thinking.

Entering the Long Passage: Adolescent Initiation

The beginnings of adolescence are marked by initiatory experiences or rites of passage, just as Alice's entry into a new phase of development is represented symbolically by her fall down the long passageway. Her abrupt and inadvertent entry into the passageway corresponds to a young person's sudden entry into adolescence at puberty's onset. Alice's unexpected transition from the everyday world of hot summer days and daisy chains to the strange underworld of peculiar creatures and upsetting experiences forces her to adapt, just as the child growing into adolescence must adapt to the new realities of changing biological, social and psychological situations. Alice's fall down the tunnel, though, is only the beginning of a series of initiatory experiences she must undergo.

"Who Are You?" Asked the Caterpillar:
Identity Formation and Physical Development

The *sine qua non* of adolescent development is identity formation. Adolescence is a time for asking questions about who one is and where one is headed in life. Alice's encounter with the Caterpillar shows that she is undergoing the phenomenon which Erik Erikson (1968, pp. 15–19) labeled an "identity crisis."

The Caterpillar, forcing Alice to reflect on her identity, asks her, "Who are you?" Alice replies, "I—I hardly know, Sir, just at present—at least I know who I *was* when I got up this morning, but I think I must have been changed several times since then" (Carroll, 1960a, p. 47). Alice's frequent changes in size have left her feeling confused; she has lost what Erikson (1968, p. 17) would call her "sense of personal sameness." During adolescence, development occurs so rapidly that it is difficult to maintain the sense of personal continuity which a stable identity requires. Many adolescents would give the same type of response that Alice gives to the Caterpillar's question.

The Caterpillar questions Alice, but he also gives her helpful advice: he tells her how to control her size by eating from the correct sides of the mushroom. If she eats from one side, she will become larger; if she eats from the other side, she will become smaller. Of course, when she takes a bite, she usually takes too much, thus becoming either very large or very small, depending on which side she chooses.

Symbolically, increase and decrease in physical size stand for psychological inflation and deflation. In adulthood, extreme oscillations in mood are rare. In adolescence, however, it is common to feel "ten miles high" one day and "about two feet tall" the next. The Caterpillar's advice is meant to help Alice gain more control of her size; symbolically understood, this is a lesson in how to avoid extreme mood swings. But, even after the Caterpillar's advice, Alice has much difficulty regulating her size; symbolizing the difficulty adolescents have in learning to regulate their moods.

Adolescents also oscillate between acting like mature adults and acting like immature children. Alice's fluctuations in physical size can be seen as symbolic of the almost hourly variability in adolescents' emotional maturity.

Alice's frequent and drastic size changes may also refer to the growth spurt which occurs in adolescent physical development. The growth spurt can result in radical gains in height and weight (height gains of four inches a year for boys, and three and a half inches a year for girls are not unusual) (McCandless and Coop, 1979, p. 29).

Such rapid acceleration in growth causes changes in body-image, and the latter changes cause changes in self-concept. The final result is an intensification of the identity crisis because the young person has difficulty maintaining a stable sense of self. Alice's changes in size, and her resulting confusion about who she is, are illustrations of the effects of the growth spurt on adolescent identity formation.

Something To Think About: Cognitive Development

Perhaps because it reflects Lewis Carroll's own fascination with logic (Carroll, 1960b, p. 13), Alice in Wonderland is particularly well-suited as an illustration of cognitive development in late childhood and early adolescence. Piaget and Inhelder (1969, p. 130) have described the shift in cognitive development occurring at the end of childhood as a change from thought which is bound to the concrete to thought which is freed from the concrete and open to the abstract. The adolescent who has attained formal operations can see the logical form of an argument and is thus not limited by the argument's particular content. Hypothetical thinking can be performed and the adolescent mind "becomes capable of drawing the necessary conclusions from truths which are merely possible" (Piaget and Inhelder, 1969, p. 132).

This newly-acquired abstract reasoning ability makes logical debate possible and even enjoyable. Adolescents are quick to point out inconsistencies and errors in the logic of an unwary adult's statements. Adults who must deal with this intellectual sword-play may find it annoying, but adolescents need verbal battling as exercise for their new cognitive powers. Through the interplay of argument and counter-argument the adolescent's developing mind sharpens its reasoning.

In the same manner, Alice's mental abilities mature as she encounters each new Wonderland experience. Her dialogues with the creatures are battles of wits that provide opportunity for practice in abstract thinking. The creatures often try to trap Alice with tricky maneuvers of logic, which, in fact, are rarely logically sound. In her early encounters, Alice is baffled by these tricks, but, as the story progresses, she begins to develop formal operational thinking and is able to fight back with the weapon of abstract reasoning. She attains this reasoning ability, however, only after she has suffered many cruel wounds from the sarcastic attacks of the Frog Footman, the Cheshire Cat, and the Mad Hatter and the March Hare.

Alice and the Frog Footman: An Introductory Lesson in Logic

Early in the story, when Alice comes to the Duchess' house and starts to knock on the door to get in, the Frog Footman, standing outside with her, makes the statement that since he is on the same side of the door as she, there is no sense in her knocking for him to let her in (Carroll, 1960a, p. 57). Although this is a perfectly logical statement, Alice is not interested in a lesson on the finer points of relative position and door-opening by a footman. She is more interested in trying all possible means of rapidly escaping this strange world.

The Frog Footman's statement is a challenge to Alice's naive approach to the world; it forces her to think about logical possibilities as she has not done before. To Alice, this lesson in logic appears to be an obstacle to her immediate goal; it seems as irrelevant to her as geometry seems to some high school students. To adolescents who are seeking immediate goals, and who have difficulty delaying gratification, many things appear to be obstacles. To Alice, the footman's statement is also an apparent obstacle, but, viewed from a different perspective, it can be potentially helpful. The Frog Footman's lesson can be a stimulus to growth, because understanding it requires that she use sequential reasoning, thus encouraging her cognitive development.

A Lesson from the Cheshire Cat

In Alice's classic encounter with the clever Cheshire Cat, she is lost and asks the cat which way she should go. The cat aptly replies that the answer depends on where she wants to get to. Alice says she doesn't care, as long as she gets *somewhere*. The cat, correctly and wittily, replies that it doesn't matter, therefore, which way she goes, because she'll be sure to get somewhere (Carroll, 1960a, p. 62).

The cat, in a practical sense, is not being very helpful. But, by replying the way it does, the cat is making Alice aware of her vagueness and is helping her to recognize the greater degree of logical precision she needs to develop.

The Cheshire Cat next introduces Alice to syllogistic reasoning. This part of the story provides an excellent teaching example for illustrating the difference between concrete and formal operational thought.

The cat claims that it is mad and Alice asks it how it knows this. The following dialogue then ensues.

> "To begin with," said the Cat, "a dog's not mad. You grant that?"
>
> "I suppose so," said Alice.
>
> "Well, then," the cat went on, "you see a dog growls when it's angry, and wags its tail when it's pleased. Now *I* growl when I'm pleased, and wag my tail when I'm angry. Therefore I'm mad."
>
> "I call it purring, not growling," said Alice.
>
> "Call it what you like," said the Cat (Carroll, 1960a, pp. 63–64).

Alice knows there is definitely something wrong with what the cat has said, but she cannot accurately identify what it is. Put into its syllogistic form, the cat's argument would appear as follows.

> Dogs are not mad and dogs wag their tails when pleased.
> Cats do not wag their tails when pleased.
> Therefore, cats are mad.

That this form of argument is invalid can easily be seen if other propositions are substituted for those used by the cat. (This method of determining the validity of an argument's form has been described by Flew, 1977, p. 24.)

For example, keeping the same form of argument, the following substitutions could be made.

> Apples are not blue, and apples have brown seeds.
> Lemons do not have brown seeds.
> Therefore, lemons are blue.

If Alice had reached the level of cognitive development where analysis of an argument's form is possible, then she could have seen, and perhaps demonstrated, that the Cheshire Cat was using an invalid form of argument. A person who has attained formal operations "is capable of dealing with the form of an argument without regard to its particular content" (Phillips, 1981, p. 163). But Alice, because she is still at the concrete operational level, is bound by the argument's content, and thus cannot deal with the form independent of this content.

The Tea Party: Over-Confidence and Impulsivity

Like the Cheshire Cat, the Mad Hatter and the March Hare lure Alice into games of wits for which she is not yet cognitively prepared. At the Tea Party, feeling unjustifiably self-confident, Alice impulsively engages in the following verbal battle with these two characters.

> "Take some more tea," the March Hare said to Alice, very earnestly.
> "I've had nothing yet," Alice replied in an offended tone: "so I can't take more."
> "You mean you can't take *less*," said the Hatter; "it's very easy to take *more* than nothing."
> "Nobody asked *your* opinion," said Alice (Carroll, 1960a, p. 71).

Here Alice becomes the victim of a logical trap, but she steps right into it. Her impulsivity can serve as a good example of adolescent impulsivity in general. All Alice has to say, when asked if she wants more tea, is: "More is only used if you've had 'some' and I've had none yet; therefore you are wrong to use 'more.' " This reply would avoid the trap. But in her moment of irritation she says more than she needs to. Perhaps the beginnings of a sense of logical form, which she had acquired from the Frog Footman's and the Cheshire Cat's lessons, along with an over-confidence in her developing abilities, led her to act impulsively and fall into the trap. She tries to be too cute.

Similarly, adolescents can display over-confidence, which causes them to engage in interactions for which they are unprepared. They are then apt to be wounded by the experience of failure and then retreat from further challenges which they could actually master. A pattern can appear in adolescence in which there is a continual oscillation between conceit, on the one hand, and a complete lack of confidence, on the other.

Though Alice's falling into the trap is painful and humiliating, its positive effects would be to encourage a more thoughtful and cautious approach to life in which one's abilities are realistically matched to one's desired achievements. That Alice has gained a more cautious attitude is shown by an encounter she has with the ugly Duchess.

The Duchess' Conundrum: Caution Comes With Maturity

The Duchess makes the following very complicated and puzzling statement.

> "Never imagine yourself not to be otherwise than what it might appear to others that what you were or might have been was not otherwise than what you had been would have appeared to them to be otherwise" (Carroll, 1960a, p. 86).

Alice, instead of impulsively blurting out a reply, as she did with the March Hare, simply and honestly admits that she is uncertain about what the Duchess' conundrum means, and that she could understand it better if it were written down. Alice is cautious, showing she has learned to discipline herself. This incident in the story can be used to teach the concept of the ability to defer gratification by restraining one's impulsivity, an ability that can appear in adolescence.

In this encounter with the Duchess, Alice thinks ahead, realizing that the Duchess' statement is an extremely difficult one that would take time to figure out, if it could be figured out at all. Alice is not afraid to admit that she doesn't understand what has been said; she does not need to pretend that she knows when she does not know. If we consider the proverb that to admit ignorance is the beginning of knowledge, then Alice's admission shows that she may be on the threshold of knowledge. Her subsequent encounter with the King confirms this.

The King and the Trial: Formal Operations Attained

Alice's dealings with the King demonstrate that she has developed greater ego strength and a more logical mind than she possessed when her adventure began. It is rather amazing, considering her recent defeats, that Alice fairly easily outwits the King. Adolescents can experience a rapid change like this in which a new level of insight and confidence is reached. A very satisfying example of Alice's newly-found logical rigor and psychological independence occurs in the following interaction between her and the King (the King had been looking

for a way to make Alice leave the trial of the knave because Alice was
challenging the King's method of conducting the trial):

> (The King) called out, "Silence!" and read out from his book,
> "Rule Forty-two. *All persons more than a mile high to leave the
> court.*"
> Everybody looked at Alice.
> "*I'm* not a mile high," said Alice.
> "You are," said the King.
> "Nearly two miles high," said the Queen.
> "Well, I shan't go, at any rate," said Alice; "besides, that's
> not a regular rule: you invented it just now."
> "It's the oldest rule in the book," said the King.
> "Then it ought to be Number One," said Alice.
> The King turned pale, and shut his notebook hastily (Carroll,
> 1960a, p. 110).

In this exchange Alice shows that she is mature enough to effectively challenge illogical statements. She does so by spotting a contra-
diction in the arbitrary and egocentric rules the King makes, and by
responding in an assertive and logical manner.

Further into the trial there is an even more impressive demonstration of Alice's developing logic when she attacks the King's attempt to
prove through a letter that the Knave stole the tarts (Carroll, 1960, pp.
110–111). The King states that, since the letter is not in the Knave's
handwriting and since the Knave did not sign the letter (an honest man,
assumes the King, would have signed it!), then the Knave must have
written it, and is therefore guilty of having stolen the tarts.

A child still at concrete operations could have been tricked by this
statement, but Alice is clear-headed and demonstrates the proper combination of emotional independence and rationality which is possible in
adolescence. She sees the inadequacy of the King's "evidence," and
realizes that there is no logical necessity in his conclusion. Alice has
transcended concrete operations and has attained formal operations; she
is now able to deal with the form of an argument and is not bound by
its particular content, as she was when she dealt with the Cheshire Cat.
Her encounter with the King exemplifies the development of both logical clarity and self-confidence in adolescence.

Confronting the Queen: Adolescent Reaction to Authority

An important reason for adolescent conflict with authority is given by Rice (1975). Referring to Piaget's ideas on the "effects of adolescent thought on personality and behaviour" (Rice 1975, p. 370), he makes this insightful statement about the formal operational adolescent:

> His ability to distinguish the possible from the real enables him to discern not only what the adult world is, but what it might be like, especially under the most ideal circumstances. This ability of the adolescent to grasp what is, and what might be, is what makes him an idealistic rebel. He compares the possible with the actual, discovers the actual is less than ideal, and becomes a critical observer of things as they are and usually ultracritical of adults as well.

Because adolescents can be especially sensitive to and frustrated by discrepancies between what is and what could be, they may become hostile, blaming parents and other authority figures for not remedying the situation.

There are times, of course, when adult authority is unfair, arbitrary, and pompous. Alice perceives that such is the case with the Queen of Hearts.

In doing verbal battle with the Queen, Alice faces a threatening and outrageously authoritarian mother-figure.

The Queen's idea of proper courtroom procedure, that is, to give a suspected criminal the sentence before the verdict is reached, is the epitome of illogic. The Queen's frequent command of "Off with his head!" is symbolic of her desire to eliminate the intellect. The Queen is thus the enemy of logic and clear thinking, the very qualities which Alice has recently worked so hard to attain. It is no wonder, then, that Alice reacts so strongly to the Queen's conduct by calling out loudly, "Stuff and nonsense!" (Carroll, 1960a, p. 113). Alice thus shows she has gained enough ego strength and cognitive development so that she can define what is correct logical procedure, and can uphold it even in the face of such an intimidating authority figure as the irrational Queen of Hearts. When an adolescent justly confronts unfair adult authority, the result may be a strengthening of the adolescent's developing ego. Alice's confrontation of the Queen provides a striking example of adolescent confrontation of arbitrary adult authority.

Alice Defends Justice: Moral Development

Alice's behavior at the trial of the Knave shows Kohlberg's concept of stages of moral development. Though her precise stage of moral development can only be inferred, Alice's confrontive behavior toward the King and Queen suggests that she has acquired moral reasoning appropriate for stage 5 on Kohlberg's scale. At stage 5 there is respect for the morality of contract, for individual rights, and for democratically accepted law (Kohlberg, 1964). Alice challenges the King and Queen because they are not upholding these standards of justice. Alice does not merely accept their authority because of their positions, as would a person still in stage 4 (''authority maintains morality''). To Alice, their authority is acceptable only if it is consistent with the underlying moral principle of democratically accepted law. Alice's behavior shows that she has attained a post-conventional moral level.

The fact that post-conventional morality and formal operational thought are developmentally related (McCandless and Boyd, 1979, p. 167) is reflected in Alice's having attained both these levels. Thus, the trial section of the story shows the correlation between cognitive and moral developmental stages that can occur in adolescence.

Mushrooms and Strange Characters: Other Concepts in Adolescent Psychology

In addition to those concepts discussed above, *Alice in Wonderland* illustrates other concepts in Adolescent Psychology. For example, Alice's eating of the mushroom and her drinking from the bottle with the note on it saying ''Drink me'' can be used as a starting point for a discussion of adolescent attitudes and behavior regarding drugs and alcohol. One apparent goal of adolescent drug use is the altered state of consciousness which drugs can produce. But do adolescents seek altered states out of rebellion, out of a lack of religious meaning in their lives, or because of a desire to escape the painful feelings involved in growing up? These and other related questions can be pursued using Alice's ''trip'' as an example.

Alice's humorous, and often frustrating, interactions with the weird characters in the story provide an example of adolescent social development. She learns how to interact with a variety of personalities, and although she has no actual peers in the story, Alice's interactions with the characters demand abilities which are essential for good peer relationships. Having successful peer relations involves cooperation, but it also involves not being swayed by peer pressure when the group consensus conflicts with one's own essential individuality. Alice learns to make up her own mind and to develop her own independent point of view even when she is pressured to conform. Her struggles dramatically depict the dilemma in which adolescents find themselves as they simultaneously attempt to have good peer relations while respecting their own developing individuality.

Sexual development, a topic of crucial importance in adolescent psychology, is unfortunately not well-illustrated in *Alice in Wonderland*. The repressive mid-nineteenth century English society may have prevented Carroll from incorporating sexual motifs into his story, plus the fact that it was first told to three little girls (Carroll, 1960b, p. 21); or perhaps Carroll's own sexless life (Carroll, 1960b, pp. 10, 13) is the reason sexual themes are not apparent. Of course, a psychoanalytic analysis of the story could reveal sexual symbolism, probably in incidents such as the descent down the tunnel.

CONCLUSION

Alice's adventures in Wonderland end when she awakens from her dream. The dream represents the unconsciousness of the pre-adolescent state of mind. The fact that Alice awakens from her dream shows that she has successfully completed her initiation and is now able to re-enter the everyday world. But she re-enters as a new person with new skills and strengths. Alice's newly-acquired cognitive, moral, and ego development enable her to rise out of the unconscious dream state and to enter a sharper, more focused consciousness. Her emergence from the dream parallels a person's emergence from the foggy semi-consciousness of pre-adolescence into the sunlit clarity of adolescent consciousness where a sense of ego control exists. It is because *Alice in Wonderland* is a tale of initiation and development that it provides an understanding of many of the basic concepts of adolescent psychology.

Suggested Reading

Carroll, L. (1960a). *Alice in Wonderland*. New York: New American Library.

———— (1960b). *The Annotated Alice* (Introduction and Notes by Martin Gardner). New York: New American Library.

Erikson, E. H. (1968). *Identity: Youth and Crisis*. New York: W. W. Norton.

Flew, A. (1977). *Thinking Straight*. Buffalo, N.Y.: Prometheus Books.

Kohlberg, L. (1964). "Development of Moral Character and Moral Ideology." In *Review of Child Development Research,* Hoffman, M. L. and Hoffman, L. W. (Eds), Vol. I. New York: Russell Sage Foundation.

McCandless, B. R. and Coop, R. H. (1979). *Adolescents: Behavior and Development*. New York: Holt, Rinehart and Winston.

Phillips, J. L. (1981). *Piaget's Theory: A Primer*. San Francisco: W. H. Freeman.

Piaget, J. and Inhelder, B. (1969). *The Psychology of the Child*. New York: Basic Books.

Rice, F. P. (1975). *The Adolescent: Development, Relationships and Culture*. Boston: Allyn and Bacon.

Index

Achilles: 22; Thetis is mother, 22

Adventure Inward - Kelsey: 209

affair, the: 176–183

agoraphobia: 86

amarrar: 228

American Indians (see Indians)

androgyny(nous): 131; 132; and mythologies, 131

anger: 40, 55, 74, 143, 166, 167, 177, 178, 195, 201, 209; children and parents, 28, 29; creative, 70; an enemy, 74, 75; genuine, 168; righteous, 51, 75; woman's, 167, 168

anima: 56, 131, 134ff, 141, 143–146, 148, 149, 161, 163, 164, 166, 217, 219, 223, chapter 11; archetype of life, 149; dark, negative, 123, 134, 135, 143, 145, 146, 161, 163; described, 134; Divine Comedy, 148; double, 179; & dreams, 134, 135, 143, 148, 236, 237, 253; & Eros, 162; & fairy tales, 135, 143, 145, 148; & homosexuality, 236; importance of, 132, 237; & individuation, 132, 148; & Jung, 131, 132, 134, 141, 148, 149, 166; & justice, 166; & moods, 143, 144, 161, 164, 165; & man's psyche, 134, 143; & old age, 253; & projection, 141, 142, 161–164; 178–180; 206; 218; possession, 143, 148, 164, 166, 168; proper function of, 148, 149; reality of, 222; & soul, 143, 150, 161, 267; & suicides, 144; & the unconscious, 148, 150, 165, 166; & writing, 144

animus: 131, 167–169; 202; angry, 167; "demon," 203; mother's, 233; & old age, 253; possession, 168

An Interrupted Life: The Diaries of Etty Hillesum 1941–1943: 214fn

Aphrodite: 101, 107, 136–138, 156, 160, 179, 181, 182, 227; & Eros, 227; & Hippolytus, 137; & masochism, 227; power of, 107, 136–138, 156, 227; & Uranus, 136

Apollo: 100, 102–104, 182; & Aesklepius, 103; archetype, 106, 109; & Coronis, 102, 103; god of knowledge, 106; god of music, 106; & healing, 106; & Hercules,

305